Advance Praise for
Harmony Express

"The Harmony Express is a locomotive read and salute to the legendary 'Oriental Express', but with Chinese characteristics. With countless hours spent on trains, Mr. Bird has done a tremendous service seeking out the nooks and crannies of the world's longest and fastest rail network, from small villages to giant, skyscraper-festooned cities, all plugged into this unfathomably rich honeycomb of rail. This buoyant and colourfully reflective book is a lucid reminder that China has a one-track mind to develop as fast as possible, even if its citizens always don't hear the whistle blow or know where the next train will go."

— Christopher Cottrell, Indo-Pacific Journalist

"In Harmony Express, Thomas Bird traverses the Middle Kingdom by rail and paints a vivid picture of a sprawling land in the lengthening shadow of Xi's rule. From rockers who blend surf, reggae and Chaoshan opera, to a rebel photographer who shares Bird's passion for riding the rails, he elaborates on a besieged liberal China. His witty, insightful and knowledgeable narrative is an essential source of information about the country's continued struggle for modernity."

— Harvey Thomlison, translator of Murong's *Dancing Through Red Dust* and author of *The Strike*

HARMONY EXPRESS

TRAVELS BY TRAIN THROUGH CHINA

Thomas Bird

Harmony Express
By Thomas Bird

ISBN-13: 978-988-8843-26-8

© 2023 Thomas Bird

Edited by Jane Kent. Additional editing by Victoria Graham
The cover photograph was taken by Walter Wang Wei
The back cover photograph was taken by Wang Lu

TRAVEL / Asia / China

EB195

All rights reserved. No part of this book may be reproduced in material form, by any means, whether graphic, electronic, mechanical or other, including photocopying or information storage, in whole or in part. May not be used to prepare other publications without written permission from the publisher except in the case of brief quotations embodied in critical articles or reviews. For information contact info@earnshawbooks.com

Published in Hong Kong by Earnshaw Books Ltd.

Contents

1. Songs of the South   1
2. Fast Train to Yesterday   39
3. Long-Haul to the Holy Hills   63
4. Bridges to Pingbian   105
5. The Not-so Express Wenzhou Service   133
6. Ghost Trains to Tianjin   181
7. Last Train to the Deep North   223
8. Rail Journey to the West   255
9. Sky Train to the Third Pole   301

SONGS OF THE SOUTH

I

Lunar New Year was no time to travel in China, a lesson learned when travelling in China during the Lunar New Year. Experience haunted me, as I nodded in and out of sleep in a third-class carriage, six people crammed onto three hardback seats, tobacco smoke befouling the air, birdseed and peanut shells piled so high you tripped over them with each visit to the universally grim toilets. Chugging through mile upon mile of frozen cabbage fields for hours, or even days, was time enough to fully grasp why old China hands timed their beach trips to Thailand during Spring Festival, avoiding Middle Kingdom madness until the disquiet settled like dust after a good spring clean.

The holiday marks the transition of the Chinese zodiac from one symbolic animal to another, a cycle that takes twelve years, along with the corresponding ten-year cycle of heavenly stems. As a case in point, Spring Festival in early 2014 saw off the water snake and inaugurated the wood horse. Along with a few fun folk customs like trying to blow neighbors up with firecrackers, the festival is associated with celebration of the family—the core in the engine of any good Confucian society. This, for the Chinese, means dinner. All well and good when you lived just a paddy field away from your mother-in-law. But rapid and uneven urbanization had stretched families right across China's 9.6 million square kilometers ranging from subtropical Hainan to sub-zero Heilongjiang. Come Spring Festival, a billion souls brave queues, congestion and general travel mayhem just to suckle on the familiar flavor of Mama's homemade dumplings. This was not just the world's biggest human migration but also the world's largest movement of mammals, vastly exceeding the 1.5 million wildebeests that roam across the great African plains annually. An estimated three billion trips were made in 2014, 266 million of them by train (rising to 413 million by 2019). There was even a word coined for this trans-continental traffic jam, *chunyun*, which combined the cheerful Chinese character for 'spring' with the equally pleasing character for 'movement' — a compound noun that vastly understated a phenomenon unimaginable anywhere else, the Serengeti included.

A wiser version of myself would have gone scuba diving in the Philippines, but news of a folk-rock music scene emerging on China's southeast coast had jiggled my rhythm stick.

Music had accompanied me across China since I'd arrived in the Pearl River Delta city of Huizhou in 2005, a green, liberal arts major armed with a cheap acoustic guitar and a contract for a rite-of-passage English teaching job. I'd played in bands from the age of 14, after a school friend had taught me the chords of G, C and D, saying "That's enough to play hundreds of songs," which appealed to my slacker instincts. But I'd never expected that there would be a market for a *laowai* guitar-slinger in the Far East. On discovering me playing a kids' song during a lesson, the school head promptly organized for me to sing *Hotel California* and *Country Roads* in a local dive bar for 100 yuan a night. I'd slowly moved up the ranks since then, and had actually played in some fairly decent outfits, while the occasional 'monkey show' — as foreigners sarcastically dub commercial gigs — helped pay the bills.

I'd also made a point of following the Chinese underground scene, hanging out in the hip record shops and live houses that proliferated as the economy boomed, always keen to see which bands were helping Middle Kingdom kids get down and boogie. The best acts were invariably from Beijing, but the enticing news that some bands from the Chaoshan region of Guangdong Province were making waves drowned out any misgivings over Chinese New Year travel, as the festival period would be the only time to catch the musicians in their home environs, as they were all based in the de facto southern capital of Guangzhou.

It was also a good excuse to travel the province as, serendipitously, the brand-new high-speed rail line linking Shenzhen with Xiamen had become operational just a few weeks before. The new line hugged the coast and connected three of the original four SEZs, the 'special economic zones' that reignited China's diffused entrepreneurial zeal in the early 1980s. It also ploughed through some of South China's lesser-known quarters, places often associated with vice and corruption. Just a month before my departure, a massive drugs bust in the village of Boshe in Lufeng, a county administered by Shanwei, netted three tones of crystal meth. I was keen to check it all out.

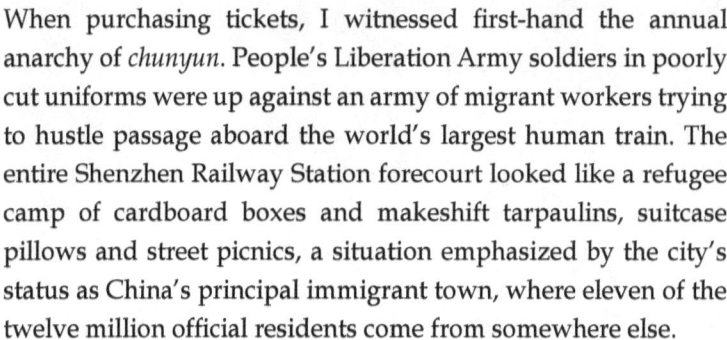

When purchasing tickets, I witnessed first-hand the annual anarchy of *chunyun*. People's Liberation Army soldiers in poorly cut uniforms were up against an army of migrant workers trying to hustle passage aboard the world's largest human train. The entire Shenzhen Railway Station forecourt looked like a refugee camp of cardboard boxes and makeshift tarpaulins, suitcase pillows and street picnics, a situation emphasized by the city's status as China's principal immigrant town, where eleven of the twelve million official residents come from somewhere else.

Yet just days later, when I taxied to Shenzhen North Railway Station, the scene was radically different. It was New Year's Day — the eye of the *chunyun* storm. A megacity virtually emptied overnight was an unnerving sight. It felt as if a neutron bomb had wiped out the entire population, while sparing the bricks and mortar.

I'd hoped to find some residual life inside Shenzhen North but it, too, was eerily quiet. A few people awaited trains but they were New Year stragglers who had failed to return for the Chinese equivalent of Christmas dinner, probably accounting for the pervasive somber mood.

I wandered around the three-year-old mega station to stroll off my morning drowsiness. It was a vast, vacuous place. There were no bookstores, newsagents or yodeling buskers, just a few fast-food chains—KFC, McDonald's and Kungfu, the local equivalent, complete with Bruce Lee mascot.

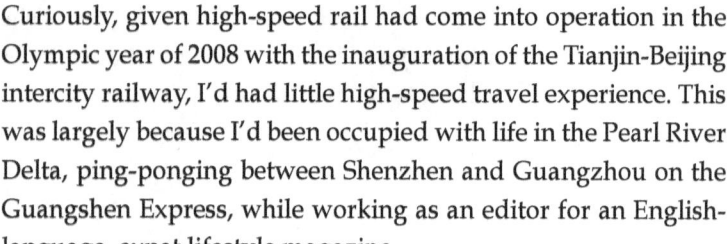

Curiously, given high-speed rail had come into operation in the Olympic year of 2008 with the inauguration of the Tianjin-Beijing intercity railway, I'd had little high-speed travel experience. This was largely because I'd been occupied with life in the Pearl River Delta, ping-ponging between Shenzhen and Guangzhou on the Guangshen Express, while working as an editor for an English-language, expat lifestyle magazine.

Built in the 1990s along a travel corridor forged by British engineers who'd connected Guangzhou (Canton) with Kowloon in 1911, the Guangshen Express was part of massive project to condense 7,500 square kilometers and eleven cities into a commutable distance. The journey afforded an attentive window-gazer real insight into the many shades of contemporary China; industrial sprawl intersected by brown estuaries that watered fruit plantations managed by tumbledown villages that persisted in the shade of towering new apartment blocks.

The Pearl River Delta might have been a manufacturing

goliath but it was also an ancient place of trade, peppered with curiosities that I explored by assuming command of the travel page. For years, I reported on the regional highlights: Bruce Lee's Ancestral Shrine in Shunde; the bizarre East-meets-West watchtowers in rural Kaiping; the ancient kilns of Foshan that once produced South China's finest porcelain. I snorkeled through the murky waters of Zhuhai's offshore islands that had witnessed the first sea battles with Europeans in the early 1500s, sweated my way up sacred Mount Luofu following in the footsteps of Song Dynasty master poet Su Dongpo and attempted windsurfing off the Dapeng Peninsula with a view of a 600-year-old walled fortress.

In that heady boom time, China was in the midst of a building frenzy. One newspaper reported the country "used more cement between 2011 and 2013 than the US used in the entire 20th Century". Just from the view outside my office window, I could believe it. I watched as new metro systems burrowed their way beneath Shenzhen and Guangzhou and intercity trains laced the Delta together, while high-speed rail stations popped up like mushrooms after the rain. I periodically checked the map of the Chinese railway network online. Every time I looked, its tentacles had spread further and deeper across the country.

The railway building blitz was made for propaganda, the high-speed trains became motifs for the dragon's rise. It was easy to get caught up in the optimism of the age.

Chinese high-speed rail development, however, had not quite been the rocket ship as it was often presented, if we take 1978 as the starting point, the year Paramount leader Deng Xiaoping first took a bullet train from Tokyo to Kyoto. This was a period when China remained frozen in Mao-time, the Cultural Revolution leaving in its wreckage a railway network only appreciated by nostalgic steam buffs. The technical gulf between Japan and

HARMONY EXPRESS

China had been as wide as the East China Sea that separated them, a disparity manifest in the quality of public transport. Speaking symbolically, Deng was quoted as saying to his Japanese hosts that he, like Xu Fu—who'd sailed from the Shanghai region to Japan over 2,000 years ago seeking the elixir of immortality on behalf of the Yellow Emperor—was in the market for a 'secret magic drug'. In essence, the medicine he craved was a cure for China's endemic backwardness.

Although his only public comment on the bullet train was, "It's very fast." Deng understood China had a lot of catching up to do. He reoriented the economy by grafting on elements of capitalism but thwarted any political reforms. With the Party firmly in the driver's seat, state planners began to look to a time when China would have its own fleet of fast trains. These would be the decades of 'high speed rail dreaming' before the State Council approved the plan in 2004, one year before I rolled across the border to Guangdong on the train from Hong Kong.

The result was the Harmony class of pearly white trains zipping across the country at 200 to 300 kilometers an hour since the first high-speed railway connecting Tianjin with Beijing was unveiled ahead of the 2008 Olympics. By the time I was third in line for a Kungfu cola in Shenzhen North, the country had already laid a total HSR track topping 10,000 kilometers. And before the Covid-19 virus brought the curtain down on my railway wayfaring days, the network had expanded to 139,000 kilometers of track including 35,000 kilometers of dedicated high-speed rail, more than the rest of the world combined.

With the Chinese characters *Hexie Hao*—Harmony Express—embossed on the carriages, the train seemed providential, a reminder of my musical quest eastwards. The D2352 Express to Xiamen almost 'landed' platform side with airplane-like elegance that felt alien to one used to travelling on old green trains, the *lüpi huochi* that did the bulk of the heavy lifting across China.

We quickly thundered through Shenzhen's manufacturing sprawl and out into the tumbledown suburbs that didn't so much end as dissolve. The mountainous topography of Guangdong meant that we were soon travelling at elevation. According to the *South China Morning Post,* the Xiamen-Shenzhen line was something of an engineering marvel with 71 tunnels and 159 bridges, although "some passengers complained their ears popped due to a sudden change in air pressure as the train sped through tunnels."

The train cruised into Huizhou South Station less than half an hour after our departure. Huizhou had been my first home in China. At the time it had felt like a remote satellite town but suddenly it felt a lot closer.

"High-speed rail is shrinking China," I jotted in my diary.

Beyond Huizhou South, we left the Delta behind and entered the rural lands of the Hakka — a Han subgroup from the northern plains who'd migrated south in steady waves over the centuries. They seldom mixed with the communities they lived amongst and Hakka was the vaguely jingoistic name given to them by the native southerners, meaning 'Guest People'.

We soared over bridges bisecting hogback hills, the morning light strobing between coal-black tunnels. The world beyond was pastoral, the domain of fallow rice fields and fish farms sparkling with amber sun drops. With each tunnel, William Gibson's famous quote, "The future is already here — it's just not evenly distributed," whooshed through my mind.

Travelling through such a landscape, it was also easy to grasp why Guangdong Province boasted such a bewildering dictionary of languages, dialects, sub-dialects, accents and mildly unnerving guttural squawks, as each village could persist on one side of a mountain and have little contact with the village on the other side.

I pulled a book out of my bag and pushed the seat back to enjoy the poetry of motion. But I was no more than a paragraph in, when a girl with pink fingernails sat down next to me. She removed a Lenovo laptop from her bag and clicked 'play' on a Japanese cartoon. She chewed strawberry-scented gum. I tried to remain focused on my book, but the anime was evidently not diverting enough as she soon began calling friends on her phone. When they tired her, she turned to me, starting a conversation in a uniquely absurd way.

"*Ni hui shuo zhongwen ma?* – Do you speak Chinese?" she pressed me to read aloud from her laptop screen where she'd typed the words.

"*Hui* – yes I can," was my monosyllabic reply.

She'd lucked out at meeting a foreigner able to read Chinese characters. I suppose she thought a bewildered expression would have indicated that I didn't know any Chinese. But it would have made more sense to ask, given that many foreigners in China speak Chinese far better than they read it.

"Awesome!" she exclaimed, giving me a pink thumbs-up. "You're not Chinese, are you?"

"Nope."

"Oh, I thought you might be from Xinjiang. Or a Mongol. You look like a Mongol."

"Do I?"

"Where are you from?"

"I'm from the UK."

"Oh, you're the first British person I've ever met."

"What a privilege," I muttered in English before mustering the decency to inquire, "And you, where might you be from?"

"Lufeng," she said of the town about 50 kilometers up ahead that had been the scene of the major drug bust a month ago.

"So you're going home?"
"Yes, I've been visiting friends in Shenzhen."
"Oh really. What were you doing there?"
"*Wan.*" *Wan* means 'to play' but it's used in common Chinese parlance to mean just about anything from gambling to karaoke to shopping.
"Then I went to Huizhou."
"Oh yes? To visit family for New Year or…"
"To play," she interceded.

We talked a little about her life. She seemed to spend most of her time travelling the province and meeting friends 'to play'. I concluded, from her expensive dress and technical appendages she wasn't self-financing this life of leisure. She was either a *fuerdai* – the rich second generation born after 1990 and accused of pursuing unserious lifestyles – or an *ernai*, some bigwig's mistress, as her porcelain-pale skin and chopstick-slender figure were the definition of beauty in South China.

The novelty of a conversation with a foreigner soon wore off, and she reverted to her computer and phone, just as the train ranged within view of the South China Sea and it was announced that we would soon be arriving at our next stop.

II

A huge billboard poster outside Shanwei Station greeted visitors with bold red characters that read, "The People of Shanwei Welcome You." It blocked the wasteland that surrounded the station from view. There was nothing, no restaurant nor hotel in sight, just the debris from construction or destruction, I could not tell which.

I boarded a bus with a few missing windows and bought a ticket for downtown. Locals chatted in a language that sounded as close to Mandarin as English is to the click language of the Kalahari Desert. Though I suspected I might be the subject of much of the banter, there was no course of action better than gazing through the cracked window panes at the decrepit housing that lined our route into Shanwei.

Appearing to detect my unease, a young man touched me on the shoulder and said, "Relax. They haven't seen a foreigner before."

"Mm, I'd gathered that," I replied, before complimenting his linguistic stripes.

"Where are you from?" he asked.

"The UK."

"England?"

"Wales, actually."

His look suggested he had no idea what Wales meant, which, I conceded, was normal. Many Chinese knew of Scotland because of the blockbuster movie, *Braveheart*. Northern Ireland won its fame—or infamy—during the Troubles. Wales (pronounced wei-er-si) remained the least-known region of the UK. Despite my singing the praises of Dylan Thomas, it was generally only football fans who knew it as the home of Ryan ji-ge-si and Gareth bei-er. But then who in Wales beyond the staff of the Happy Gathering on Cowbridge Road could point to Shanwei on a map?

"And where are you from?" I inquired.

"I'm a local," he said, nodding his head towards the town beyond the space where a window should have been.

"Are you back for New Year?"

"Yes, I work, in Cambodia."

"Oh, I've been to Cambodia. Interesting place. What do you do there?" I asked, a tad surprised.

"I work in a casino."

"Ah, well that sounds glamorous. But I thought Cambodia

was quite poor"

"Well it's not really a casino, it's more like an online betting company. Our clients are mostly Chinese."

"Then why did they build it in Cambodia?"

"Because gambling is illegal in China." He said this in the candid way Chinese often told me about rule-bending, with a tone that expressed *this Neanderthal just doesn't get it*, which was pretty true.

He introduced himself as Eric Huang. He was built like most local men, short but well-proportioned. He sported John Lennon-glasses and the kind of clothes typical of many urbane Chinese, namely unflashy local configurations of Western high-street brands. His English fluency, he told me, was acquired in the unlikely location of Hunan Province, where he'd studied Business English after failing to find a more coveted place in a Guangzhou institution. He now worked as a translator at the betting company, making sure their English-language materials were all in check, giving the enterprise an air of international gravitas despite their business being focused around the dubious earnings of a wealthy Mainland Chinese clientele, I surmised.

"Where are you going?" he asked.

"I'm going to visit friends in Haifeng but I'm early. I heard Shanwei's old town was interesting, so I thought I'd check it out. I hope this bus stops near there."

"It does," he said. "To be honest, I have nothing to do. Do you mind if I accompany you?"

"That would be great."

A few stops later and Eric ushered me off the bus in a dilapidated downtown of somber new tower blocks nestled between even more somber old tenements.

"You know, I think the more tones a language has the more beautiful it is. Cantonese sounds nicer than Mandarin because

Mandarin only has four tones, but as Southern Min has one more tone than Cantonese, it sounds the best."

"Where does that leave toneless English?"

Eric chuckled but I soon realized his linguistic jingoism was just a bridge to what he really wanted to talk about.

"This place hasn't changed in fifteen years," he complained.

I had to agree the rusty bicycles, Lifan motorbikes and grubby storefront workshops conjured up a China already forgotten in the Pearl River Delta boomtowns, though that only made it more interesting to walk through.

"Why do you think that is?" I asked.

"It's partly policy. The government has really focused on developing the Pearl River Delta, Guangzhou, Shenzhen and all those rich places. But it's also corruption. This place stinks. Chaoshan people are famous for doing business, but you have to leave to make money. I think that's kind of ironic."

I asked Eric about the drugs bust in Lufeng.

"Lufeng is near here," he noted. "Another ten minutes on the high-speed train will take you there. That place is crazy, the villagers have AK-47s."

The Chaoshan region was renowned for corruption, but its residents were also known to be deeply traditional, maintaining musical and religious practices that had largely disappeared elsewhere. I hoped to see evidence of this, particularly as it was still the New Year holiday, but the dusty main street alluded to little ceremony bar a few red lanterns and New Year banners suspended between crooked lampposts.

All that changed as soon as we veered from the main drag into a labyrinth of alleyways near the harbor. Outside a small Buddhist shrine we came upon a lion dance troupe. It was made up of young men, probably in their last years of high school, sporting the cool hairstyles, ear piercings and tattoos that a typical gang of Hongkongers might exhibit. Their fashion sense might have been disseminated by Hong Kong TV but the New Year traditions were rooted in centuries-old tradition, I soon learned, when a heart-shuddering blast of firecrackers announced the beginning of the ceremony. To the accompaniment of gongs and thumping imperial drums, the troupe, led by a dancer wearing a Laughing Buddha mask, set off touring temples and shops where Shanwei locals donated money for a prayer-dance to ward off bad spirits at the onset of a new lunar epoch. All we had to do was follow, zigzagging through streets flanked by tiny businesses fronting lopsided buildings, interspersed with some quaint old fishermen's houses.

Shouting over the noise, I asked Eric Huang why tradition was so fiercely guarded.

"We're just stubborn," he replied, as we walk past rows of houses with their front doors left wide open, leaving living rooms in full public view. "People here have little sense of privacy," he explained of the communal mentality, adding, "Over New Year, people with the same surname will gather together to celebrate."

Eventually we arrived at Shanwei's largest temple, the Tianhou Ge, to scenes of rapture so fantastical and fanatical it was hard to believe we were still in the ostensibly atheist People's Republic. The air burned hot with the ash of lucky money and other offerings to ancestors, including joss paper cars, villas, mobile phones, stereos and just about any other luxury you could forge via origami. Hundreds of locals congregated, all busy communing with a pantheon of saints and sages.

I wondered aloud what the Party powerful would make of such 'feudalism'.

"I guess most people are praying for fortune in business in the coming year," Eric said of the regional mercantile instinct.

We waded through the chanting congregation, many

prostrating themselves before effigies and shrines. "And many are praying for a grandson," he added. "You know local people don't like daughters."

I asked Eric if he felt Shanwei people were religious.

"Definitely superstitious," he said.

Belief in divination grew evident as we rounded the side of the temple to a line of tables where fortune-tellers were busy predicting people's future, employing every means imaginable, from palm and face reading to consulting astrological charts of mind-boggling complexity.

At first, we went unnoticed but after a few minutes snooping around, some locals began to point and stare at the outsider intruding into their supernatural world of ceremony and noise. When an old lady berated me for taking pictures, Eric and I saw it as a sign from heaven to depart.

We made our way above the incense smoke line by climbing a nearby hill topped by a towering white statue of Mazu, the Goddess of the Sea. Here we won ourselves a full panorama of Shanwei, its fishing fleet crowding the harbor flanked by verdant hills, the ancient and chaotic old town by the sea, the new high-rise beckoning people inland.

I was content to absorb the view but it was almost midday, spurring Eric to ask me if I'd like to have lunch at his house.

"I'm vegetarian," I said. "Will that be a problem?" Vegetarianism is invariably a problem in southern China.

"That's fine, on the first day of New Year we don't eat animals."

"Oh really? Why is that?"

"It's tradition, not to kill at the beginning of a new era. We should begin each year with kindness."

Eric's hometown Tianqian was located on a small peninsula. Alighting the minibus, I observed what had probably been some kind of market town in its day. All the homes were decorated with red ribbons suspended above the doors, a local New Year's tradition meaning good fortune, I was told. The noise and smells of chickens and pigs emanated from people's gardens, while black oxen stippled the surrounding rice fields that had yellowed through the cool, dry winter months.

As we walked towards Eric's house, I asked if those contracted by the government to fix the roads often stole the money.

"The *government* steals the money!" Eric exclaimed.

There was evidently no refuse collection service and litter blighted the land. Packaging was piled up in mounds at the end of the street like a plastic funeral pyre readied to burn.

Eric's home was conversely clean and well-furnished.

"My father is a chef," he explained.

Mr Huang and I were introduced but his father was not particularly confident speaking Mandarin, and clearly a little unsure what a Welshman was doing in his kitchen. After all, it was hardly a daily experience to meet an out-of-towner, never mind and *out-of-country-person*, as 'foreigner' is literally translated. But he was clearly a good cook and soon started dishing-up locally grown radish, a soupy tofu dish and garlic-fried cabbage. We were joined by Eric's mother and his two younger siblings, one of whom, Huang Yuqing, was studying for the dreaded *gaokao*, an infamously cruel set of examinations Chinese high school students had to pass in order to get into university. She practiced some simple English with me.

"Where do you hope to study?" I asked.

"I want go Guangzhou," she replied, giggling timidly. "I no want leave Guangdong."

I'd heard Chaoshan people were known for having big

families and discussed this with Eric's father, noting that they had had three children since the one-child policy had been implemented.

"That's nothing," he said, slurping down some soup. "In Lufeng, couples commonly have seven or eight children."

"That's why they do illegal things," Eric added in English. "How else could they feed such big families?"

Eric's father then dropped a satirical idiom, "In heaven there is Lei Feng, in hell there is Lufeng," to illustrate how the town was viewed locally. Lei Feng was a propagandist's socialist hero in the mode of Alexey Stakhanov, a moral exemplar the Party wished the masses would venerate.

After lunch, Eric took me on a tour of Tianqian. We strolled down the main street and cut through a damp and stinky wet market vending all the exoticisms for which Guangdong was famous: snakes and dogs, seafood, rare birds in miserable cages and a selection of tropical fruits like durian and lychee. Eric picked out a hard fruit, akin to an unripe pear in texture and recommended I try it. "This one is good, I'm not sure of the English name." I took a bite. It tasted like an unripe pear.

Eventually, we came upon the King Temple, evidently the heart of town. There was a square shaded by a sacred banyan tree beneath which a crowd had gathered to watch a game of dice. Money was on the table and a policeman was watching the game intently while puffing on a cigarette.

Feeling I'd taken in all the attractions Tianqian had to offer, I bid Eric farewell and we walked to the bus stop together. While we walked, he suddenly opened up about his concerns for his future. He had fallen for a local girl and was currently trying to woo her. A friend wanted to open an English school in distant Guizhou Province and he was wondering if he should invest. I only had hackneyed advice, "Just follow your heart."

III

Ren Ke and Ah Mao were waiting for me outside Haifeng's government offices. "Hey, Xiao Fei!" they called, offering up the warm smiles Chinese always deliver to a visiting friend.

I had first encountered them a month before, backstage at the MIDI Festival—a major Chinese rock assembly that began in Beijing in 1997 and had spread nationwide. After my band's sound-check, I'd been introduced to Wu Tiao Ren, the folk stage's headline act. Already a fan of the group's first two records, I quickly befriended Ren Ke and Ah Mao, the founding members, as well as veteran rock drummer Lao Wei, who had been recruited for their second album *Some Other Scenery*. A few weeks later, I'd got in touch to tell the boys I was heading east.

"*Lai, lai, lai,*" was the reply, essentially, "Come on by."

Ren Ke was dark-skinned, somewhat effeminate, with the air of a beat poet. Ah Mao was tall and fair for a southerner. He carried himself with the no-nonsense attitude and sharp wit requisite of an artist who grew up in a world where many contemporaries made a living manufacturing toasters for Walmart.

We collected Ren Ke's improbably cute girlfriend Han Ting from a nearby apartment the boys had converted into a practice studio. She seemed relieved to have someone new to speak to, as the band's rehearsal space had left her with only menthol cigarettes and books for company.

With the light fading, we decided to check out the town and get a bite to eat before the boys got back to their music, so we all hopped into what Ah Mao called, 'a Haifeng-style taxi'— essentially a metal box with motorbike wheels.

"Before they built traffic lights here, this junction was like India," Ah Mao called over the lawnmower engine, as if that would somehow reassure me.

I distracted myself from the prospect of impending death by

engaging Han Ting in conversation. After all, along with me, she was an outsider, a bookish city girl who appeared even less comfortable in these strange environs than I did.

"How are you enjoying Haifeng?" I yelled at her as we hurtled down the road like a rogue shopping trolley some truant kids had launched down a hill.

"After ten days here I'm fed up. I'm tired of all the family rituals," she hollered back.

"Where are you from?"

"I'm from Guangzhou."

"So you're Cantonese?"

"Half. My mother is from Hunan."

"That's unusual," I said, pointing out that migration between the provinces would have been limited during her parent's generation. But it was commonplace since Deng Xiaoping's economic reforms, with Hunanese migrants flooding Guangdong looking for work opportunities or to marry wealthy Cantonese businessmen. The so-called Xiang ladies had a reputation for being beautiful but notoriously ill-tempered. By contrast, Cantonese women were mild-mannered and generally more urbane, it was said. I wondered what her mixed heritage meant for Han Ting.

"My mother is a tiger," she yelled, as we swung around a corner, narrowly avoiding a collision with another motor-trike. "She always has the last word in our house. Round here they treat women badly, they're second class, not like in Hunan."

We finally aborted the three-wheeled death sentence outside a pink-tiled building.

"Even though we went to the same school, Ah Mao and I first met in 2004 at a music concert," Ren Ke said, pointing to what amounted to a car park set before a metal shuttered door. "Then we had separate bands, we weren't particularly familiar with one another."

They led me down a few forlorn streets to Haifeng Middle School, which they both had attended and regarded with a bit of nostalgia.

"I haven't been back for ages," Ren Ke said, staring at the school while watching some past episode of life play out on a cerebral screen.

"I first heard rock n roll in 1994 when Tang Dynasty played in Hong Kong," Ah Mao told us. He was referring to the legendary televised concert in which some of China's most dynamic acts burst from behind the bamboo curtain to stun a closeted Hong Kong audience, which had little idea Beijing was brewing such potent musical medicine. "In Guangdong, we could get Hong Kong TV if you pointed your aerial in the right direction. After I saw that show I decided to grow my hair long. This used to annoy my teacher, who berated me in that classroom over there for being disruptive."

It was strange to see these two high school dropouts in this setting. Just one month before, they'd headlined the folk stage while rock legends, their youthful idols Tang Dynasty, headlined the main stage.

I'd learned of their love of books when we'd first met, but neither had attended any kind of higher-education institution. "Chinese education is rubbish," Ah Mao said kicking a Coke can out of the school gates. "When we come back here people don't understand the path we're on. They just want to talk about business, buying houses or having kids." He pointed at some junk drifting through a puddle like a miniature boat. "You know in Haifeng everyone litters. Even people driving BMWs."

While Wu Tiao Ren rehearsed the following day, a friend named

Cuba was assigned to show me the town. He was teddy-boyish, with cropped hair and furry sideburns. He told me he made iPhone art. As I had no idea what that meant exactly, I asked instead, "Why do they call you Cuba?"

"Because they say I look like a foreigner," he explained, matter-of-factly.

He did have a curiously Hispanic lilt and in the right revolutionary attire, he could have stood shoulder-to-shoulder with Che Guevara and no one would have called him out.

With Han Ting, we set off in the drizzle to experience what Haifeng offered sightseers. We found its principal historic attraction, the Red Palace. "It dates back to the Ming Dynasty," Cuba said through a cloud of blue cigarette smoke. "But it's been renovated a few times." In its latest incarnation, the Red Palace was home to an exhibition celebrating socialist revolution. "I don't know how much is true," Cuba conceded. "These are just Communist Party fables."

Behind the temple we found a brilliantly weathered hospital dating back to 1921, when China had been a chaotic and factionalized Republic ostensibly led by the Kuomintang Party, or KMT. Not long after World War II ended, the communists saw the KMT off to Taiwan, where they re-constituted the Republic of China. Whichever version of China one prefers, what's certain is that the architecture of the Republic was vastly superior to the socialist box architecture that followed it. Unfortunately, the hospital was sorely neglected and though its flaking exterior gave it an antiquated charm, it was tragic to see such a delightful building decaying in the mercilessly damp Guangdong climate.

Beside the hospital, Cuba showed us a small outbuilding.

"When I was four I lived here. My father's work unit took care of this place."

"What are these?" I asked, pointing at some framed big

character posters.

"These are from the Cultural Revolution."

"How terrifying," said Han Ting "This one says 'Kill all the landlords'."

"These proclamations are like Hitler's," Cuba scoffed, and lit another cigarette.

We entered an adjacent park deserted except for a few elderly folk playing cards in a pavilion. The park commemorated local communist hero Peng Pai and there was a commemorative statue of him looking dapper in a suit, his hands on his hips. Peng was murdered in 1929 in Shanghai after the purge of leftists in 1927 ended the brief Nationalist–Communist alliance. Wu Tiao Ren had penned a song *Peng Ah Pai* in tribute.

> *He came out from a cavern. Trees and weeds were sparse.*
> *It was like his heart had been taken out. He just dusted himself off.*
> *He was just hanging around, 'till he reached the old bridge.*
> *KMT guys patted him on the shoulder, and said,*
> *"Hey, man, what are you doing?"*
> *"Nothing, I'm just waiting for someone."*
> *"Waiting for someone? I'm afraid you are waiting for your death."*
> *He thought, "If I had a pistol, I would kill you both!"*
> *"Don't be angry, sirs. Would you like a cigarette? Or I can sing a song for you?"*

As we walked back into the anarchic streets of Haifeng, it felt strange to think just how swiftly we'd straddled the ages: The remnants of imperial China nestled beside the Nationalist and Socialist periods of the 20th Century. Since the late Qing there'd been imperialism, republicanism, factionalism, civil war, world war, revolution, communism, isolationism, Maoism and belatedly state capitalism, albeit rebranded 'socialism with Chinese characteristics'. Yet history was distinctly missing in the architecture of the vast majority of Haifeng's buildings. The drab apartment blocks that dominated the cityscape appeared far older than they were—in China, everything, it sometimes felt, was temporary, as if foreshadowing yet another epoch. Recent news had reported Shenzhen's intention to relocate 4,000 factories to the area. The glass edifices of China's new opulence would surely follow.

We eventually arrived at the last remnants of the city wall, marked with the ominous 'chai' character meaning 'slated for demolition'. Cuba joked that was why the West called the Middle Kingdom 'Chai-na' before asking in resignation all dissenters exhibited when confronted with the all-determining power of the state, "What can we do about it?"

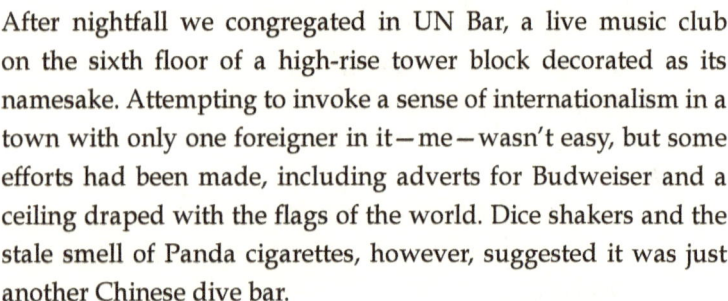

After nightfall we congregated in UN Bar, a live music club on the sixth floor of a high-rise tower block decorated as its namesake. Attempting to invoke a sense of internationalism in a town with only one foreigner in it—me—wasn't easy, but some efforts had been made, including adverts for Budweiser and a ceiling draped with the flags of the world. Dice shakers and the stale smell of Panda cigarettes, however, suggested it was just another Chinese dive bar.

The who's-who of Haifeng society seemed to have turned up for Wu Tiao Ren's performance, not the typical grungy twenty-somethings you usually met at gigs. Girls wore their finest frocks, relatives sported their Sunday best. I was ringside at Haifeng's big night out. There was scarcely a free seat when Ah Mao and Ren Ke finally took to the stage.

It felt a tad unnerving to be the outsider in such circumstances. But as the band hacked into their frantic set, all eyes were drawn towards the stage and I could drink myself into a contented state of delirium without eliciting too much attention.

The band had cultivated a really unique sound. Their harmonious vocal style recalled the high-pitched call-and-response technique of Chaoshan opera, the native classical music on China's southeast coast. By contrast, Ah Mao's rhythmic, monotone guitar playing was closer to the folk music of China's northwest, which was heavily influenced by Central Asian styles. Throw in the rich cadence of Ren Ke's accordion work and you had a product most musicians could only dream of, a blend of discernible influences that had not trapped them in any established canon but left him free to push boundaries. Put simply, Wu Tiao Ren sounded like Wu Tiao Ren.

The drunken scrawl in my diary from that evening was difficult to transcribe, "There's reggae, surf-guitar and Chaoshan opera in one musical phrase... Haifeng collides with a wall of sound... The boys' combined musical personality exceeds the sum of its parts..."

There was no doubt, the excitement of the gig, coupled with the alcohol, was getting to me. The Chinese musical landscape was so dominated by bubble-gum-pop that it was simply thrilling to hear something not produced for the ubiquitous karaoke parlors.

Late in the evening, I stumbled up a flight of stairs onto a rooftop terrace to get some fresh air. Through the drizzle and fog, the neon billboard signs illuminated bad plumbing fixtures protruding from walls, tangled electric wiring hanging from lampposts and anarchic traffic. Emanating from the bar below was the seminal sound of contemporary Chinese music, more intense, and to my mind more important than almost anything

I'd heard in years. In a world so sorely lacking in originality, Wu Tiao Ren had found a fresh recipe somewhere deep inside the sonic cookbook. It was a feast.

IV

How the night ended will be forever lost in a Haifeng haze. I vaguely recall an outdoor barbeque stand, toasting large bottles of Tsingtao with friends, friends of friends and whoever else was around. My phone records show I'd called the Hunan girl I'd been seeing in Shenzhen around midnight. A guitar had been passed around, promoting something of street-side jam. But the only lucid memory I have was the announcement that we would soon be arriving in Chaoshan Station stirring me from my high-speed slumber.

A shuttle bus got me to downtown Shantou, where, hungover and lost, I stopped for a bottle of water at a roadside shop from where I gauged the scene. It was one that resurrected Charles Dickens's opening to *Bleak House*. "Fog up the river, where it flows among green aits and meadows; fog down the river, where it rolls defiled among the tiers of shipping and the waterside pollutions of a great (and dirty) city." It wasn't that Shantou was poor — the garish skyscrapers and profusion of cars suggested the contrary. But the tall buildings were austere and charmless, already severely dated when compared with the skyline of Shenzhen and other first-tier cities. People on the street were nervous and unfriendly, wearing poorly fitting factory surplus, jigging between the traffic, cocooned in their own heads. Everyone smelled of pleather. Many men lingered on street corners like hustlers in a New York gangster film, smoking cigarettes while looking for someone to hit up for cash. Waterways were fouled; the air choked with an unholy haze and green vegetables had been planted on any strip of unused wasteland.

I walked around for most of an hour trying to find a ride to the harbor. Eventually, I flagged an unlicensed cab. The driver was a foul-mouthed migrant from Anhui Province. His shirt didn't quite cover his girth, which protruded like a pigskin belt. He smoked constantly, lighting one cigarette with the last and without opening the windows properly, indiscriminately caking me in ash. I asked him what he thought of Shantou.

"This is a rubbish city," he said. "It's so corrupt. Everyone with money leaves and banks their cash in Hong Kong. I haven't seen progress in ten years. City mayors fulfil a two-year appointment, then they disappear, fuck knows where, maybe jail, maybe Beijing."

"Isn't this a Special Economic Zone?"

"So they say."

I told him I'd heard there were serious graft issues, particularly in Lufeng.

"That's the fucking obvious. Lufeng is the worst. It's full of drugs — those farmers are worth tens of thousands of yuan."

Not wanting to be seen giving cash to the traffic police, the driver dropped me off 100 meters from the harbor. I walked down the hill.

A rust-colored ferry soon sailed into sight, so overcrowded and dilapidated it appeared to be defying the laws of physics by remaining afloat. The train had brought me a long way from the Pearl River, where Turbojet hydrofoils connect cities like Shenzhen and Zhuhai — the two SEZs that flowered.

The ferry gate opened and cars, motorbikes and pedestrians pour off chaotically, driving headlong into those attempting to get aboard.

I joined in the pandemonium, rationalizing that I had no choice but to wrestle my way onto the vessel. While the last motorbikes were still revving their way onto the stern, a baritone horn blew as we set sail.

———∽∽∽———

I had wanted to visit Nan'ao Island since I'd first heard Toy Captain's debut album, the deliciously branded *South Island, Marine Flavor Was a Nice Feeling*. The record, which chronicled the myths and real-life stories of a remote island somewhere off China's southeast coast seemed to capture the timbre of subtropical Guangdong with a collection of what could only be described as Chinese sea shanties. Over the years, I'd caught Toy Captain at various shows and festivals, but the chance to visit singer-songwriter Li Yihan at home, was an opportunity I couldn't pass up.

The harbor on Nan'ao Island was just a terrace of wooden huts selling dried fish and angling equipment next to a gravel car park. I called Yihan to announce my arrival, then sat down to wait beside some old wooden sampans bobbing in the swell, a timeless scene were it not for a giant construction project discernible through the sea mist. The concrete aqueducts reaching from the waves were the beginnings of a bridge that would one day anchor Nan'ao to the Mainland.

"Sorry we're late," called Long-haired Li across the car park.

His Shanghainese girlfriend Jiajia, wearing a long blue hippie dress a yoga follower might sport in Bali, accompanied him, along with a sprightly young cousin named Wu Gui.

As we got in the car, I asked Yihan what he thought of the bridge.

"We're all worried and we don't like it, nobody wants it, but what choice do we have?"

Our route traced a narrow lane between the sparkling sea and the island's whaleback interior. The only possible obstacle would have been one of the many water buffalo crossing the tarmac. Each village we passed through was impossibly quaint, while the shrine-dotted hills suggested religion was as important here as in Shanwei. Though the island was officially just another county of Shantou, it looked like another world from the chocking city I'd just left.

The Li family home was a charming, two-story fishing cottage adorned with sturdy old fixtures and fittings—wooden clocks, framed photographs, built-to-last tables—rare relics in the disposable age of IKEA. There was a courtyard out back centered on a well with an outhouse toilet at the rear. It reminded me of a real home passed down the generations, made all the more cordial by the extended family congregating for dinner when I arrived, including Yihan's sister and her moon-faced twin baby daughters.

I was ravenous. Though Yihan's mother lamented my vegetarianism—a gripe she maintained throughout my stay—she still managed to knock together some great tofu and vegetable dishes. We washed down the banquet with Yihan's dad's home-brewed sweet red wine, which kindled a lethargy that might have steered me straight to bed. But Yihan was eager to show me Nan'ao and insisted we ride over to the village harbor on scooters.

The gunpowder mist of New Year fireworks hung across the water, distorting the starlight and veiling the fishing fleet with a ghostly hue. It smelled sulphury but the fresh salty air reinvigorated me.

"It's like a dream world," I said, looking at the junks bobbing in the half-light of the moon like a ghost fleet, eyes painted on their bows, a tradition, so they could 'see their way forward',

Yihan explained

"That's what I said when I arrived," agreed Jiajia.

The evening grew all the more surreal when we encountered a procession of fishermen bashing gongs and drums and parading Daoist and Buddhist effigies from Nan'ao's temples.

There was a real carnival atmosphere, with dance groups of schoolchildren performing between traditional harlequin saints, those cartoon deities that humorless European missionaries described as pagan idols, but which I loved.

After the procession, we drank a nightcap on the balcony while Yihan introduced a song he'd been working on.

"It's about the plight of migrant workers in China. I read a newspaper story about a man who fixed air conditioners. He fell off the building and died. He was saving to get married. It was such a tragic loss, so unfair."

He began to play a melancholy ballad, Jiajia was near to tears.

The next day, following a hearty breakfast of local radish and mushrooms, eggs and more tofu, all washed down with kung-fu tea, the blood in my brain slowly began flowing again. So much of China's land was farmed with the indiscriminate use of fertilizers and pesticides that one became accustomed to chemical-tinged fruit and vegetables. It was only in largely self-sustaining places like Nan'ao that food, like culture, retained a wholesome quality.

I chatted with Jiajia.

"Up until recently, local women had to eat separately from men," she told me. "Even today, most of the responsibility to maintain the home falls on women."

"Why is there only one twin baby today?" I asked, noting the lone toddler in a high chair.

"The mother took the other one back to Guangzhou early this morning. She can't raise two at a time so she has to leave one here for the grandparents to look after. When she comes back, she'll switch the babies, so they'll take it in turns to live with their mother."

"But that means the twins won't grow up as twins."

"*Mei ban fa*," said Jiajia with a shrug, using the ubiquitous 'no way out' mitigation applied whenever one encounters a tough situation.

Wu Gui joined us and we set out on scooters to explore the island. By the afternoon, I was totally enamored by the lofty meadows grazed by skinny brown cattle, the blissful bays and soaring, forested hills topped with pavilions and temples.

Near the coast, we found the *Songjin* — the Song Dynasty well from 1276 AD. "The Southern Song court fled south when the Mongol hordes conquered Hangzhou," Yihan told me. "The Emperor and his entourage passed through Fujian and came here. That's why the women in Nan'ao are so beautiful. They are the descendants of Song nobility and their concubines."

He pointed to a sandy bay. "The beleaguered Song soldiers had been hungry after months of war and travel, so the Emperor prayed to the gods to turn the sand into rice. But a beautiful girl walked by just as the sand began to transform, distracting him. That's why Nan'ao's sand is so white. It's almost rice."

Yihan's stories blended historic fact, local legend and personal embellishment but they brought to life the magical worldview of Nan'ao. Had I been travelling alone, I would have missed them altogether. As he put it, "People come here for seafood and sunshine, and they miss all of this."

Yihan was an amateur historian, collecting black-and-white photographs of Nan'ao and comparing them with scenes of today. Back at his house he showed me letters from island natives who'd emigrated overseas. Walking through a village one afternoon, he salvaged some antique furniture discarded by unsentimental villagers.

Laoyuan was a crumbling warren of old fishing cottages populated exclusively by elderly people. The young had all left to chase their fortunes in Shantou or the Pearl River Delta.

We sat and listened to some Chaoshan opera with two fantastically wrinkled ladies busy mending fishing nets. "I like to listen to their stories," Yihan said. "It gives me inspiration for my songs. This grandma is over ninety, imagine what she has seen."

"Lots of women live to be a hundred in Nan'ao," Jiajia added. "Because the food is fresh and life is natural. But there are not so many old men because they all smoke heavily," she said, glaring at Yihan, a hopeless nicotine addict.

They say it's good to leave a place when the weather changes and I departed as a howling tempest bombarded the island. Except for some discarded plastic bags and bottles, Nan'ao's environment was in pretty good shape. Yet I wondered how long it could remain this way. During our motorbike tour of the island, we'd visited Qing'ao beach, which was already fronted by a row of McMansions. "This is the main tourist beach," Yihan had explained. Banners lining the road espoused property developer's intentions to build second homes for Guangdong's well-to-do. With the bridge's completion, Nan'ao's fate, I sensed, would be sealed. Like Shenzhen's native villagers, locals would probably sell the land and move away. The specter of development added urgency to Yihan's work, cataloguing local culture and singing about it in the Nan'ao dialect.

"You know this language is slowly dying," he'd told me. "People move out in search of work, marry people from elsewhere, settle down and their children grow up speaking Mandarin."

The rain made boarding the ferry a perilously slippery affair. As we sailed towards Shantou, I took my last look at Nan'ao, realizing this storm-pummeled islet was faced with a wave that could very easily envelop it and the centuries past: the tide of progress.

V

Old and dilapidated Chaozhou exuded far more charm than gilded Shantou and I liked it immediately. Good cities always straddle fine waterways, in Chaozhou's case, the chocolate brown River Han. Though the suburbs were composed of bleak, Soviet-style flats, the historic city center was jammed with interest. As I walked beside the maroon-colored waters, the vaporizing drizzle collecting over its surface conjured a haunting mist, which exalted the historic splendor of the wood and stone Guangji Bridge. Some of the ancient city had been renovated, and was clearly targeting sightseers, a spattering of whom shopped for handicrafts and local ginger tea, which was 'good for fevers', the sales staff all claimed. Sensing the early signs of a cold, I walked away with more ginger tea than I could reasonably carry, having been charmed by a beautiful salesgirl.

I spent the afternoon stumbling around temples, from the imposing Confucian Temple to the ethereal, candle-lit Kaiyuan Temple. But it was the maze of backstreets that proved most intriguing: row upon row of tiny shops housing artisans' businesses. Tea, porcelain, brass utensils and other locally produced items were all being hawked from shop houses. "It's a Chinese Birmingham," I jotted, recalling its 19th Century moniker, 'the city of a thousand trades'.

Were it not for the rain, I could have wandered, happily lost, until it was time to take the train. But the heavens defied my wanderlust and I took the train, my shoes sodden with the soup of puddles, my nose running like the Han River.

After nightfall, only the blur of amber street lamps was discernible beyond the carriage. Raindrops traced their way across the window, then fell into oblivion. I dreamed of CC, the Hunan girl I'd been romantically involved with, on and off, for two years. She'd been married when we met, separated from her partner, but periodically reunited. I was caught in the middle, yet also stuck outside — as *waiguo ren* (outside country people) so often were — a barbarian at the city gate, forbidden from entering the inner realm where the most intimate of Chinese affairs played out. It felt both good and bad to be away from the drama, racing across the invisible state line that separated Guangdong from Fujian. But I also feared my absence might be viewed as neglect. Afterall, it was always easier to run from your troubles. The fact you inevitably brought them with you was only remembered after dark, when you reached another alien station and sought a bed for the night.

Alighting at Xiamen North, I promptly taxied to Sanqiutian Pier. I'd booked a room on another offshore island, Gulangyu, which was far closer to the Mainland than Nan'ao. But when I arrived at the hostel desk, the staff looked at me like a cat that had just watched a rabbit disappear inside a magician's hat.

"What booking?"

With no private rooms available, I was forced to shack up in a dorm with some chatty university classmates. They had little intention of sleeping early and had wedged the window ajar for fresh air.

I awoke feeling like a mummy unearthed from a peat bog and

waited at least an hour for the winter sunlight to de-ice me.

It took several cups of ginger tea before I was able to waddle out the hostel door and attempt to locate a shop selling toiletries so I might take a shower after many days of travel with only the most rudimentary of washes.

I promptly got lost in the tangle of winding lanes. Flowers cascading from window sills perfumed narrow streets, curating a pleasant ambience for a road-weary wanderer questing after some Longliqi soap. I passed villa after villa, engendering the surreal sense that last night's train had somehow punctured the fabric of space time to deliver me to colonial Hong Kong before they built any skyscrapers.

Shops were piled high with imported Taiwanese novelties like Sun Yat-sen cigarettes and dried fish. But getting any necessities proved difficult.

"Got any shampoo?"

"You want a balloon?"

"Soap?"

"No soap, we have a shell necklace for your wife..."

The sole soap-vending convenience store, I eventually discovered, was just outside my hostel. I'd come full circle. But my early morning tour proved a blessing in disguise because when I re-emerged after a glorious shower, the island was packed with tourists streaming off the ferry like an invading Mongol horde—the curse of New Year travel confirming I was very much back on the beaten track after my musical diversions.

———∞———

Gulangyu's tourist appeal was born of European trade. In 1745, the Qianlong Emperor had introduced the 'Canton System' whereby all foreign trade would be channeled through one easy-to-manage entrepôt, namely Guangzhou (aka Canton).

The system survived almost a century until tea-addicted Great Britain, which had rectified its massive trade deficit with China by hawking Indian-grown opium, fell out with China's stifling bureaucracy. Lobbied by opium traders like William Jardine, Parliament sent in the gunboats in 1839, making short work of Chinese war junks. In 1842, the first of what China still called the 'unequal treaties' was signed in Nanjing, leading to five coastal cities being opened as treaty ports including Xiamen, or Amoy, as it was known back then. Xiamen, like other treaty ports, was divided into concessions where foreigners lived lives apart from China, puffing cigars in gentlemen's clubs, playing tennis, praying in their own churches, subject to the laws of their homeland. Gulangyu became one such surreal setting for this experiment in semi-colonialism.

Since the 1980s, the occidental architecture had made the island a huge draw for the growing numbers of happy-snapping tourists keen for a bit of foreign exoticism minus the long plane ride. I tagged along on a guided tour to get a gist of the Chinese view.

"Everyone knows the Opium War, right?" the guide asked. "Well, this was the British consulate building," he said, pointing to a red brick building bearing a Happy Year of the Horse banner. "Just up ahead is the German consulate that was built in…"

I traipsed behind the guide trying to photograph regal consulate buildings and Japanese mansions while navigating a seemingly endless human stream. Travel fatigue soon began to set in. The man flu I was coming down with—a Chaoshan-born disease that combined the symptoms of a mild cold with a heavy depression—was coloring my experience. Feeling suffocated, I retreated to a restaurant, ordered a fried rice and downed a couple of beers.

Afterwards, dazed by too much midday booze and too little

sleep, I stumbled along the coastal road lined by stall after stall of Taiwanese knickknacks. When I eventually asked why so much stuff came from Formosa, a vendor said, "Just across the water, that's Taiwan."

He was referring to an island just beyond the horizon, not quite Formosa in its entirety but Dadan, part of the Jinmen archipelago. He showed me a postcard with a close-up view. There was a white sign bearing the slogan, "Three principles of the people unite China" in traditional characters.

"Sun Yat-sen said that," he explained. Sun holds the prestigious Father of the Nation title on both sides of the strait, though his three 'mins' or principles of the people Nationalism (Minzu), Democracy (Minquan) and Well-being (Minsheng) have decidedly different interpretations depending on which side you of the strait you were standing.

"You can take a boat trip to get a closer look if you'd like," he said. "My brother works for the tour company..."

"That's OK," I told him, and stumbled back to the hostel for a long siesta.

I departed Gulangyu early the next morning for Xiamen. This had been the original location of foreign settlement, as a few old buildings attested, though, as Xiamen pioneer Revered P.W. Pitcher wrote in *In and about Amoy*, the first expats didn't last long. "There are streets so narrow that you cannot carry an umbrella," he complained. And added, "Several well-defined and distinct stenches greet the sense of smell at every step." Indeed, it was the city's notorious filth — or a Western perception of squalor — that prompted the imperial interlopers to retreat to offshore Gulangyu.

Conversely, the roads I walked were broad and long. Although the 'well-defined and distinct stenches' of modern China, namely gutter oil, construction materials and petrol fumes, pervaded the streets, I was grateful for the space.

I wandered up the main commercial drag, Zhongshan Road. It was noticeably affluent compared with Chaozhou, ordered when compared with Shantou. But the shops were uninteresting chain stores selling mass-produced garments. Halfway down the road a screen had been erected airing a black and white 'Red' movie: early socialist realism propagated on a road with at least two McDonald's.

Across town, the Overseas Chinese Museum proved to be a gushing exhibition of Chinese heroic efforts abroad, with one point of interest: "In 1881, Canada constructed the longest railway that traversed the North American continent. Among the 17,000 Chinese roadmen, more than 4,000 laid down their lives for this construction project." It reminded me that while railway development stalled at home, Chinese coolies traveled from ports like Xiamen to construct the great railroads of the 19th Century, including the American Transcontinental Railway that helped forge and define the territory of the United States, and the Trans-Siberian that did the same for Russia.

Walking back towards Zhongshan Road, I stumbled upon a disused railway track that had been turned into a pedestrian path of sorts, connecting some lovely public gardens festooned with flowers and hissing with bugs. I decided to follow it, just to see where I'd end up.

Eventually, the track came to Hongshan Tunnel, a subterranean passage-turned-gallery chronicling Chinese railway history. It covered the evolution of the railway from the import of steam trains from the USA, Russia and Japan, through the East Wind diesel locomotive age, before concluding with the contemporary high-speed rail era

Unclear whether life was imitating art or vice versa, after I'd walked a few kilometers further, I caught sight of old locomotives parked on an adjacent track. It was great to get up close with these handsomely painted workhorses of Red China. Further ahead, I could see a high-speed train nosing its way out of a station. I ask a passing female soldier where I'd arrived at, exactly.

"That's Xiamen Station," she said.

There was a legion of migrant workers busily expanding the building, presumably to cater to the increase in high-speed rail traffic. Even the pedestrianized railway line I was following didn't quite finish. It just blended with the station's tracks in a messy and incomplete manner. As was so often the case in China, it was a work in progress, with no clear end in sight.

FAST TRAIN TO YESTERDAY

I

With a first-quarter moon still holding its own in the pale morning sky, I digested the imposing sight of Beijing West Station. It was planned in the 1950s, though only completed decades later, once the country had emerged from the chaos of the Mao-era. Evidently, architects were feeling nostalgic for the trappings of civilization vandalized during the Cultural Revolution, as the towering structure was crowned with some elaborate Ming roofing.

Inside, the station felt more like an ant colony than a Ming palace as Chinese summer vacationers rushed about, shepherding children and talking loudly. Many were evidently bound for Lhasa or Sanya, exotic tourist favorites at the very ends of railways.

Browsing the souvenirs stands, I stumbled into a veritable museum of ornamental tea flasks shelved beside bags of premade Peking duck and golden talismans bearing portraits of Party leaders. One store was vending kids' toys including a baby doll that crawled to the soundtrack of *Little Apple*, the hit pop song produced by the Chopstick Brothers.

"How much is the musical *wawa*?" I asked the saleswoman.

"Twenty-two kuai," she replied enthusiastically.

"I'll give you fifteen," I said.

"No, twenty-two is the lowest price, come on, handsome brother, buy one for your girlfriend…"

I had to admire her tenacity, even if a gift that weird would certainly be the death knell of any relationship. It's hard to imagine manufacturing something so absurd, though if you could imagine it, someone somewhere in China was making it. In the famous travelogue *Riding the Iron Rooster* (1988) Paul Theroux observed "the Chinese were perfecting a technique for making-do and mending," a sentiment that haunted me, for a country that had long been the analogue of thriftiness had become a place of such wasteful abundance that a doll with an MP3 player in its belly was on sale for less than the price of a pint of beer in Wales.

———∞∞———

My move north had been prompted by the breakdown of my relationship with CC in the south. I adapted quickly to capital life, finding a flat-share overlooking the ancient heart of the city. When at home, I slipped into the life of a hutong weasel, frequenting the boozy rock dives and hipster cafés that dotted downtown. But guidebook jobs and travel magazine assignments frequently drew me back into the provinces by train.

China railways were assuming a grander form in my mind, something more than just means to get around and see the country. The previous year, I'd travelled to Hainan Island aboard the Z201. Just past Guangzhou, it changed track and at the coast, enshrouded in darkness, the carriages were uncoupled and shunted onto a ferry. I crossed the Qiongzhou Strait sitting on a second-class railway bunk bed eating a pot noodle. On the north shore of Hainan, the train carriages were promptly coupled back together, before completing the journey to Sanya some thirty-eight hours from its departure point in wintery Beijing.

While dipping my toes in the warm, jade-colored waters of the South China Sea, I'd thought about how a humble Chinese train had taken me from the frozen central plains to an island; from China's heartlands to its southern frontier; from temperate to torpid latitudes—traversing "the many China's of China" my friend, the author Murong, often spoke of, along the way—worlds within worlds, all wired together by the iron road.

This epiphany evolved further when hiking in Hunan Province amidst the pillar rock formations of Zhangjiajie National Forest Park. Atop a towering karst peak, I encountered a chirpy Scotsman who, gazing at the otherworldly vista, observed, "This really is the country of superlatives, isn't it?"

Back in Beijing, I vowed to expand the scope of my quest: to see how the land of big numbers translated into the railway travel experience: to ride her longest, fastest, oldest and slowest trains just to see where they took me, and whom I'd meet on and off the rails.

The statistics of China's railway network were, of course, mind-boggling, which made the country from the perspective of *waiguo*—the outside—look megalith. But from *guonei*—the inside—it could conversely feel intimate, a billion bursting souls, each with a story to tell. These dualities seemed to converge on Chinese railways, the national arteries feeding all the organs of this complex, multifaceted beast. Statistics measured in track length or kilometers-an-hour told one thing about China, while the man in the third row of the second carriage of provincial train service could speak of quite another. It was the incongruity of it all that so tickled my travel bone.

A loudspeaker announcing the train's impending departure awoke me from my ruminations. After the ritual pushing and shoving that preceded any Chinese railway journey, I slumped into my allotted seat. The train was soon imbued with the scent of a thousand different pot noodle flavors as we cruised out of the capital, passing a locomotive dragging a caravan of green carriages heading in the opposite direction.

The old train was a reminder the Harmony class I was travelling on was very much a newbie. Construction of the original Beijing-Guangzhou (Jingguang) railway, which the high-speed line traced, had been prioritized after the Sino-Japanese War in 1895. From 1897 to 1905, French and Belgian firms hastily completed the Beijing-Hankou (Beihan) section. But due to diplomatic wrangling, fiscal woes and political tumult, the Guangzhou-Hankou (Yuehan) section was constructed at a snail's pace, completed only in 1936.

The original north–south line might have taken forty years but China moves faster these days. Construction of the Jingguangshen high-speed line had begun in 2009 and opened in sections every few years since. The line already connected Beijing with Shenzhen via 2,000kilometers of high-speed track, the equivalent of a fast train linking New York with Miami in little over eight hours. And as of 2019, the line would be extended to connect Hong Kong to Harbin, creating the longest high-speed rail corridor anywhere in the world.

Hebei Province was soon rushing past the window as we raced towards Henan at over 300kilometers an hour. The twin provinces north and south of the Yellow River covered much of the region known as *Zhongyuan*, the central plain. This was the hallowed land that birthed Chinese civilization, although a casual observer wouldn't know it from the vantage point of the carriage windows. The view was yellow in color as we whizzed by endless wheat and cornfields. There was little wildlife visible and irrigation ditches bubbled with the run off of chemical fertilizer. Tellingly, few spent their summer holidays roaming these parts, a pity perhaps, as the plain is dotted with enough historical wonders to rival Egypt or Greece. The state-run newspaper *China Daily* had just published an article listing the ten most important archeological finds of the previous year, and six of them were from *Zhongyuan* ranging from Tang-era salt-boiling sites in Huanghua city to a massive royal tomb in the ancient capital of Luoyang dating back 2,600 years.

As I was enroute to Hong Kong to promote a guidebook I'd helped pen about Luoyang, I felt a certain solidarity with the flatlands we were traversing.

Notwithstanding the eons of human habitation recorded here, the landscape was unrelentingly monotonous from Shijiazhuang to Zhengzhou, as if somebody has made a sepia film of a field and cut it into a loop. Only the blur of villages aroused my attention, brown brick farmsteads organized into uneven rows between maize and soya bean plantations. I could distinguish feral dogs; there were people wearing overalls driving blue motor-trikes burdened with more hay than you could legally fit inside a middle-sized British lorry. These were the fifty percent, the poor men and women tasked with feeding the rest of the billion, yet we seldom intruded on their domain; high-speed trains were bound for cities, not villages.

Like the moon orbiting the earth, it served China well to operate a two-speed economy—two parallel worlds, one indentured to the other. When not growing food, the poor labored for the urban rich, building their tower blocks and laying their railway tracks, infrastructure that was organized like 19th Century European colonies, ensuring that 'never the twain shall meet'. Rural and urban China were such distinct entities that when Chinese peasants were contracted to labor in the cities they were referred to as 'migrants' just as Eastern Europeans in the UK or South Americans in the US. The household registration system made sure this apartheid was even legislated, marking people from birth as either a rural or an urban Red subject.

For a traveler like myself, this class segregation made the

prospect of leaping the great divide to visit Ah Lan's home village enticing, and it was to this unknown destination—not the familiarities of Hong Kong—that my thoughts drifted.

Ah Lan was the wife of Long-haired Wu, my *xiongdi* or 'brother', which in Confucian terms meant we're bound by a lifelong pledge to help one another. We'd met years before in Ping Pong Space, a French-run live house in Guangzhou where Long-haired Wu had been performing classic Chinese rock numbers.

After the set, Wu introduced me to his family, his ex-model wife Ah Lan who towered over both us, and their son Liaoliao, who, at the tender age of three, was already serving a rock n roll apprenticeship in bars where his father performed. We quickly bonded, the beginning of an enduring friendship, and a few years later they honored me by making me the godfather—*gandie*—to their second son Diandian.

Just before I moved back to Beijing, Long-haired Wu relocated the family to the Songzhuang Art Colony on the eastern outskirts of the capital. But the poor air quality of the north prompted Ah Lan to take the kids south for the summer.

I asked if she fancied some beach time in Shenzhen.

"I'll buy the ice cream."

But she had other plans.

"Actually, I need to take the boys back to my home village, you couldn't help could you? Managing the two of them on my own is really difficult, they are so naughty."

I agreed willingly to a Jiangxi Province vacation.

"Great. It will be amazing; you'll probably be the first foreigner to set foot in my home village."

As we rolled into Hebei Province across the Jianghan plain, I noticed electricity pylons, phone lines, expressways and railways all flowed towards the provincial capital Wuhan like rivers feeding a mighty lake. The tri-city appeared truly monstrous on our approach, a goliath of new China.

A hundred years ago *Colliers Magazine* dubbed the Wuhan tri-city area 'The Chicago of China' for its prodigious industrial output. This was manifest in acrid pollution exacerbated by the soul-sapping heat, as Wuhan, Chongqing and Nanjing were known as the Yangtze River's three 'cauldrons'.

The double-decker Wuhan Yangtze River Bridge completed in 1957 and glimpsed as we journeyed south, re-enforced Wuhan's image as the buckle on China's proverbial waistband where its two halves — the rice-growing south and wheat-growing north — ostensibly met.

Indeed, the saying 'all roads lead to Rome' could be easily be Sinicized if you substituted 'Rome' with 'Wuhan'. For though the central plain was China's cultural center, this was the real middle of the Middle Kingdom.

Some way past the Hunan border, the train rocked me to sleep. I snoozed my way around Dongting Lake and through Yueyang, only peeling my eyes open again when we arrived in Changsha South Station.

After my ritual stroll on the platform, I returned to my seat to enjoy the scenery of the Nanling Mountains that had long separated Guangdong Province from the rest of China. The train burst through this terrific mountain range into lush forests, overhanging limestone karst hills and deep gorges — a world apart from the monoculture of the central plain. The land was untamed and primitive. A village of antiquated stone cottages that was organized around an ancestral hall and fishpond caught my eye. Two banyan trees flanking the settlement. As if to complete an image usually embossed on a Ming teapot, a farmer wearing a bamboo hat was working the land. He didn't even look up at the fast train rocketing by. I wondered if he ever did.

HARMONY EXPRESS

II

Hong Kong days raced by like a neon-hued typhoon. I made it to my designated venue to talk up Luoyang and hawk a few guidebooks. But between handshakes, book signings, business card exchanges, hits of caffeine, shots of alcohol and sobering laps of the hotel pool, my mind's eye kept focusing on the promise of that other China, not 'The Mainland' Hongkongers spoke of with varying degrees of suspicion, but the vast arcadian expanse that persisted beyond the clamor of modern megacities, *Nongcun*— the countryside.

Having seen friends, and stocked up on books in Kowloon, I boarded the border-bound train at Central, crossing the Lo Wu border at sundown, before busing the remainder of the way to a satellite town east of the Pearl River Delta's rolling sprawl to rendezvous with Ah Lan.

Like Shenzhen North, Huizhou South Station was oversized and architecturally devoid of place or meaning. Modern Chinese power architecture. The capacious interior, however, was easily repurposed as a football pitch. The sight of a foreigner running back and forth in the company of two mini-Johnny Ramones, Diandian, a four-year-old, and Liaoliao at nine, didn't quite mesh with the general scene. Staid Chinese men seldom played games with their kids. Instead, they stared. There was even a term *weiguan* which combined the character 'enclose' with the character 'to look' to describe the national habit of encircling something out of the ordinary and gawking. Yet the kids ignored the spectators and we burned off some serious energy before the announcement to board the D2322 called full time on the match.

"Come on!" called Ah Lan who was dragging suitcases brimming with the belongings of three human beings, in addition to presents for the family — bags of dried figs, rice cakes, a portable radio for her dad — essential in a culture where gift-giving was sacrosanct. It was an eye-opener for a bachelor accustomed to wandering the back provinces with just a backpack for company.

Once settled, the train began racing eastwards towards Chaoshan following the same line I'd taken through Guangdong when visiting the folk band Wu Tiao Ren and singer Li Yihan. Diandian was going through a stage in his development that prompted him to climb over everything, the carriage chairs, the luggage racks and principally, me, so it was a relief to know I'd seen the scenery before, as I wouldn't be seeing much this time around.

"Do-do-do," he said, climbing my shoulders, "why is your nose so big?"

"So I can smell you in the dark."

He swung upside down, hanging off my arm like Spiderman.

"Do-do-do, why are your eyes so round?"

"So I can find you when you run away."

This intellectual discourse continued until—after umpteen bags of sunflower seeds, nuts, crisps, chocolate biscuits, spillages, trips to the bathroom to wash faces, trips to the bathroom to wash hands, trips to the bathroom to pee, trips to the hot water dispenser, trips for the sake of trips, periodic tantrums, apologies to nearby passengers, and further apologies to nearby passengers—both children fell into unconsciousness so serene it was as if the batteries had been removed from a baby doll that crawled to the soundtrack of *Little Apple*.

In the absence of infant diversions, all was amplified: the purr of the train wheels, the aroma of spicy dried tofu and hot tea. We'd left Guangdong and were now looping through Longyan county in southern Fujian Province. It was a Hakka stronghold famous for its donut-shaped fortress villages known as Tulou. American intelligence had once mistaken the Tulou for missile installations, but beyond the window there was little to evoke the specter of competing superpowers. This was the realm of Fujian's famous tea groves bound to the folds of the hills in an image that seemed rendered by *Shennong*, the god of agriculture, for our viewing pleasure.

I noticed Ah Lan casting her eyes far beyond the passing scenery.

"The kids are asleep," I told her. "Are you looking forward to seeing your family?"

"I miss them so much; I was so young when I left home for Shenzhen and so much time has passed. I should go back more often."

"How old were you when you left?"

"Sixteen, I followed my older brother down south, he found me a job in a factory making DVD players."

"How was that?"

"It was awful, so tiring, the machines were dangerous and the boss was really cruel."

"I never knew you'd been a factory girl."

"It was my first job in the big city, but the whole time I missed my home village, you'll see, it's so beautiful there. I've never felt bad about growing up in the countryside, for me it was the happiest time."

"How long did you work in the factory?"

"Two years. At least until I met a man who said I was tall and good looking, he helped me get better work."

"Doing what?"

Ah Lan turned from the window to face me: "Have you seen those girls standing outside fancy hotels and restaurants clapping?"

"Yes," I replied, thinking of the made-up country lasses in long red dresses employed to lure male clientele into venues, a bold expression, if ever there was one, of China's bottomless human well.

"Well that was me, way back then, at least before I met Long-haired Wu."

"How did you two meet again?"

"I was modelling at an event; he was performing with his band. He saw me on the catwalk and, you know, he only dates tall girls. He told his friends. 'I'm going to get her'. At first I didn't like him, he never washed his clothes and smelled bad but slowly he wooed me, well, I was only twenty-one, he was this big city guy."

"And you've been together ever since."

Reflections of her past turn Ah Lan's eyes glassy. I can't tell how she feels: regretful, nostalgic, fortunate, all of the above. She shakes her mind free of cobwebs. "That was a long time ago," she said, mustering a half-smile.

We alighted at Nanfeng Station just as the southern sky was turning amber with the sunset to welcome us to a county known by the excellent moniker *juzicheng* – Tangerine Town, on account of its principal crop.

After a late dinner at a roadside barbeque restaurant, we procured a car from Ah Lan's half-sister for the final leg of the journey, which took us from the main road onto an unlit, potholed track.

"If it were daytime, you could see the mountains," Ah Lan said, clearly nervous about what impression her remote home village would make on me. But beyond the window, there was only a draft of plants scents and intermittent hoots of night animals pervading the varying shades of darkness. She, of course, could have no idea how happy I was, to know what a coup I felt I'd pulled off just to have eluded the city limits for

HARMONY EXPRESS

Nowheresville, Jiangxi Province, PRC.

Ah Lan's parents were waiting up for us as we stumbled into the village, sleepy children in tow. There was little outward emotion as the family was reunited. As typical in Confucian culture, the unsaid words sounded the loudest.

"How are you, Xiao Fei?" inquired Ah Lan's mother Yu Sifeng, pouring me stewed green tea while pushing cigarettes and snacks in my direction.

"Tired," replied her father Cheng Chaoxian, on my behalf.

Cousin Maomao, the six-year-old daughter of Ah Lan's brother, was asleep on a downstairs bed, so we talked for a few minutes in low voices before I was shown to my room.

The next morning, the sun climbed over a nearby hill and began cooking my bare skin, forcing me to get up.

Blank walls confronted me, jazzed up by a peeling poster of Taiwanese girl group S.H.E. There was a noisy electric fan, probably manufactured in the 1980s, but little else of material value.

Finding my clothes, I stumbled downstairs and out into the light of the day. On both sides of the narrow stone street, the residents of New River village were already wide awake, working away in small groups, peeling the skin from marble-ball sized lotus seeds while gossiping merrily in a dialect from Mars. More than the change in environment, the first thought in my languid brain was how jovial everyone was compared with big city denizens, exchanging a currency of laughter and smiles across the narrow cobbled-stoned passage that constitutes the main street.

"Come help, Xiao Fei," said Ah Lan, who was sitting with her parents in the doorway, as I imagined she'd sat as a child. She showed me how to break the lotus head and remove the edible pearls from the green seed pods, which ones to keep and which to discard and how to peel away the thin layer of film before placing the seeds to soak in a bucket of water. It took me around two minutes to peel one, while the villagers nimbly picked through the pile in seconds.

"We don't eat these, we can sell them for a lot of money," Ah Lan explained. "Restaurants in Beijing and Shanghai serve up Nanfeng's lotus seeds. They're famous. They're used in traditional medicine too. Did you know they can cure impotence? My mother says she can cook up a batch for lunch just so you can try them," she added.

"Do you think I have difficulties in the bedroom department?"

"Haha, no, Silly, I mean they make you more virile," she said, flexing her arm to demonstrate, "and they help boost longevity."

"Sounds great, I certainly don't want to die young," I said, realizing that even in the remotest corner of the Middle Kingdom, the old Confucian maxim, "How delightful it is to have friends visit from afar," implied I would be spoiled.

When I inquired the whereabouts of the toilet, Ah Lan warned, "This will take some getting used to," and led me down a path at the edge of a paddy field to a small outhouse that smelled as if it hadn't been cleaned since the Tang Dynasty. It was buzzing with flies and baked by the summer sun into something resembling a poor man's sauna.

"You have tissues, right?" she called.

"I'm fine," I replied, though a garden hose and rubber gloves would have been far more suited than a handful of pocket-worn Kleenex. There was no light except for a few shafts of sunlight between the wooden boards, which made positioning one's bottom over a wooden hole some meters above a steaming pit of feces quite tasking. All manner of creepy-crawlies were nipping at me and when I removed my t-shirt so as not to overheat, the snacking became a banquet. The outhouse doubled as a tool shed and when I attempted to leave, I managed a short scuffle with a rake while my left shoe got stuck in a significant mound of animal dung.

When I reappeared into the fresh morning air, I was filled with a sense of relief and achievement. Time would tell whether I'd contracted Japanese encephalitis, an incurable brain swelling pathogen endemic to damp paddy fields in rural East Asia, but at least I'd made it out alive.

This sense of elation dissolved when I noticed a man wearing a bamboo hat, a cigarette dangling from his lower lip, eyeing me like someone confronting an alien who had just crashed a spaceship into his chicken coop. I was as red-faced as the war god Guan Yu, tattooed by insect bites and glistening with sweat.

It was wretched to consider that I might well be the first European this poor farmer had ever laid eyes upon and I suddenly realized why the British had felt the need to invent the 'stiff upper lip', particularly as they explored and conquered remote corners of the world, when, presumably, moments like this were commonplace.

Mustering a sense of imperiousness, I said, "Good morning," purposefully before putting on my t-shirt backwards and strolling back up the slope to Ah Lan and her gaggle of lotus seed-peelers.

———∽∽———

"There you are Xiao Fei," said Ah Lan, "come on let's go to Purple Cloud township. It's not far, they have a market every three or four days."

"Why every three or four days?"

"It depends on the moon."

Purple Cloud township was the local hub. There was market where rows of vegetable stalls vended the eclectic mix of edible plants that only the Chinese could glean from the land, outside the local post office and school. Ah Lan stopped to chat with every Tang, Deng and Hali she encountered. There was a real sense of a homecoming, the customary 'long time no see' greeting echoing around the marketplace. Each conversation hinged on the well-being of family.

"Hey, Xiao Fei, meet my second cousin," Ah Lan said, "and this is my maternal great aunt, and this is my third brother and this is our neighbor but I call him second uncle..." Everyone we encountered was either a blood relative or special family friend and after five minutes I was entirely lost as to who related to whom and how.

"Is this Long-haired Wu?" asked one old-timer, earnestly.

Ah Lan broke down in laughter. "Hey, Xiao Fei, they think you're my husband."

I had to wonder how much I resemble a middle-aged Sichuanese ink painter, before realizing these people simply saw what they wanted to. A foreigner was, perhaps, unimaginable, but everyone knew Ah Lan married a weird-looking outsider.

III

I fell into a gentle routine in New River village. While I wrote my diary in my room, Diandian would seek me out either to remove money from my pockets for sweets, or to rest his head on my chest and promptly pass out, exhausted from playing. It was a patent reminder of how free and feral children could be in the right setting. Diandian, Liaoliao and cousin Maomao disappeared on their bicycles for hours on end without arousing any parental concern, in a country where child abduction, was a real issue, with around 70,000 kidnapped each year, due, in part, to a traditional preference for boys. Unlike Chinese city kids, the trio enjoyed essential experiences, like water fights with the neighborhood children or pitching in with fun farm chores.

Some mornings I sat with Ah Lan's dad Cheng Chaoxian and drank tea on the portico. He was a tall man, with sunken shoulders and a sun-browned head lined by years of toil in the fields. His posture was of someone who long ago saw the futility in arguing with the world.

"Were you born here in New River village?" I asked him, imagining he'd spent his whole life on that very porch.

"Oh no, no, I was born far away, in Chengjia village in Zhejiang Province just six years after liberation," he said, applying the Party's preferred euphemism for their victory, as if it marked Year One in the reign of Emperor Mao. Which, I suppose, it did.

"Then why did you move here?"

"We had no choice. In 1969, they built a dam and flooded our ancestral homeland, so we all moved to Jiangxi together, the whole village. That's why people from the other villages call us *Old Zhejiang;* we don't speak their dialect."

"That's true," interceded Ah Lan, "I was born here. I've never lived in Zhejiang and I still can't speak the dialect. It's always hard for me to explain to people I meet outside where I come from when I speak Zhejiangnese but my household residency card says 'Jiangxi'."

"We built this place ourselves," continued Cheng, "every brick was put down by one of us, now the young are leaving to work in the city. With this generation, the village will die."

I couldn't help but associate New River village with a Marquez's Macondo. It was a place that was just fifty years old yet it felt like it had been there forever. Day-to-day life was largely removed from the wider-world beyond the bamboo-coated hills, but somehow, I sensed the fragility of rural life, too, a feeling that this could all be blown away like dust in the wind should the powers-that-be deem it necessary.

"What was it like here during the Cultural Revolution?" I asked.

"I've seen leaders come and go but they don't affect us much, we're poor, who cares about us, who cares about this place?" I wondered how genuine his answer was but saw little reason in attempting to unearth whatever sorrows Cheng may or may not have buried.

Ah Lan took me to visit some of the local scenic spots, first an isolated lagoon where I swam, "Better than a shower," she called from the lakeside, then Gelian Rock, a bulbous set of sandstone karst rock formations that protruded from the surrounding forests like giant tomatoes in a celestial salad bowl.

As we ascended the hillside, Ah Lan imagined out loud what tourism could do for Nanfeng county. "We could build guesthouses like in Yangshuo and Dali and take people hiking, show them the real China. Do you think foreigners would like to come?"

"Of course they would, this place is stunning," I replied, though in my heart I knew what tourism-with-Chinese-characteristics would do to the place, shuddering at the thought of grand resorts supplanting the bamboo groves and wild places.

Soft evenings were spent wandering along the river's edge where the local aunties did their exercises to the accompaniment of Mandopop jazzed up with a dance beat.

But it was the canopy of stars hanging in the night sky that attracted me most and I spent so much time looking at them I strained my neck muscles.

"What are you doing?" asked Ah Lan.

"The cosmos, we seldom see any of it in Shenzhen or Beijing," I replied, arching my back like a wannabe yogi.

"Look at the moon."

"Huge, isn't it?" I said, my head still tilted at as close to 90 degrees as my spinal cord would reasonably allow. "It feels so close."

"No, Silly! Down here," she said, gesturing to the river.

She was right, the orb's reflection was shimmering in the water, recalling a popular image in Tang poetry, particularly that of Li Bai's: "*Below the moon a heavenly mirror, While clouds unite to raise a mirage,*" he wrote in *Saying Goodbye to Jiangmen*. And, "*While the autumn moon falls into the waves of the river. What can you do as the east is turning white?*" concluded *Tune of Raven's Perch*.

According to legend, Li Bai was said to have died while drunkenly trying to scoop the moon from the Yangtze River, and although this was an unlikely end, the image of the moon as a sacred beacon signposting destiny was a seductively romantic one.

We sat down by the water's edge from where Ah Lan threw pebbles that cast waves across the yellow orb in the water. Gradually, she grew pensive: "*Nongmin* is an insult in China but I always admit I'm a peasant. Why try to hide it? I feel so fortunate to have grown up here, I learned a great deal from the land: I took care of the pigs, chickens and the buffalo. I was a real country gal with a good reputation for hard work."

The buffalo were gone, replaced by noisy motor-ploughs but much else remained as it had been when Ah Lan was younger, unchanged in a country hell-bent on changing.

"Sometimes I wish I could come back, I love it here, the air is clear and the people are so friendly. But my husband can't bear it, he thinks they are all hicks."

By her own admission, Ah Lan didn't get much formal education but when we walked in the meadows, she proved quite the expert.

"That's *yecai*," she said pointing to some fern, "you can fry it up with garlic and it's good for your health... don't touch that plant, it looks good but it's poisonous..."

I found myself behaving like a Boy Scout, curious about the former owner of the snakeskin drying on the path between the paddies and fascinated by the butterflies, bats, frogs and especially the birds we encountered, the purple heron and graceful cattle egrets. I was also a touch envious of Ah Lan's rural ease when compared with my clumsiness. As a child of suburbia, I felt as ill-equipped for country life as I was in the urban jungle. Perhaps that's why I became a wandering scribe, destined to bounce from one to the other.

Before we'd left Beijing, Long-haired Wu had warned me, "My wife comes from a village where the road ends, there's nothing beyond it," and he was right. I liked the place all the better for its isolation. It wasn't just another kind of place but another kind of time.

IV

Gua Huazai, a family friend of local Jiangxi stock, swung by the Cheng household to drop off some vegetables and we got chatting. He was plump and bald like a laughing Buddha, if only the Lord of Light sported a bold red New York City t-shirt. He'd spent time working as a security guard in various east coast cities and was quite well-informed, if a touch self-effacing.

"You must come by for dinner," Ah Lan said. Everyone who passed through New River got an invite, but Huazai accepted, arriving later with a bottle of grain liquor under his arm that was labeled 40 proof.

"It's hard being back home," he told me over dinner and periodic shots of firewater, "my parents are giving me a lot of hassle about being unmarried, my mother is ashamed, Chinese parents just want grandkids."

"Huazai is like you, Xiao Fei," Ah Lan said, "unlucky in love."

"Can't find the right one, aye? I know the feeling," I commiserated.

"I have nothing to offer, no education, no real skills, just two hands," he complained, waving his giant paws at me. "In China, there are more men than women, especially in the countryside, so who's going to go for me?"

We drank to romantic misfortune and though much of the evening was lost in the befuddlement of boozy babble, I must have asked Huazai to take me hiking as he returned the following day with his motorbike and a plastic bag containing two bottles of water.

"Come on, I'll show you the local variety of bamboo."

I was a bit unsteady after the night's liquor session but couldn't very well decline a venture that I had sought.

The mystical strain of bamboo the locals talked about was a real curiosity. When I'd been a university student of Chinese, I'd read an essay about a man who, seeing bamboo scaffolding withstand a typhoon in Hong Kong, became obsessed with the plant, a type of grass. He went on to discover the plethora of traditional purposes for bamboo, as furniture and housing, ornaments and clothing, food and medicine. The article seeded an interest I'd maintained over the years and every time I stumbled upon an article about bamboo—admittedly not very often—I'd read it, cultivating an archive of facts to bore barflies in any expat pub.

"I bought a pair of socks made of bamboo in Suzhou," I yelled at Huazai as we motor-biked between a sea of rippling rice.

"Oh really?"

"Yes, and a bamboo toothbrush. You should get one, they're biodegradable."

His mute reply suggested disinterest. "Bamboo is the only grass to adapt to a forest environment, it is the world's fastest-growing plant, scientists have recorded 92cm a day... Did you know a giant panda can eat up to 20 kilograms of bamboo in 24 hours?"

We crossed the valley and passed Huazai's house, a wooden structure overlooking a ravine, looking like a hillbilly home in the Appalachians, complete with a porch for a dungaree-wearing uncle to play his banjo. His father was at home and we were introduced, before pressing forward to dirt tracks where we left the bike and continued on foot.

Back at New River village, the houses had been made with tamped earth and wooden beams holding the structure in place much like the Tudor style. Many had been painted white and looked quite picturesque. But amongst the hills, people were living in rotten wooden dwellings, "homes scarcely fit for swine," as Long-haired Wu described them when narrating his wife's origins.

"The Zhejiang folk down in the valley have better houses than we do, because Zhejiang is more prosperous than Jiangxi," Huazai explained of the local class system.

Every household we passed invited us in for tea and cigarettes. Often Huazai had to translate as many didn't speak Mandarin with any fluency.

Outside, one village we came upon a stream channeling through a deep gorge, our path flanked by forest. It was as humid as the Devil's own Turkish bath and I suggested we should probably turn back, sweat having doubled the weight of my clothing.

"Keep going, up ahead there's the special bamboo grove I want to show you. I know you love bamboo."

We struggled until we come upon a vast forest of bamboo shoots as tall as houses and swaying in the hilltop breeze like a crowd swaying to a love song.

"Take a look at our special bamboo," Huazai suggested, holding a shoot back and welcoming me into the woods as if it were a VIP suite.

Superficially, the bamboo looked like any you might see in rural south China, but on closer inspection I saw it was striped several shades of yellow, brown and green. It was a beautiful pattern, testament to the limitless expressions nature can conjure.

"We call this seven-colors bamboo," Huazai said proudly, placing his hands on his hips and beaming like a Bodhisattva.

I stepped amongst the giant grass trees and tried to take a moment to experience what the Japanese refer to as Shinrin Yoku, 'forest bathing'. I absorbed the earthy scent of the woods. The bamboo grew in dense clusters that creaked loudly when they swayed and drowned out the sun just a few steps from the perimeter. Only splashes of light helped guide my passage. Spider webs bridged the patterned bamboo shoots while the ground was layered with multi-storied moss and fungi. Large ants were on the march carrying leaves and twigs, while overhead birds chattered amongst the swaying leaves of the bamboo canopy. The architecture was incredible, every niche filled, like a Shenzhen of the natural world, with each individual playing a minute role in maintaining an economy that reached from the earth to the heavens.

V

Ah Lan was on edge. "I'm worried about my father," she confided in me. "He goes off, sometimes for a whole day with just two steamed buns. My mother is concerned too. He never stops working, doing this and that, even when there's nothing to do and he should rest. They're too old to be farmers now, I wish we had some money to give them."

"When will the tangerines be ready?" I inquired.

"Harvest isn't until September."

"Tell them I want to come back and help out with fruit picking."

A loud laugh burst from her. "You'd be no help at all, I saw you with the lotus seeds."

"That's an unfair comparison, citrus fruits are much easier to pick."

"Tangerines worry me, too," Ah Lan continued, "There's a lot of corruption in China's fruit market, the middlemen squeeze the farmers, the market is saturated and if you don't sell them soon enough, they go off."

I had nothing to console her with but a sympathetic smile.

To avoid any tantrums, we didn't tell the children we were leaving. With bags packed, we bade farewell to Sifeng and Chaoxian.

"Come again," said Ah Lan's mother, with unfaltering warmth.

"Don't worry, I'll be back to help out with the tangerines," I falsely assured her.

By the time we got to the car, Ah Lan was crying. I realized that while I'd been on an adventure, she'd been on an emotional trip of her own, with worries running as deep as the village well. Despite my affection for the area, the poverty the villagers lived with couldn't be overlooked. The tangerines and lotus seeds were destined for city supermarkets, while modern services like healthcare or education were all but absent. There was never any money about. When one of the villagers had read out loud a wanted poster offering financial rewards for suspected criminals, I was made aware, not just of how lawless China's countryside can be, but also how uneducated it is, as he was reading it to his illiterate kin. And while I'd marveled at the abundant wildlife, the farmers complained the protected birds were eating their crops.

We didn't speak as the car crept away into the darkness. I noticed the moon above was shrinking again.

"Thanks," Ah Lan said, eventually.

"For what?"

"For coming here."

"All I did was hang out and eat other people's food."

"It was nice."

"Come on," I said, "it's been a privilege. Anyway, best focus on the road ahead. We've got a train to catch."

LONG HAUL TO THE HOLY HILLS

I

In the centre of a roundabout a large billboard poster boldly proclaimed, "Changchun: Driving Northeast China". This was China's Motown, an epithet drawn from the local motor industry rather than its rhythm n blues scene. The wheels started turning in 1956 when four-ton Soviet-style Liberation trucks began rolling off the assembly line at Changchun's First Automobile Works, heralding a new automotive era. Predictably, like so many new eras communism had been charged with curating, China's automobile industry stalled like a Hillman Imp with some dodgy battery cables. Progress had been glacial until the 1980s when the Party powerful began sweet-talking foreign car companies to sign-up for joint ventures. A potential billion new gas-guzzlers was an enticing prospect for wolfish auto executives, even though few Chinese could afford their own set of wheels back then.

Twenty years later, when I rolled into China, "The Bicycle Kingdom" moniker was still splashed across tourist t-shirts while Katie Melua's chart-topping refrain, "There are nine-million bicycles in Beijing," was on radio playlists. Yet this two-wheeled world wasn't destined to last much longer. In 2008 China's auto industry surpassed America's to become the world's largest and though per capita ownership still lagged far behind, Chinese consumers became almost as car-crazy as their counterparts across the Pacific. As skies blackened with yet more smog, few put two and two together. Owning a nice motor became so important as to be deemed prerequisite to marriage, a sentiment expressed by Ma Nuo, a contestant on the television dating show *If you are the one*, who, when asked by a prospective suitor if she'd like to "ride on a bicycle with me", responded, "I would rather cry in a BMW than smile on a bicycle." Tellingly, Changchun's First Automobile Works no longer produced cumbersome trucks but Volkswagens, Audis and Toyotas, as well as some suspiciously derivative models of its own.

The streets of Jilin Province's car-loving capital were laid out in straight lines and right angles. For the automotive-class of Changchuner, these prosaic boulevards offered ideal terrain to cruise around in their Wind Rover SUVs. But for a lone traveler, one who believes you must walk a city to get acquainted with it, Changchun was paved to hell. It was so devoid of reference points than even in a grid-planned city, I managed to get lost. No matter where I walked, dusty tea shops and 'happy ending' spas were all I encountered. On every second road, I negotiated pavements soaked with brake fluid as grease-stained mechanics hunched beneath the bonnet of a Trumpchi or a Chery QQme, while comparably greasy eateries dished up brunches to late-risers.

I veered from the main thoroughfares in vain hopes of stumbling upon something to kindle my interest. But if the streets weren't clogged with cars, they were potholed and flanked by rundown tenements. The pavements were in terrible shape, presumably because everyone parked on them. Electricity wires dangled from crooked poles outside backdoor bars and KTV lounges bearing Korean-language neon signs. Beneath an elevated dual carriageway I followed the cracked path along the banks of Yitiao River, where the water flowed low and muddy. A mountain bike was discarded down there, like an apple core.

Rural China periodically intruded on the scene — a beekeeper selling honey from a street-side hive, bees swarming around her head; a sun-browned farmer wearing a baseball cap selling apples from a cart drawn by the sorriest looking horse in the world.

After walking for what felt like days, I chanced upon the Confucian Temple thronged with tracksuit-clad teenagers listening obediently to instructions from a teacher with a megaphone. Policemen turned me away, perhaps the city's only tourist, unwelcome in one of its few historic buildings.

Walking back towards my hotel, I stumbled upon one more curiosity, a church, wedged between the concrete cubes that constitute architecture in Changchun. I rubbed my eyes in bewilderment.

It was not that churches didn't exist in China; over 90 million people were registered Christians, more than the entire population of Germany, and many more were unregistered believers who attended underground 'house churches'. But it was rare to see a church of such vintage. According to a stone plaque, this was St Theresa's Cathedral, built in 1889.

The interior was painted a cold white. Romanesque pillars supported a high ceiling. The décor was familiar to anyone who grew up in Europe: stained-glass windows, white candles and a wooden cross on the pulpit before which a woman was droning a prayer in the same way Buddhists chant.

"Oh, Hello Father, I didn't see you there."

The priest awarded me a Christian smile, combining compassion for thy neighbor with a sense of self-satisfaction at having won eternal membership into the in-club.

He gestured for me to go ahead and approach the altar.

"No, I'm not..."

"Please, foreign friend, please..."

"I'm fine here at the back, enjoying the scenery, great candles you've got here..."

"Please..."

I realized I wouldn't win this one and it was neither the place nor the time to confound the man with questions such as "Why did the god of Abraham choose to ignore illiterate ancient China in favor of some wily desert tribes?" or "The Christian Taiping Rebellion, not so good for China, huh?"

"Please friend, go on..."

I walked several rows forward then slid into a pew and bowed my head. Before me was the *Shengjing* — the Holy Bible — with gold Chinese characters embossed on the front of a leather hardback. I peeled back the first few pages and read: "*Shen shuo you guang, jiu you le guang* – And God said, Let there be light: and there was light..."

It was a pretty accurate translation, I concluded, before putting the book back. I couldn't pray, even in a city that needed a good prayer. "What should I do?" I asked the Jesus effigy. The woman in front was still bobbing her head devoutly. Seeking something to gaze at, I removed the Bruce Chatwin book I'd covered in pencil notes on the train ride up there. Clasping it in my hand, I softly mouthed the sacred words: "*What Am I Doing Here?*"

I'd almost cancelled my overnight train ticket to Changchun some weeks before. The city was located at the very heart of Northeast China (known to history as Manchuria) — a huge swathe of the country I was yet to explore. But before I'd set out, the Beijing International Book Fair had rolled around, luring various literati types to the capital including photographer-turned-guidebook-publisher Magnus Bartlett.

Bartlett and I had met at my speaking gig in Hong Kong. I'd been on a podium nervously preparing my Luoyang speech when he'd engaged me with the five-star opener, "So you think you're a bit of a travel writer, aye? Well, then you must know Bruce Chatwin? I was his photographer back in the 1980s..."

My relationship with Bruce Chatwin was like a romance with a girl who lived faraway, one marked by long periods of estrangement and occasional reunions. I'd been set *The Songliners* as an undergrad, which led me to *In Patagonia,* which I thought was a more complete work. I liked his novels less than the slim, if philosophically weighty, travel vignettes. Did I know Chatwin? We were acquainted.

But Bartlett was no Chatwin wingman and had left an impression all of his own, a bespectacled septuagenarian with a roller coaster mind often travelling in two directions at once. A non-Chinese speaking Sinophile, he enunciated each word with the brand of English only British public school can engender, that 'layer of slime' upper-class accent that embarrassed Chatwin, who'd boarded at Marlborough College.

Like the famous travel writer, Bartlett was possessed with the capacity to grow intimate with strangers quickly, beguiling them with a library of stories to rival those of the finest raconteur. And over a pot of dragon well tea, he was keen to talk, not just about books but photographs as well.

"Look at these," he'd said, removing some analogue treasures from an envelope. He had on him several strips of film which, when held to the light, revealed the mountain town of Lijiang in distant Yunnan Province back in 1985.

"It's another world isn't it?"

"Isn't it just," Bartlett had whispered, clearly pleased with his own work. "China in those days was so innocent."

I felt like I was seeing Lijiang for the first time, although I'd been there a decade before as a backpacker. I'd heard it had become a bit of a tourist circus in the years since, however.

Which was why Bartlett's images of the fabled Himalayan Naxi town pre-tourist boom were a real boon. James Hilton's Shangri-La, before neighboring Zhongdian pinched the epithet, Peter Goullart's *Forgotten Kingdom* in all its pastoral glory.

Lijiang had enchanted more than a few wandering scribes since the West 'opened' China, and, in particular discovered the inland arcadia that was Yunnan. There had been plant hunters like the aptly named Scotsman George Forrest, while Austrian-American botanist, anthropologist, linguist and all-round grouch Joseph Rock had documented the native Naxi people for National Geographic, eventually producing *The Ancient Nakhi Kingdom of Southwest China*, which three decades on, Bruce Chatwin made "our excuse for coming here" when he visited on behalf of *The New York Times*. The article published in 1985 as 'In China, Rock's Kingdom,' while an extended version, 'Rock's World' appeared in *What Am I Doing Here?*, a collection of Chatwin's essays and articles I found in the Beijing Bookworm.

"I originally engaged Bruce," Bartlett had explained of how he'd met Chatwin. "And ended up visiting him at his flat in Eton Square in 1983, he impressed me. Bruce was incredibly well-read. I was trying to persuade him to write a foreword to one of my guidebooks. Anyway, he and his wife Elizabeth came out to stay with us in Hong Kong and we had a glorious few days. My wife Margarita adored him, he was so charming. He charmed everyone. We eventually went on the Yunnan trip: me, Bruce, his wife Elizabeth and the legendary art dealer Johnson Tsang, who came along as our translator."

Bartlett regaled me with their journey, flying from Guangzhou to Kunming then the stage-by-stage bus journey up the Himalayan foothills in the days before the train.

"You didn't see many cars, just Red Flag sedans and trunks brimming with timber roaring down the hill at a hell of pace. I remember Bruce had a bottle of whisky, which we passed around. And I had a cassette with some Little Richard, which the driver let us play. The people on the bus thought we were all mad."

The film Bartlett had brought to show me contained three striking images of Chatwin in Lijiang: Bruce pedaling a sit-up-and-beg bicycle on a country road, getting a bare-razor shave in a local barber and looking at a map with a camera around his neck while sporting a pair of Nike jogging bottoms. His fallen-angel good looks were unmistakable, the setting fittingly primordial for a man whose writing sought to delve into the nomad spirit of our hunter-gatherer selves.

"When Bruce met the doctor," Bartlett continued, "They bonded immediately."

He was referring to Dr Ho, about whom Bruce wrote, and in typical Chatwinian fashion, turned into a star. Ho had featured in all his guidebooks since.

He rummaged in his bag for a tiny notebook, "I think I have the page, ahh, here it is." He read: "snowflakes the size of a hand. Rain joining sunset to sunset. The wind quick as arrows... Commands quick as lightning. And the bandits lose their gall... Their black flag falls to the earth... They run for their lives... Heads heaped like grave mounds... Blood like rain... The dikes choked with armor and rattan shields. The trail of foxes and the trail of jackals, have vanished from the battlefield..."

"What is that?"

"Isn't it beautiful? It was written on the stone drum outside Lijiang. Johnson translated it on the spot while Bruce scribbled it down."

I recalled Chatwin's assertion that "everyone needs a quest as an excuse for living."

I'd began dreaming of walking in Chatwin's Himalayan footsteps and considered changing my travel plans entirely when I noticed online that Changchun was the start point of the K2288, China's tenth longest railway service in terms of distance and second in terms of time. It took 60 hours, primarily owing to the 39 scheduled stops it had to make to roll from the northeast to the southwest. Few ever rode it from end to end, but perhaps I could.

The train was not scheduled to depart until 7:09 p.m. that night, which still left time to kill in Chinese Motown. Ignoring the Changchun World Sculpture Park — which looked to be a soul-destroying "ninety-two hectares of natural landscapes and cultural landscapes conceived under the theme of friendship, peace and spring" — the city was a one-site-wonder. That site, bizarrely, commemorated the epoch when this relatively young city became the capital of Manchukuo, a pseudo-Japanese colony from which the Japanese launched their full assault on China proper in 1937.

The tour of the Imperial Palace of Manchukuo began with a strong dose of the unexpected, namely, a race track. Leaning on the fence I watched some jockeys clad in brightly colored racing outfits bound around between cigarette breaks. They jumped over bales of hay as they galloped. But I couldn't shake a sense of the surreal imbuing the place. You just don't see many jockey clubs in the People's Republic. Even the colonial race course in Shanghai was turned into People's Square. The regional equestrian obsession was entirely of Hong Kong provenance, a strange love child born of the British penchant for sports clubs and the Cantonese passion for gambling. Yet here, over 2,500 kilometers north of Happy Valley Racecourse, I admired the trim lawn, surrounded by a dirt track and enclosed by a neat white fence.

The entrance to the palace was a sturdy Russian-style gate,

with pillars at each side supporting an arched roof adorned by two golden dragons and the characters *Xing Yun Men* – The Gate of Good Fortune. It was an architectural juxtaposition that hinted at the strange mélange to come, for there was no discernible theme to the campus of buildings, the styles of Russia, China and Japan having been blended like fusion cooking, although the overall effect was not inharmonious. In fact, it was rather more homely than the overbearing palaces one typically encountered across China.

The principal building was the Tongde Hall, which had been converted from an old salt tax collection office, nicknamed the Salt Palace among cynical locals. The interior was decked out spectacularly with thick carpets, lavish curtains and patterned wallpaper. There was even a throne room from which Puyi pretended to govern. I later learned that a dance scene from the Bernardo Bertolucci movie-biopic *The Last Emperor* had been shot inside, and given the décor, it was easy to see why a producer had warmed to it.

The dance scene, like Puyi's reign, was largely fictitious and he actually spent most of his time in the smaller Jixi Building. It had been the Jilin-Heilongjiang Exclusive Transportation Bureau before it was appropriated as his living quarters. Despite an affiliated Buddhist shrine, it retained the character of a Russian manor, replete with grey brick walls, a lime-green sloping roof and an ostentatious balcony supported by annular pillars that flanked the front door. It was within these walls that Puyi's neglected wife Wang Rong sought solace in opium, a habit that helped end her life at age 41.

Puyi, too, wrestled with medical ailments both real and imaginary, including rumors of impotency, addiction to pharmaceutical drugs, fits of extreme anger and a nasty case of hemorrhoids. He also became fanatically religious, reading

Buddhist scriptures for much of the day, as well as obsessing over hygiene by ordering his staff to hunt and kill all the palace flies.

I imagined how Chatwin might have spun the bizarre story of Puyi's life — probably as a fable lamenting the decline of the once great horse-riding caste that became sedentary and bloated and inevitably lost the Dragon Throne.

The jingoistic History of the Occupation of Northeastern China Museum on the palace grounds was of limited interest. Only a black and white photograph of Chairman Mao facing Puyi caught my attention. The pair were apparently sharing a joke. But the convivial outward expression of the men veiled an epoch-making message: the Mandate of Heaven had passed from the Qing to the Reds. Victory emanated from the Chairman's expression. Born of southern peasant stock, Mao Zedong reigned for 25 years until his death in 1976. Highborn Puyi died from bowel cancer in 1967, a humble gardener, deprived of the royalties from his autobiography he'd authored at Mao's behest. That book, *From Emperor to Citizen: The Autobiography of Aisin-Gioro Puyi,* was on sale in the museum gift shop, buried between some Russian *Matryoshka* dolls, and a mound of Mao's Little Red Book. I purchased the last English-language copy to go with my Chatwin book. After all, I had a long train journey ahead.

II

Industrial Changchun hadn't offered much for a traveler, but it was at least a fine place of departure. To experience China's finest train journeys you must begin at her extremities. And it felt cathartic to be leaving Chinese Motown via train because the city actually grew up during the railway age. Even then, Changchun Railway Vehicles still manufactured a catalogue of railway tools and components including half of China's high-speed train carriages.

My home for the next two and a half days, however, was no bullet train. I was taking a green train, top bunk, right in the middle of carriage, forcing me to climb up the metal pegs with my bags in tow. It was a maneuver I'd performed before but I still ended up swinging around like a chimpanzee that had just been released into the jungle after a lifetime of pampered domesticity at the zoo. Hurling the bulk of my luggage onto the overhead racks, I lay down and browsed the first pages of *From Emperor to Citizen* until the train jolted into motion. When I was confident the ferment had dissipated below, I clambered back down to get acquainted with my new travel companions. This was good etiquette on Chinese slow trains. The rationale was simple. We'll all be living in confines as intimate as criminal cellmates for some time to come, so why not turn the bottom bunk into a sofa and share tea and conversation while you do your time?

"My name's Mr Lu and this is my daughter Yingying," said a man wearing an Almost Heaven, West Virginia t-shirt. He told me he was from Lianhua village on the eastern edge of Inner Mongolia, just north of Changchun. Lianhua means lotus flower.

"What a nice name for a place," I told him, knowing villages beyond the Wall were often grim, impoverished by bad soil and worse weather.

"What kind of business do you do in Lianhua village?" I ask.

'*Yumi*'. Lu said bluntly, 'corn'.

The skin around Mr Lu's eyes was wrinkled like that of an elderly man's, though he was only 43. He constantly massaged his wrists and fingers, arthritis perhaps.

"Where are you heading?" I asked.

"We're going to Jishou, in Shandong Province. She's going to teachers' college," he said, gesturing proudly to Yingying who appeared indifferent. Her fingernails were varnished and she sported cute ankle bracelets. Whether a career as an educator would help liberate her family from the land was unclear, she could end up teaching via smart screen in Shanghai or with chalk and board in Lianhua village. Whatever fate had lined up for her, it was pleasing to see her doting father seeing her off to college, and via train, no less.

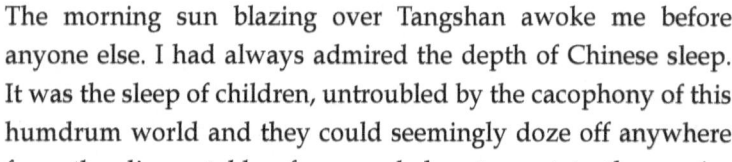

The morning sun blazing over Tangshan awoke me before anyone else. I had always admired the depth of Chinese sleep. It was the sleep of children, untroubled by the cacophony of this humdrum world and they could seemingly doze off anywhere from the dinner table of a crowded restaurant to the service counter of a convenience store.

As morning music flooded the carriage, we circumvented Beijing via its sister city Tianjin, then skirted back into Hebei Province.

"Breakfast, breakfast, breakfast," chanted the first trolley pusher of the day, "*mantou*, steamed buns, rice-porridge, *youtiao*..."

Two squat men who occupied the bunks opposite began to awake from a deep slumber. It required some serious groans and stretches before either man looked fit enough to make it to the bathroom unaided.

After getting the morning's first nicotine hit, they returned to the carriage bearing great balls of white dough—the northerners preferred choice of carbohydrate, namely *mantou*. It was a poor man's pudding, one that would fill you up until lunchtime without leaking any nutrients into the bloodstream. Yet notwithstanding their heavy-duty breakfast, both men were incredibly lean, muscle and flesh hanging off narrow skeleton frames like scarecrows grown crooked from years in the wind. I soon learned their names, Mr Pan and Mr Wang.

"I overheard you talking yesterday. Your Chinese is not bad, foreign friend," said Mr Pan, clearly the most self-assured of the pair.

"Really not bad," agreed Mr Wang, whose upper-lip carried a thick moustache just like that of the famous revolutionary Dr Sun Yat-sen. "Egg?" he asked, offering me a brown egg that had been boiled in tea, by the look of it, for many centuries.

"I'm fine," I said, noting the bag of vegetarian pot noodles I'd stockpiled in Changchun before departure.

"Where are you from?" Pan asked.

"The UK."

I anticipated a comment about the Queen or football but instead he said, "*Fukelan qundao*," and mimed a machine gun.

"What?"

"*Fukelan qundao*, Madame Thatcher sent you there to fight." He mimed a machine gun again.

"Oh the Falkland Islands. I see. Well I was just past my first birthday when that took place so…"

"You British are always fighting, in India, even in our China…"

"Well that is true but you know, it was a long time ago and…"

"The sun never sets."

"What?"

"That's what they say about your Empire, isn't it Old Wang?" Mr Pan turned to face Mr Wang.

"Right, the sun never sets," Wang confirmed, spitting pieces of tea egg onto his lap.

"The sun never sets," Pan repeated.

"But it has set…" I appealed.

"No, you still have the Falklands plus Australia, Canada,

New Zealand..."

Pan spoke in bullet points. I couldn't ascertain whether his tone was accusing or if he simply wanted to show off the knowledge he must have garnered from a geography book dating back to Puyi's time. We discussed Britain's long history of ruining just about everywhere else's history with Pan adding the pronoun 'you' before 'British' as in "you Brits" to suggest I'd personally had a hand in the imperial project. Eventually his energy wavered and I was able to turn the conversation around.

"So where are you both heading?" I asked.

"Back home," replied Pan.

"To build a school," added Wang.

"And where is home?"

"Anyang."

"Wow, you're from Anyang!"

"You've heard of our hometown?"

"I've been there. It was the capital of China during the ancient Shang Dynasty. That's where the Chinese script originated, at least, so they say, there's an amazing museum with unearthed Zhou-era chariots and tortoise shells engraved with primitive characters..."

"You know a lot," said Pan, who appeared bemused by my interest in the vestiges of antiquity that cluttered his corner of Henan like the rubble of a palace after a gas heater explosion.

"It is true, they dug up the oracle bones round our way, right Old Wang?"

"Right, oracle bones and a royal grave."

"Yes, that was near Old Li's house, he couldn't farm for months while the archeologists from Peking University messed around with his fields."

"He lost a fortune."

The pair nattered about a host of archeological finds

unearthed in their neighborhood as if these were simply day-to-day occurrences, like finding an old five-pound note stuffed down the back of the sofa. Perhaps you just become complacent about historical treasures when you hail from one of the cradles of civilization.

"That sounds amazing, which ruler did they unearth?" I inquired, fishing for a scoop.

"I couldn't say. We come from a poor township far from the city, there's not much there now, just sunflowers," said Pan. "We won't stay long, build the school and then go back outside, maybe Beijing or Tianjin to find some more work."

Travel writers often head to remote destinations to write about the last wandering tribes that are unbound from the corruption of sedentary life, a pretension of which I'm as guilty as Chatwin. But China's migrant workers were the true nomads of the age; their destiny was ever determined by the changing winds of the economy. Perhaps as many as 100,000 Tibetans roamed the plateau, a number that paled in comparison with the tens of millions of Chinese one met on the railroad, ever seeking fresh pastures scattered across the vast realm they called simply 'outside.'

As we inched across the central plain, I noticed Pan and Wang growing restless.

"Why is this train so slow?" Wang complained aloud, after returning from his umpteenth cigarette break.

For me, there was pleasure just being aboard this transnational caravan, exempting me from the need to plan a day and motivate myself through it. But for these men, impatient to get home and get to work, it was a tedious mode of return. They simply couldn't afford to travel 'for travel's sake' — the act of moving Robert Louis Stevenson described as "the great affair".

"What are the trains like in your country?"

"Slow, not much better than this one and there aren't any beds, of course."

"Why not?"

"The UK isn't that big; you don't really need to sleep on trains."

"Not that big? The Empire where the sun never sets!"

"Well it's slightly larger than Henan Province if that gives you some perspective…"

"Your high-speed trains are pretty good then?"

"Um, we don't actually have one."

"What? We have them here in Henan. I took it once; it was much better than this sluggish piece of crap," he said, slapping the wall of the carriage.

"I like the green trains…"

"Why don't you build a high-speed train in the UK?" Pan asked, exhibiting tones of disbelief. I could feel myself getting sucked into a bewildering conversation about the Dickensian state of the British railways. His perspective was doubtlessly rooted in China's Marxist interpretation of history that saw the British not just as imperialists but 'railway imperialists', pushing the iron road on a reticent 'Johnny Chinaman' who believed the souls of the dead would be disturbed by the roaring trains.

"You should get China to build one, we'll do it," he persisted.

"I can imagine," I said, thinking Pan and Wang and their kin would happily lay the tracks, faster and for far less money than any European laborer.

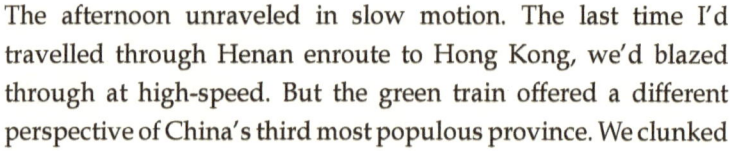

The afternoon unraveled in slow motion. The last time I'd travelled through Henan enroute to Hong Kong, we'd blazed through at high-speed. But the green train offered a different perspective of China's third most populous province. We clunked from Xinxiang to Jiaozuo to Guanlin—an unending series of everywhere you've never heard of, counties that just happen to be inhabited by millions. If it were an independent country of its own, Henan would be the 16th most populous country on earth, just behind Vietnam. Every inch of the good earth was given to cultivation. As Chatwin put it in *Heavenly Horses*, "As the Chinese people have multiplied, their field system has crept over the face of China like a skin rash." And while the Chinese had innovated some remarkable agricultural techniques over the centuries, the menace of chemical fertilizers was clearly wreaking havoc with the ecosystem, making Chatwin's 'skin rash' metaphor evermore germane. Whenever I looked up from Puyi's memoir, I caught sight of a peasant wearing goggles and mask busily spraying his crop with something clearly labelled *duwu* – toxic. Headlines of exploding watermelons or garbage-tainted tofu or pesticide-soaked strawberries had become so commonplace they were really the new normal. Ah Lan's husband Long-haired Wu had even written a song about it, with lyrics that went, *"Polluted food, we've eaten so much, tainted alcohol, we've drunk so much, we're treated like pigs and dogs…"*

As darkness began to settle, I whiled away the idle hours chin-wagging with the train crew.

"I've been a cop for Thirty-seven years," boasted a policeman lounging against the window, "but I bet you can't guess my age," he said. He had, to his credit, maintained a full head of black hair though he was clearly beyond his salad days.

"Thirty-six?" I suggested, to a chorus of laughter.

The waitress had short, functional hair and a brilliant northeast accent, which she boomed at everyone, no matter how close or far they are from earshot. "Hey, foreign one, you'll have to order something if you want to sit there!"

"That's fine, I'm bored of tea anyway, get me a beer and some egg fried tomatoes with rice."

I watched her convey my request to a cook with a huge belly protruding beneath chef-whites so brilliantly stained they looked like a work of abstract impressionism. Soon, a steaming hot plate of fried food, a bowl of rice and lukewarm can of lager were before me, a real Chinese train banquet, sorely missing from the high-speed trains.

The waitress chatted in the casual way Chinese have with strangers. "I'm two years from retirement," she said.

"Wow, that's quite an achievement. What do you plan to do?

"Italy!" she remarked, with certainty that made me jealous.

"Italy?"

"That's right, foreign one. I like old things, I want to explore ancient Rome and try Italian food, I hear it's very tasty."

"It is very good, pizza, ice cream, frothy cappuccinos, pasta..."

"Chinese noodles are much better than Italian noodles," she said, reminding me many Chinese travel with the bravado the English employed when they embarked on their Grand Tour of Europe, intent not so much to learn, as to prove to themselves that their birthplace was far better.

"Parts of Henan, cities like Luoyang and Anyang, are older than ancient Rome," I said, gesturing to the sun ebbing over the plain.

"Listen, foreign one, I've been working on this train longer than you've been alive. I have a plan. My husband and I are going to Italy."

I couldn't blame her. A Roman holiday was certainly deserved after a lifetime crisscrossing China. My muscles were already aching from inactivity and boredom permeated by the long hours when my eyes were too tired to read. But the Changchun crew appeared relaxed, sharing cigarettes and jokes and time. This band of people was fated to travel back and forth across an earth flattened by the inflexibility and inevitability of the national timetable.

As another train rattled by on the opposite tracks sounding its horn, I thought about all the other railway crews who were idling away the hours in the restaurant car, perhaps dreaming of Paris or Athens or somewhere afar that had taken root in the psyche. China Railway Corporation was the world's fourth biggest employer with over two million on the payroll. That was the population of Latvia.

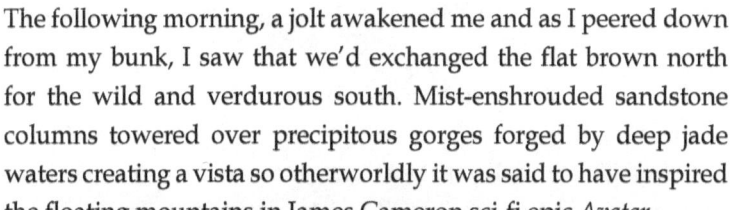

The following morning, a jolt awakened me and as I peered down from my bunk, I saw that we'd exchanged the flat brown north for the wild and verdurous south. Mist-enshrouded sandstone columns towered over precipitous gorges forged by deep jade waters creating a vista so otherworldly it was said to have inspired the floating mountains in James Cameron sci-fi epic *Avatar*.

The craggy terrain of the Hunan-Guizhou borderlands was a land of historic contention, inhabited by 'upland anarchist tribes' like the Miao, Dong and Tujia, people who have long resisted Chinese dominion. It was also the home turf of my favorite Chinese author, Shen Congwen, himself of mixed ethnic heritage, who hailed from nearby Fenghuang and whose masterwork *Border Town* described the free-spirited inhabitants of kingdoms China swallowed long ago, but was still struggling to digest. The novella's protagonist was Cuicui, a country girl who "grew up under the sun and the wind, which turned her skin as black as could be. The azure mountains and green brooks that met her eyes turned them clear and bright as crystal." These mountains and brooks remained quilted by a crochet blanket of 'nationalities' embellishing the vista with a real frontier vibe. It was a region that would have doubtlessly appealed to Chatwin's imagination, for as his biographer Nicholas Shakespeare noted in the introduction to *In Patagonia*, he "was always attracted to border countries: to places on the rim of the world, sandwiched ambiguously between cultures, neither one thing nor another".

In the dining carriage, I met the first foreigners I'd seen in days, an attractive couple of Italian backpackers.

"Where have you been?" I asked.

"We've been travelling for some time, first in India, now China. We just travelled from Zhangjiajie to Fenghuang. Now we want to go to Dali, I hear it's nice there?" the woman half-asserted, half-asked.

"It is nice. Sounds like an epic journey. How are you enjoying your China trip so far?"

They glance awkwardly at one another. "The people here, 'ow you say in English, I can't see any light in their eyes," said the man, somewhat disparagingly.

"Did you prefer India?" I inquired, wondering if the delirium of the boisterous subcontinent preceded disappointment in guarded China. It was a touchy subject as India was widely perceived to be China's great rival and there had been border skirmishes just months before.

Both nodded enthusiastically.

"What about the food?" I asked, "Chinese or Indian?"

"It's hard here because we can't communicate, we can't order what we want..."

"Maybe you should befriend the waitress?" I said, pointing to the carriage's Manchurian Matron.

"We can't speak Chinese."

"I don't think that matters," I said, watching her bellow at every unwitting traveler who strayed into the restaurant carriage

"Can you help us order?" asked the girl staring blankly at the Chinese-language menu card.

"Sure? What do you want?" I asked, scanning my eyes down a list of staples: sour and spicy julienned potatoes, Kung Pao chicken, jasmine tea...

"Do they have coffee?"

III

Kunming sat on a plateau 2,000 meters above sea level and the air immediately struck me as crisper than in the heavy north.

I left the station just as the sun peered over the horizon. My limbs were as stiff as a robot's, my hair as greasy as a Sichuanese fish supper but there was a great sense of satisfaction at having completed the journey — a 4,000 kilometer diagonal brush stroke across the country from the Long Spring to the City of Eternal Spring.

At the exit, a horde of touts offered minivan rides to exotic locations, while vendors hawked breakfast buns and flatbread. Mandarin collided with a myriad of other tongues to conjure a Yunnanese soundscape distinct from monolingual Changchun. Yunnan was home to twenty-five of China's fifty-six recognized ethnic minorities, some, like the Naxi of Lijiang, were unique to the province. As more than thirty-eight per cent of the provincial population claimed to be of one 'nationality' or another, Kunming was a real melting pot, a blend evident in the dazzling dresses of some women congregated outside the station.

Negotiating my way through the hullabaloo, I walked towards a side-street lined with budget hotels, the words 'hot shower' motivating each step. But every hotel turned me away, echoing the 'no foreigners' mantra.

Eventually, I met a more conversational hotelier and was informed that the police had warned everyone not to admit foreign travelers in the run-up to the Party Congress.

"That's ridiculous," I protested, "This is a tourist town. Where am I supposed to stay?"

"The five-star international hotel down the road."

"That's what everyone keeps saying. I can't afford it."

"I don't know," he said, offering me a consolatory cigarette, which I popped behind my ear to be polite.

"Listen pal, if you come to my country, you can stay in any hotel you want," I appealed.

"Where are you from?"

"Great Britain, you know, the Empire where the sun never sets," I said, trying to amplify my significance.

"Ah yes, a fine place."

"Won't you help a friend from afar?"

"David Beckham, Queen Elizabeth, British people are good," he confirmed, puffing a lungful of smoke into the dawn light.

"Well what if Beckham or the Queen came here, would you turn them away?"

"They wouldn't come here, Comrade. They'd be staying in the five-star international hotel."

After some effort, I managed to find lodgings at a youth hostel. I spent the next few days in the company of old friends who treated me to Yunnanese fare, revitalizing me for the next leg of my journey. I would travel on one of China's most attractive railways, a track that ghosted the ancient tea horse road via staging posts like Dali before terminating at the Naxi capital, Lijiang. For centuries, pony caravans delivered lowland tea to highland Tibetans whose fibreless meat diet required its digestive properties. The merchants then returned bearing Tibetan brass wares and yak hides to be sold at the Flower and Bird Market in Kunming. Add to this wonderful tale of inter-ethnic trade a sublime climate nurturing bucolic stepped farmland framed by snow-dusted Himalayan peaks and you have a perfect rail trip. Except that China Railways, in their infinite wisdom, ran all three uphill services at night.

Darkness had fallen as I reached the station. Travelers were being herded one by one through a turn-stile, tickets and IDs scrutinized repeatedly in the sight of gun-brandishing SWAT teams.

In March 2014, eight individuals drew knives in Kunming Station, killing thirty-one people and leaving hundreds injured in one of China's most brutal terrorist attacks. Security personnel shot four dead at the scene while four were captured. Their trial lasted one day, three were sentenced to be executed, one to life imprisonment. State media branded them 'Islamic extremists, though they may well have been Uighur separatists who have long campaigned for independence in the corner of China they call East Turkistan. This, and other ethnic skirmishes, had provoked the Party to ramp up railway security exponentially, so it was a relief to get inside, even if there was nothing to do but browse ethnic knickknack stalls.

All my fellow passengers went to bed as soon as they boarded the train. But sleep didn't come easily to me. I listened to the creak of the wheels as we edged our way in the darkness. This was a slug of a locomotive, taking nine hours to cover three hundred kilometers, all uphill, winning it the title of China's slowest mainline train. As I lay there restless somewhere on the ancient tea horse road, I wondered what might remain of Chatwin's China.

IV

Lijiang's old town had become a new town. Venturing through the winding cobblestone lanes, I discovered all of the street-facing shops were vending tourist tat on an emporium scale. Everything had a made-in-a-Guangdong-factory feel about it.

In a square, bored Naxi women were twirling around before a gawking crowd of holidaymakers. The show went some way to resurrect Paul Theroux's observation, "For the Chinese, the minorities in Yunnan are somewhere between hillbillies and zoo animals."

Some of the Han Chinese shopkeepers had donned Naxi costume to invoke a sense of the exotic, raising serious questions about what actual 'intangible cultural heritage' UNESCO was charged with protecting, unless capitalism was on their list.

Thankfully, Lijiang's commercial dimensions dissipated north of the old town, giving way to a valley of flower-lined roads and cornfields peppered by traditional whitewashed farmhouses topped with fantastic roaring cat tiles — the Naxi people's eternal protector.

I found Joseph Rock's adopted home village Yushu set on a grassy slope in the shadow of the Jade Dragon Snow Mountain and comprised entirely of stone houses, some still bound together by dry earth.

When Chatwin had visited Joseph Rock's home, it had been occupied by a local named Li Wenbiao, who'd shown the curious foreigners around. It had since been turned into a half-forgotten museum looked after by an elderly Naxi man threading a wicker basket in a courtyard. There were purple and pink flowers in the garden, testament to the botanical riches that first drew Rock north from Burma. Two ground-floor rooms exhibited the marvelous photographs he had taken of the Naxi in all their tribal regalia, along with his turgid books about them, while upstairs his bed, desk and oil lamps had been meticulously conserved. It was a haunting homage to a man who, as Chatwin put it, "gave his life to recording the customs, ceremonies and the unique pictographic script of his Nakhi friends".

Chatwin's Lijiang story actually began in Baisha. "It is a cold, sunny Sunday in Yunnan. On the plain below Jade Dragon Mountain, the villagers of Beisha are letting off fire-crackers to celebrate the building of a house, and the village doctor is holding a feast in his upper room, in honor of his first-born grandson."

That village doctor he referred to was He Shixiu, a local brainbox who'd studied medicine at university in Nanjing. Chatwin — never one for spelling people's names correctly — called him Doctor Ho, a sound based on the local dialect, and the name had stuck.

"Where does the doctor live?" I asked a wrinkled lady in prime Naxi costume who was selling barbequed corn.

Following her finger, I walked along the cobbled street, intoxicated by the perfume of wildflowers, the gossip of elderly Naxi ladies who still sold mud-coated vegetables by "weeping willows and a quick-water stream" as Chatwin wrote.

The Jade Dragon Chinese Herbal Medicine Clinic was a wooden structure with stone foundations and a heavy tiled roof bearing down upon the willow-shaded street. An ancient woman, Doctor Ho's wife, I learned, was sweeping the portico with a bamboo broom. The exterior walls were festooned with newspaper cuttings as well as letters from famous clientele.

I stepped inside and saw the doctor sitting meekly behind a medicine counter reading a heavily worn book with a magnifying glass.

Doctor Ho's son, He Shulong, was busy entertaining foreign tourists with his father's exploits. Shulong appeared in Chatwin's article as the 27-year-old father of newly born He Deshou. Now he was almost sixty and evidently the man of the house. The backpacker crowd stood attentively in a circle while he gave his sales pitch: "Doctor Ho was banished to the countryside but in the high hills he discovered many plants that could cure sooooooo many diseases," he said, sweeping his hand like a thespian, adding long pauses and high tones to his exaggerated English enunciation for dramatic effect. Yet despite his best efforts, his storytelling sounded rehearsed, at times confused, as if he'd told these tales so many times he'd forgotten what the original oration was about.

Once the clinic crowd dispersed, I explained to Shulong that I was following the trail of Bruce Chatwin. I wanted to show his father Bartlett's photos but Shulong immediately sprang into performance mode.

"Look here, you can see the faaaaaammmmmous travel writer Bruce Chatwin," he said pointing to various articles and photos collected in a corner including several editions and translations of *What Am I Doing Here?*

"Michael Palin came here tooooooooo, he British, also very famous, from BBC."

Shulong then pointed to a very early Yunnan guide, published by none other than Magnus Bartlett. "This book was by Patrick Booz, he teacher in Kunming, first foreigner come here in 1970s when the China ooooooppppennn up."

I realized Shulong wouldn't be easily prized from the script as he began reeling off a list of VIPs who have visited the practice like someone reading the ingredients on a breakfast cereal box. The clinic had become a veritable shrine to the Doctor's international celebrity, the seeds of which Chatwin inadvertently planted.

"Can I show Doctor Ho some pictures of Chatwin in Lijiang?" I asked Shulong when I eventually got a word in edgeways.

"My father will be 96 next month, during the Mid-Autumn Festival."

"That's wonderful, but do you think I can show him these pictures?"

"Okay. But I have to interpret what you say into Naxi language, he's ooooolddddd and deaf."

While Shulong explained my mission, I approached the renowned apothecary and readied my pictures. His white medical apron, I noticed, was adorned with trinkets from abroad: a Canadian flag, a souvenir keyring from Holland.

"You can speak to my father," said Shulong.

I laid out Bartlett's photos before him. "This is Bruce Chatwin in Lijiang," I said while his son interpreted into Naxi.

I saw his eyes moisten though his expression didn't alter.

"You can see here, he's getting a shave, and that's Bruce on a bicycle. I wonder if you know where that might be?"

The doctor examined the picture but said nothing.

"Tell your father these pictures are unpublished, very few people have seen them before."

Shulong failed to elicit a response.

I packed up the pictures and thanked the doctor for his time. Suddenly, in near-perfect English, Doctor Ho proclaimed, "Chatwin liked Joseph Rock. That's who I learned English from. He was my father's good friend. They were exactly the same age. I'm sorry Bruce died; he had AIDS. What a pity. I wish I could have given him medicine. Are you in touch with his wife Elizabeth? Please tell her I'm still alive and thinking of her."

The doctor fell silent again, returning to the antique book. I then bade them farewell. But just as I left the practice, Doctor Ho received another current of energy and called after me, "Come again in 10 years, I'll still be here, you know why? I have a philosophy, don't drink or smoke, exercise every day and most importantly, be happy."

Framed by trees and festooned by prayer flags, Yufeng Lamasery was a gentle, woody place. Chatwin deemed it "the loveliest" though Rock called it "a home of rats".

Inside, I chanced upon a bespectacled tour guide with greying hair and a devious smile, one who spoke English as well as Doctor Ho.

"Some tea, foreign friend?"

"Honestly, I'd love a cuppa," I told him.

"I'm Richard," he said, "Richard He, local Naxi international expert guide number one."

I took his card and followed him into a room where an enormous Tibetan was seated, chatting with a small Chinese congregation over tea. Richard He had brought along a client, a Shanghai-based American businessman. The man appeared disinterested in this enchanting spot. "I had a few meetings in Kunming, and a couple of days to spare so I thought I'd take a vacation," he said, implying he'd much rather be jet-skiing off the coast of Thailand.

The red-robed Tibetan poured tea and held court. He spoke no English but told me in Mandarin, "I've just come back from a pilgrimage to the Labrang Monastery in Gansu. You should go, foreign friend, it's beautiful."

Later that evening, watching selfie-stick wielding tourists pose before the North Gate of Lijiang's commercialized old town, I found myself wondering why I wasn't in a Tibetan Lamasery in Gansu. Everything felt wrong. I resolved to change tack, to realize Chatwin's 'nomadic alternative' in spirit, not just tick off locations he and Bartlett visited like a sightseer.

Fishing He's business card from my wallet, I made the call.

"Hello Richard?"

"Who is that?"

"Thomas, we met earlier at the Lamasery. Thomas, Xiao Fei in Chinese, you gave me your card."

"No I didn't."

"Yes you did, I have it here," I then read aloud, "Richard He, local Naxi international expert guide number one."

"Are you free tomorrow? Free to be my guide?"

"Yes, where would you like to go? What about Lake Lugu? There are many beautiful women there, I can get us cheap coach tickets now if you'd like."

"No, I don't want to go where the tourists go," I begged. "Let's just hike into the mountains, to distant villages. Take me off the map."

"Off the map, I see, let me think. Okay, I know the way."

"You know the way off the map?"

"Yes, of course, I'm local. Where do you want to meet?" Richard asked me, without flinching.

"By the Black Dragon Lake?"

"Okay, see you tomorrow at nine."

"Eight, Richard, I want to leave early."

"Nine is early, don't you think?"

"No, I would like to leave at eight."

"How about half-past eight?"

"This isn't a negotiation Richard"

"Okay, quarter past eight tomorrow, Black Dragon Lake, see you then, haha."

———∽∽———

Richard met me 8.45 a.m., still chewing on the last mouthfuls of breakfast.

"Oh, it's you. Well, never mind," he said.

"What do you mean, 'Oh, it's you'?"

"I thought it was the tall man in the restaurant by the South Gate, his wife was beautiful, I think they are rich."

"I'm sorry to disappoint you."

"It's not your fault."

We bused to Jade Water village from where Richard guided me down a path to a roadside hedge.

"This way is a very good place to start, I think," he said, arching his leg over the thorny brush and walking headlong into the undergrowth.

"There's just bush, nothing else. Are you sure you know where you're going?"

"This is part of the ancient tea horse road," Richard called back.

"Really?" I yelled, struggling to follow him through the nettles and brush.

"Yes, it was never actually one road but many paths, all leading to Lhasa. To those crazy Tibetans. They needed tea you know? All they eat is meat. Yak, yak, yak. No tofu, no cabbage, nothing."

"Why do you think Tibetans are crazy?" I asked as we reached a vague suggestion of an earthen track.

"They are mad, always fighting with the Chinese and with themselves. If you go to Tibet, you will see what I mean. Anyone who lives up there in the cold where nothing grows must be crazy."

"Aren't Naxi people descended from Tibetans?"

"Yes, we come from over the hill. But that was a long time ago, a thousand years past. Naxi people are better, friendlier. You see Joseph Rock and Peter Goullart stayed here, we're hospitable, not like those cannibal Wa people, they'd wear your skull like a hat."

He contemplated our route for a while then did an about turn in motion and mindset. "But Tibetan culture is strong, they still wear their traditional clothes, still read their language. We Naxi saw money and cars and abandoned our gods."

A discernible pass gradually evolved from the undergrowth snaking through a thick evergreen forest. On this pine-perfumed trail we discussed the minority peoples that populated the region and I soon learned that Richard would, at some point, remark on the quality of the women, who were invariably "troublesome" or "dangerous" or "dishonest" but always "beautiful".

"You walk well for a Britisher. Americans can't walk, they wouldn't make it this far, there's something bad in their food, all those hamburgers and what not."

"There must be some good American walkers."

"No there are none. French, they walk well, they are active, there must be many mountains in France."

"The Alps?"

"The what?"

"Never mind."

We circumvented a mountain lake hanging on the hillside like a celestial swimming bath, the wind sending ripples across the emerald waters and tickling our hot cheeks cold. It was a good place to pause and catch our breath.

"Why have you come to Lijiang?" Richard asked me as he glugged tea from his flask.

"I'm researching a story about Bruce Chatwin, who came here in 1985."

"Aye, 1985." Richard contemplated the year, counting on his fingers and muttering to himself. "I would have been twenty-two. Was he the American teacher?"

"No, an Englishman, a writer.

"Sorry I don't remember him."

"He visited Doctor Ho."

"Hahaha, the doctor, he likes to talk. So does his son, those two are always talking. What did, um, Blues Shatwig do?"

"Bruce Chatwin, he was a writer, he was interested in Joseph Rock."

"Did he like plants? That whole hillside there is a protected area, full of rhododendrons and several kinds of pine trees, you can get money for pine nuts if you collect them. Abalone mushrooms too, the Japanese love them and wild medicine to sell to the Cantonese, they'll take anything."

"Chatwin liked the idea of botany but he wasn't methodical enough to be a plant hunter, he was really a story hunter, a collector of tales."

"Sounds interesting. So he came here?" Richard asked, pointing to the forest slope we were ascending.

"What, this exact spot? Probably not."

"Ahhh, so we are lost?"

"No, we're walking. Chatwin was a great walker. He considered it a kind of poetic act, something spiritual that could cure all ills. Hang on, I have the quote here," I explained, opening my notebook. "Here it is: 'walking is a virtue, tourism is a deadly sin'."

"I like that," Richard said, repeating the sentence over and over.

As the mountain path climbed up a steep gradient, I was less inclined to chat, but Richard, though almost twenty years my senior, continued to talk like someone with a mild case of Tourette's.

"My wife is very stupid, always arguing with me, my son, he works in insurance, he also doesn't help, life is hard, family is tiring, society is like a spider's web, don't you think? Maybe

I'll meet a new wife, a nice Yi or Lisu woman. Naxi women are opinionated but Yi and Lisu are very simple. I want a simple life, not like Bo Xilai, he is in prison now…"

Bo Xilai was the charismatic mayor of Chongqing once tipped for the Politburo glory until his career came to a spectacular end after Chongqing's police chief sought asylum in the US Consulate in Chengdu, claiming Bo, and Bo's wife Gu Kailai, had been involved in the mysterious murder of a British businessman called Neil Hayward. It was an extraordinary cloak-and-dagger tale and a major PR dent for the Party's respectability, which resulted in Bo being sentenced to life imprisonment. To this day, speculation enshrouds the official narrative. Was Bo's fall part of a broader power struggle? How did a foreign consultant who went to school in Harrow reach such high levels of influence?

But as the Chinese saying goes, "The mountains are high and the emperor is far away," and political intrigue felt like a distant thing as we crossed one of the great peculiarities of the Himalayas, a tabletop grassland as flat as a lowland meadow. Skipping through the tall grass we encountered a shepherd whom Richard talked to while his goats bothered me.

"Everything is fine, we're going in the right direction," he reported back.

"But where are we going?"

"You said anywhere there are no tourists."

"Right."

"So this is the correct way."

We hiked until late afternoon, when we emerged in a pastoral valley. After tramping through fruit orchards we found a single-lane road leading to a lost horizon of massive snow-covered mountains.

"That's Shangri-La," said Richard.

"Are we going there?" I asked, feeling an intense magnetism

towards the rooftop of the world.

"It is so far away, maybe three hours driving, you Britishers, sometimes stupid."

"Then where next?"

"We should go back; it will be getting dark soon."

"Back to Lijiang? We've been hiking for seven hours, if we turn back now we won't make it back until, well, gone midnight!"

"A car will come along eventually."

"Richard, we've been walking down the hill for the last hour or two and not one vehicle has passed us except a one-seat tractor. Unless you plan to ride that man's mule over there..."

"We can't ride a mule back, there's two of us, stupid!"

"What about those houses over there?" I asked, pointing to a tiny hamlet suspended on the edge of a vast ravine.

"Those villagers are Yi people, not Naxi. They're like gypsies, happy-go-lucky; give them fifty yuan and they'll gamble and drink it away in minutes. They won't have any cars down there."

"I mean, do you think we can stay there, pay a villager for a spare room?"

"No, let's go back to Lijiang, I want Naxi-style tofu for dinner."

"I thought you wanted to find a new wife, maybe there's a nice Yi woman in the village," I said.

Richard thought for a moment, stroking his moustache with his thumb and forefinger. "Maybe, we can try."

We walked down the road until we reached a collection of woody houses with backyards populated with pigs and chickens and muck-coated children. Packs of dogs roamed the streets howling as we passed.

Richard called, "*Nihao, you ren ma*? – Hello, anyone at home?" then turned to me and said, "they're still in the fields, there's nobody home."

Eventually, he lured a village elder out of his front door. He recommended an old widow who lived down the road and was short of money.

Richard knocked on the door and after some negotiation we won a lodging.

The lady of the house wore a green headscarf. Enormous silver earrings had stretched her earlobes while her skin was as wrinkled as a sundried tomato. She spoke only a language of monosyllabic squawks that even Richard struggled to decipher.

In the courtyard, a tap piped ice-cold groundwater to the surface, the house shower and sink.

"She told me we can wash," Richard said, already splashing his face and twitching with the cold.

Our hostess stirred a pot hung over a fire in a kitchen blackened by smoke in a scene reminiscent of a medieval witch's lair. There was no chimney. Potatoes were the principal crop and we watched as this old Chinese-gypsy woman peeled and cooked the spuds.

Richard turned to me and whispered, "She's nice isn't she?"

"Very kind."

"No, I mean beautiful." He chuckled like a school boy, raising his eyebrows above the frames of his glasses.

"Isn't she a little old for you?"

"I like older women, you can trust them."

"She's covered in mud."

"She's a farmer, hard-working, I like…"

"To each his own, Richard."

I couldn't ascertain what was being said throughout the duration of our supper though it appeared Richard was attempting to woo this poor Yi woman, while she was fiercely resisting his advances, at times shouting at him and waving her finger.

"She says I'm no good."

After a banquet of spicy spuds, boiled eggs and sticky white rice washed down with a few glasses of the suicidally strong rice wine, we stepped out into the courtyard to watch the galaxy explode.

"We're very high," said Richard. "Just look how low the sky is."

I was allocated a rigid wooden bed but fell into a sleep of a thousand sleeps, the rest only hearty hikers enjoy. I could have snoozed well beyond the dawn, but a village choir of cockerels won't permit indolence. Despite their chorus, I hugged my blanket hoping for an extra hour snooze until Richard burst into my room in his underwear shouting, "Cloud river, cloud river!"

"What the…"

"Cloud river, come see, quickly. Britisher."

"Outside, the whole valley, cloud river." He dashed out the farm gate door.

Against my better judgment, I followed suit. But he was right. The ravine had filled with a cotton wool stream, a ghost dragon that relegated my full English lexicon to a gasping "Wow!" sound. I stood dazed and amazed as this Himalayan specter enveloped the whole village, cloaking us in a damp white Tibetan veil.

For days, Richard and I wandered Lijiang's peripheral valleys, places centuries away from the modern tourist conveniences of the old town.

We found our way to Shigu or 'Stone Drum', a picturesque market town next to the first bend in the Yangtze River where Chatwin saw "a cylinder of marble in a pavilion by the willows" engraved with a Ming-era war poem that Johnson Tsang had translated.

As we crossed corn fields and tobacco plantations, traversed rickety river bridges and marched up antiquated stone paths, I found myself warming to the ex-high school English teacher turned hapless tour guide, even if he'd taken to singing sentimental pop numbers like *Take Me To Your Heart* and *My Heart Must Go On* while we walked.

Richard hadn't initially grasped where I wanted to go, namely, the opposite direction of everyone else. Yet he'd converted to the nomad creed quickly, following his nose up hill trails to dilapidated Red Army barracks or through wild valleys inhabited by the brown and handsome Lesu people who nurtured fields of barley hanging from the hillside like library bookshelves.

Deep into our third day of our destination-less adventure, dark clouds converged in skies that had been azure blue.

"It's going to rain, Richard."

"Keep going, Britisher, don't be a loser like Bo Xilai, follow me to Shangri-La."

On the peak of a hill, two karst rocks appeared before us, forging a giant V-shape.

"Walking is a virtue, keep going and we'll reach Shangri-La!" Richard asserted once more waving a wooden stick like a sword and marching towards the growls of Himalayan thunder like a soldier heading into battle.

Conversely, it was I who had to call it a day, urging Richard to turn back for Lijiang before the weather turned ugly.

"Okay, okay," he conceded, "but I must come back, I need to know where that trail goes."

On the sodden road back to Lijiang, Richard invited me to stay at his house, an offer I accepted willingly.

He lived in a wooden quadrilateral dwelling with a courtyard in the middle. It would have been a nice place were it not caked in cobwebs.

"Don't break them," Richard ordered, "I like spiders; it interests me to watch them work."

Richard's kitchen hadn't seen a mop since his wife left. He ate directly from the frying pan to avoid washing-up. On the wall he'd fastened a map of Lijiang from the 1970s. Noting my consternation, he joked, "What do you think of Lijiang's international tourist office number one, haha?"

His son Harry He came home at nightfall. He appeared like a typical Chinese twenty-something occupied by a regular white-collar job. When Richard took a shower, we chatted for a while.

"I studied in Chongqing but wanted to come back home, in China, family is important," he told me.

"Why didn't you continue your father's travel business?"

"I want a quiet life, not like his. You know my father is a paradox, he's received a lot of Western influences over the years but in his heart he's just a Naxi villager, there's lots he doesn't understand."

He soon retired to play online games, his hobby, he told me.

"My son is angry with me," Richard confessed later that night. "It's very terrible. He's trapped between his mother and me. And I've had some problems with the local Party bureau; they say I'm not a good comrade. I think it is just jealousy, I'm the international tour guide number one, flying the flag for our village. They should make me the propaganda chief!"

V

There was no train to Shangri-La, just two bus routes. One short and direct, the other a village hopper that wormed its way through the old mountain trade routes taking the better part of the day. As Richard recommended one more stop, "god's country" I took the latter bus.

At Tiger Leaping Gorge, all the tourists alighted, leaving just a few people on the bus. The driver turned to us—two Tibetan women wearing turbans, a remarkable backpacking deaf couple from Zhejiang and me—and said simply "eat" while miming the process with invisible chopsticks, evidently concerned that some, and perhaps none of us, would understand him. He hastily reversed into a car park outside a grubby restaurant strip.

I ordered some egg-fried rice to try and stabilize an unhappy stomach that had been tasked with digesting several days of wild country meals. A few mouthfuls provoked the inverse reaction and I was soon clinging to the walls of latrine suspended over the Jingsha River where whatever one discharged fell some meters in plain view of other restaurants to become fish food.

"This wouldn't happen to Chatwin," I lamented as I shuffled back to the dinner table.

Except it would. He just wouldn't write about it. This was partially his ghostly narration style and partially the intrepid explorer persona he carefully cultivated, though by all accounts he was a clumsy traveler, prone to sickness, a talker as much as a walker.

It was the most recurrent criticism of Chatwin one read, a sense of being short-changed by the absence of ardor that is so central to serious travel and travel literature. As Paul Theroux complained, "Life was never so neat as Bruce made out."

Chatwin was possessed with a remarkable capacity to arrive somewhere at just the right moment and unwittingly change it. Like Patagonia or Alice Springs, Chatwin's spell had made a pilgrimage site of Jade Dragon Chinese Herbal Medicine Clinic, even if the family has since grown drunk on celebrity. "We locals don't seek his help" a Baisha villager had said to me as we'd watched lines of Western tourists arrive for a taste of Doctor Ho's miracle cures for various ailments.

There was a telling line in Magnus Bartlett's correspondences with Chatwin. I removed the letter from my bag and read, "I do sympathize with your skin problem, I had something similar a few years ago in a less visible but in some ways rather more critical locale and it gave me a good deal of angst until it was sorted out."

What Bartlett could not have known then was that Chatwin's skin rash was a symptom of the HIV virus he'd already contracted, probably in New York. Bruce never spoke openly about the disease until close to the end, having been quite unable to confront this grim misfortune or admit to his homosexuality that had made him a victim of the 'plague' that ravaged gay communities in the 1980s. Instead, he concocted stories to explain his symptoms, remarking after his China tour that he'd eaten "raw Cantonese whale" or "a thousand-year-old egg" and thus contracted a rare Chinese fungal infection.

"It annoyed me that he blamed his ill health on China," Bartlett had said to me, the only negative thing he had to say of their great Yunnan adventure.

The mini bus driver ordered us aboard. We were soon snaking up hills with vistas so beguiling that every bend rounded invited another gasp.

I alighted at the tiny village of Baidi in Sanba township. The one reason to make this seven-hour detour was Baishuitai. Richard had told me the "White Water Terraces are very beautiful." They were in fact a holy place for the Naxi, as the mystic founder of their Dongba faith had settled here to spread his new religion.

In the pearly white pools of calcium and spring water

stepping down the hillside, the Naxi also saw a heavenly mirror of the paddy fields they farmed.

I passed a man selling incense beside a statue of a Naxi icon, a rather cartoonish effigy of a Crowned King. Following a line of Tibetan prayer flags, I eventually found myself in a stepped assembly of chalk-white ponds where I encountered some unlikely pilgrims, twenty or so Americans, wading knee-deep in the crystalline waters. They'd imbued the air with the smell of hairspray. Several of them appeared to be pressed into jeans several sizes too small.

"Mind if I join you?" I asked one of them.

"Sure thing, buddy."

I removed my socks and shoes and stepped into the cold, calcium-rich waters.

"It's pretty cold."

"Yeah, you get used to it," she said, then turned away. "Hey Bobby, would ya pass me my phone, honey?

"What are you doing all the way out here?" I asked a young boy wearing a baseball cap who looked to be no older than eighteen.

"We teachers at a new International School in Lee-jan," he said, in textbook southern drawl.

"There can't be many expats down there?"

"There's like fifty in total, but we don't just teach white kids."

I learned that the crowd were all China newbies from states like Georgia, North Carolina and Texas. Their concerns were uniquely provincial, "I can't wait to get a car out here," said one, "I miss my doggy," said another.

None, when pressed, expressed more than a passing interest in the Naxi, or indeed, the Chinese, though they did all wish to study the Chinese language.

It dawned on me as I waded through the Naxi people's holy

water that I'd infiltrated a company of Christian missionaries, evangelicals spreading the Word via the proxy of an International School.

Shunning any theological debate, I waded away from the crowd to enjoy the Himalayan panorama from another bizarrely beautiful, snow-white paddling pool. I lingered until my toes turned blue.

On the way back down the hill, I stopped at the Dongba shrine and purchased a handful of incense sticks. "Take these old man," I said, planting them before the Naxi Crown King and setting them alight, "you're going to need them."

BRIDGES TO PINGBIAN

I

I'm not the first person to have struggled to leave Kunming. Back in the 1970s, Communist Party officials in Beijing first got wind of Yunnan's capital charms when those exiled there during the Cultural Revolution refused to return home.

Cloudland, where I shacked up to write up my notes, was located down a colorful backstreet and boasted a large courtyard shaded by the canopy of a fantastic tree flowering purple and indigo, as if it were still spring. The city's reputation as a place of 'eternal spring' stemmed from an enviable climate conjured by its high altitude and moderated by Dian Lake, an enormous body of water flanking the western suburbs that ensured the mercury never plummeted into the sub-zeros or hiked beyond the low-30s, not bad in a country where shirt-drenching summer humidity, ear-biting winter dryness, coastal typhoons, sand-sweeping prairie winds and sky-tainting 'airpocalypse's were the norm. Every *waishengren* or 'outside province person' I spoke to, including my friend Dora from Shandong, cited the weather as a key factor in the decision to up-stakes and relocate inland. As I went about my day beneath cobalt blue skies, I could see and taste and feel why.

Like most Mainland cities, Kunming had expanded like an inflatable castle throughout the fat years. But downtown remained surprisingly walkable and suffused with diversions. I lost long afternoons ambling around leafy public gardens like Cuihu Park where city elders gathered to sing revolutionary hymns, their songs colliding over a lake peppered by a thousand migratory birds that appeared happy to suffer the cacophony to flap about in this gorgeous setting.

The half-decaying, half-gentrified stone and wood dwellings lining Old Street led to the Flower and Bird Market, a thronging, urban bazaar where the kind of flowers that had adventure-botanists George Forrest and Joseph Rock scouring the hills a century ago were readily available street-side: rhododendron, orchids and yulan magnolias were just some of Yunnan's native flowers to colonize the gardens of the world, their nectar perfuming the air with a raft of scents alien to most of China's choking urban centers.

I surveyed shops piled high with Pu'er tea from southern Yunnan and Tibetan silverware from Shangri-La; brass-plated bamboo water pipes used for the popular local pastime of bonging tobacco, as well as jade and amber trinkets with semi-precious stones from the mines of Myanmar.

Dinner was always a cause of celebration in China, especially Kunming, which, to my palate, had some of the best food in the country, even though it never made most Chinese friends' hit list. Yunnan was excluded from the big leagues, China's Four Major Cuisines and the expanded Eight Great Cuisines, probably because of the 'impurity' of it, that there was fruit in the rice or rice in the fruit. There was even cheese on the menu, *rushan* – the Bai people's grilled fermented milk cakes, how very un-PRC. But this oversight was certainly a symptom of Han chauvinism rather than a proper culinary critique, for the province was considered ecologically 'hyper diverse' and inevitably produced an extraordinary range of edible exoticisms. For a mushroom fiend like me, dining out meant banquets of forest fungi: porcini, green-headed mushrooms, dried beef mushrooms, pine mushrooms, two-tone fungus, black truffles and so on. If you could name a 'shroom, someone in Yunnan was almost certainly frying it with garlic and coriander.

Hand-pulled wheat noodles also made a cameo appearance on the Kunming menu, and Dora and I regularly rendezvoused for lunch near the doorway to the Nancheng Mosque. Before Dora introduced me to the Muslim Quarter, I hadn't associated the Southwest with Islam, but it turned out that the religion had made a major incursion in support of Kublai Khan's forces during the 12th Century.

Dora's Hui friend permitted us to sit in her headscarf shop and chit chat over afternoon tea until nightfall, after which I sought out after-dark distractions.

One night, I went on a date with a coffee-skinned ethnic Dai girl who took me to a swing dancing class in an upstairs craft brewery, the kind of place that would be the domain of belly flaunting traders in Guangzhou or anxious embassy staffers in Beijing. But in Kunming, it was the habitat of an unpretentious band of Mandarin-language students, English teachers and Chinese returnees from overseas who'd traded high Shanghai salaries for the charms of laid-back Yunnan. There was even a beer called Xi Dada IPA, named after CCP Chairman Papa Xi, a *jeu de mots* you probably wouldn't get away with on the East Coast.

A sizable French community added good cafés to the roster of reasons to hang around in Kunming, garnishing the Yunnan stew with an unexpected dash of Parisian pepper. As something of a lapsed Francophile, who'd spent a semester in France as an undergraduate, I was naturally intrigued by Kunming's French connection.

The current crop of restauranteurs, it turned out, were not the first-generation Gauls to call Yunnan home, as several garishly yellow colonial villas across city indicated. Their story actually began in the 19th Century south of the frontier where French forces had been expanding their hold over Indochina. It was the discovery that the Red River was the best route to the lucrative tin deposits in Yunnan that brought them to the very edge of heaven's dominion. In 1883, after being lobbied by Vietnamese elites, the Qing court dispatched troops into Tonkin, where they engaged the French in skirmishes. Diplomatic wrangling followed and failed, leading to a decisive French naval attack on the Fuzhou Dockyard three years later.

Victory at sea spurred the French to build a railway inland, the Kunming-Haiphong Railway or *Le Chemins de Fer de L'Indo-Chine et du Yunnan*, the legacy of which was chronicled at Kunming North Station, a mustard-colored station building topped by a retro clock tower that housed the provincial railway museum. The language on gallery walls was rich in Marxist vitriol. The French "war of aggression against China in 1883" led the "stupid Qing government" to sign an "unequal treaty", which gave up Chinese suzerainty of Vietnam. After the first Sino-Japanese War ended in 1895, the French were then said to have "blackmailed" the "weak and incompetent" Manchu rulers into consenting to the construction of a railway from Vietnam into China "under threat of war".

To critics, the Kunming-Haiphong Railway reeked of colonial overreach, comparable to the British experience in Kenya during the construction of infamous Lunatic Express. The initial estimate of 70 million francs was pushed up to 95 million francs. The cost in human life was horrific as countless coolies died while laying tracks equivalent in length as that from Paris to Perpignan. An uprising against working conditions saw thousands of laborers executed by the French.

Yet for good and for bad, the railway transformed Yunnan, as the museum's historians concede with sentimental chagrin: "On the vast Yunnan Plateau, the jingling bells of caravans echoed along the ancient tea horse road for thousands of years when in 1910 the Yunnan-Vietnam railway completely changed the traditional means of transport... With colonial greed and plunder, it mercilessly ripped open the southwest door of China..."

Despite "plundering China's sovereignty like tigers and wolves" with their "blood-soaked" railway, the train connected the region's mineral resources, exotic flora and unique wares with the markets of the world via the port city of Haiphong, bringing investment to one of China's poorest provinces. It was also a major engineering feat; crossing such mountainous topography it required 155 tunnels and 425 bridges. *The Times* called it an 'engineering marvel' on its completion in 1910 and compared it to the Suez and Panama canals, according to the museum.

The most famous of the bridges along the track is afforded special reverence, namely, Paul Bodin's *Viaduct de Faux Namti*, an 'inverted V' steel bridge that crossed a narrow gorge above the Sichuan River. Lauded for its esthetic beauty and its innovative design, photos of the bridge dominate several gallery walls.

The Chinese love of giving inanimate objects symbolic names like Elephant Trunk Hill in Guilin or worse, Penis Rock in Shaoguan, and have duly dubbed Bodin's viaduct Renzi Bridge as it appears to resemble the character 'ren' meaning 'person'. They had even made a replica in the museum's main hall, one so bad it looked as if the local kindergarten had knocked it together.

I hatched a plan to take the French railway to Vietnam with the hope of chugging across the Renzi Bridge along the way, only to learn from my friend Master Fu that passenger travel ceased on the Chinese section of the French railway in 2005, the year I arrived in China. Merde!

"It's still worth exploring. You can see parts of the French tracks from the window of the new train," Master Fu said over dinner. "There's a stone bridge here, a tunnel there... the tracks get quite close to one another in some places."

Master Fu had been a train driver but now spent his retirement years photographing the vestiges of the French railway. He was something of an authority on the track. He was also an excellent character to behold, with intense eyes and wispy grey mutton chops. He was blessed with a fantastic chuckle and spoke Mandarin with a strong hint of the nasal Kunming dialect, despite being born of a northern family, which probably accounted for his height. "You'd better get down to Mengzi, that's the best place to see some French heritage sites, but it would be difficult without a car," he added.

Fu had brought along his friend Cui Xiongtao for dinner, a talkative tour guide who had been to 50 or so countries, spoke several languages and had more hobbies than a trainspotting stamp-collector who worked in a record store. One of his passions was the study and documentation of the Kunming-Haiphong Railway.

"There are a few branch lines of Dianyue you could check out and even ride," he suggested, applying the local name for the track that combines the character 'Dian' — an ancient kingdom of Yunnan — with Yue, the 'Viet' of Vietnam. "The branch lines were built just after the trunk line was completed to exploit mines in the region. But they're a bit fake. You know, when the Chinese government opens somewhere up to tourism, they often get the history wrong."

"Still, it would be fun to roll through southern Yunnan on an old train," I said. "Unfortunately, I already have a ticket to Hekou. I have to leave tomorrow for a border crossing. My visa stipulates I need to leave China every 90 days."

"When you come back to China you could stop off at Jianshui," Xiongtao suggested, before detailing an itinerary only someone working in the tourist industry could conjure.

The two men showed me photos of remote stretches of track framed by tropical vegetation, populated by ethnic minorities in fantastic traditional dress, while French stations stood reminiscent of a half-forgotten epoch when the cockerel ruled the roost in *Indochine*.

"What about the Renzi Bridge?" I asked them, now quite excited by the prospect of a new quest. "Can one still see it?"

"That's really far from anywhere, in a distant valley in Pingbian," Xiongtao said candidly.

"By public transport from Mengzi it might take a few days if you could do it at all," Fu added. "But it's still there and Pingbian really is beautiful."

———∽∽———

Quilted in jungle mist and ringed by plant pot hills, Hekou marked the end of the line in southwest China. It was a hodgepodge place, devoid of any serious charm. It struck me as a quintessential border town, one where every second person appeared to be passing through and every second product came from the country just across the river. One local confessed to have swum to Vietnam before. "We used to do it all the time, locals never bother with the formalities of the border crossing." I'm not surprised. The town of Lao Cai was so close that if a Vietnamese farmer sneezed, I'd have caught a cold.

The Chinese checkpoint was typically austere, with one Gestapo-like cop asking me, "Why are you going to Vietnam?" his pointless question etched with a tone of condescension many Chinese reserved for their Southeast Asian neighbors.

I played dumb and shrugged. "Why not?"

A Friendship Bridge connected the two countries but these Communist neighbors weren't the best of pals. They even went to war as recently as 1979, both claiming victory in the conflict, though many lives were lost and little was achieved. In fact, it's probably fairer to say they both lost.

Crossing the bridge, I was tasked with dodging mini women wearing bamboo hats and mini men in Ho Chi Minh-style pith helmets. They looked as if they'd been dressed by the Vietnam tourist bureau.

Each Vietnamese merchant was given a shakedown by Chinese border guards, much like school bullies roughing up the hippie kids for their lunch money. There was a lot of shouting and miscommunication, neither nationality apparently versed in the other's language.

Thankfully, the Vietnamese side was far more relaxed — chilled out Southeast Asia, at last. Due to the exchange rate, I swiftly became a millionaire, the first wad of Vietnamese dong splashed on a Hanoi-style ice coffee to celebrate my arrival in the 'Nam before flagging a cab to the station.

From the onset, the place was evidently running in a lower gear than Yunnan, just as Yunnan was slower paced than eastern China. There were no maddening lines, incessant passport checks, bag scans or hurried crowds to scrummage with, just a mahogany desk staffed by some impossibly pretty tellers. I was almost taken aback by the ease with which I could rent a mobile bed bound for Hanoi, though at 300,000 dong, my illusions of wealth wouldn't last much longer.

After nightfall, we were ordered politely across the tracks to board the Hanoi-bound train. The walls of the sleeper cabin were decked in wood and it smelled like a log cabin. Outside, the night critters serenaded us until, with a shunt, we rolled gently into the dark night along colonial French tracks laid over a century ago.

I decided to spend a few days slumming it in Hanoi. Like an old suit, the Vietnamese capital had a lived-in quality to it. It's older quarters appeared very similar to a southern Chinese city, albeit, one with a lemongrass twist. There were birds hanging in cages outside shops named with Chinese characters, dishes that looked and tasted more Cantonese than Thai, shrines to Daoist saints and Zen Buddhist temples. Perhaps the most pronounced evidence of Sinicized Annam — the Peaceful South as the Chinese "protectorate" was once known — was the 1,000-year-old Temple of Literature dedicated to Confucius, its interior decorated with stone steles, door lions and imperial drums, its doorways embossed with classical Chinese script *Wen Miao Men*, literally Culture Temple Gate.

Although Hanoi had clearly absorbed much from the Chinese, as well as the French, the city was easy on its own feet, eclectic most certainly, but with a personality of its own conception, like Wu Tiao Ren or any other good band where you could hear the influences without feeling they were in any way derivative.

In the city's live music venues, Hanoi Rock City near Lake Tay and The Doors near Hoan Kiem Lake, I lost several evenings. The latter seemed to me a spooky name given how many songs the psychedelic Los Angeles quartet had supplied to Vietnam war movies. It was at the bar that I met a girl called Phuong, named just like the character from Graham Greene's *The Quiet American*, who took me on her scooter to see some of the sights: the Red River crossed by the incredible Long Bien Bridge and the manifestly dangerous Train Street, essentially a residential quarter where a locomotive ploughed through thrice daily, passing so close to people's houses that you could hear them singing *The End* in the bathtub.

It was along this track that I concluded my mission to Haiphong at the very end of the Dianyue Railway, leaving Hanoi via Long Bien Bridge, which was bombed so many times by the Americans its existence at all was a miracle.

I'd followed the Red River in stages since passing Xiaguan in Yunnan's northwest. In Vietnam it diverged into a hundred earthworm-like estuaries meandering into the Bay of Tonkin, where the French once battled the Chinese, across a marshy plain. The scene reminded me of what the Pearl River Delta might have looked like before they paved paradise, although glimpses of several crude factories befouling the air suggest an ominous future for a region already courting heavy industry away from Guangdong.

My terminus station, Ga Haiphong, was a peach-colored colonial station that introduced me to what was a far Frencher place than Hanoi. I strolled along broad Parisienne-style boulevards lined by coffee shops and regal yellow villas sporting brown wooden window shutters. Haiphongers appeared to have adopted the French work ethic, too; both museums were closed for a three-hour lunch break and just about everyone was eating out.

With little else to distract me, I bought a ferry ticket to Cat Ba Island and spent my remaining days writing up notes at a beach shack over-looking the spectacular karst islands of Halong Bay.

———∞———

Hekou, on my return, was warm and wreathed in mist. But the Chinese dress for the season, not the weather. "Everyone is in puffer jackets and trousers," I noted in my diary, "though I still have sand in the pockets of the beach shorts I bought on Cat Ba Island."

At the station, I noticed two policemen escorting a prisoner onto the Kunming-bound train, his legs and arms in heavy chains, his head concealed by a hood as if he was bound for the gallows. Whatever this man had done, the cops weren't taking any chances. Aboard the train, a black curtain was hung to separate the makeshift prison wagon from the rest of us, which cultivated an uneasy atmosphere for a lone *laowai* in Bermuda shorts.

I was grateful to alight just two hours north at Jianshui Station though the sense of disquiet lingered.

"Are you from Xinjiang?" my cab driver asked while staring at me rather than the blacktop we're rolling over.

"No, I'm from the UK. I'm a *waiguoren* – a foreigner."

"You really look like a Uighur," he asserted. He was on edge because of unrest in Xinjiang, a so-called autonomous region dominated by Han Chinese.

"I don't think so," I said, looking at myself in the wing mirror, a brown-haired dwarf when compared with the typically lanky build of a copper-skinned Uighur men.

"I thought you might be from Xinjiang because we have a lot of Muslims in Jianshui."

"I didn't know that," I replied, catching a vague whiff of baijiu from the man's breath. "I'm here to check out a railway."

"Oh yes, lots of Muslims in Yunnan. His bloodshot eyes examined me like an X-ray machine.

"I'm no expert on Islam in China," I told him.

"There are many, we have a Hui people district. I can take you there if you want, it's on the way to your hotel, a shortcut, kind of."

He veered off the main drag down a gravel track into a sizable neighborhood. Sure enough, the women there all wore head scarves, there were halal butchers and the rooftops wore crescent moon crests like Arabian weathervanes.

"Why does everyone have such large front gates?" I asked.

"Because they're rich, the Muslims here have money and they don't want to share it."

"Really?"

"Oh yes. They don't drink or eat pork like us Han people," he explained. "So they can save a lot of cash."

I wasn't about to argue. The high gates and walls looked more like security concessions than expressions of wealth, especially as we emerged from the Muslim quarter into an ostensibly Han Chinese area, evoking a strong sense of ethnic segregation.

"Is there much intermarriage between the Han and the Hui?" I asked.

"No fucking way, not at all, they don't like us, nor we them. They keep themselves to themselves. After all, we enjoy a drink."

Growing uneasy, I resisted further talk, counting the seconds until we pulled up outside my guesthouse.

After paying my fare, I rounded the car to grab my bags from the boot. Heading towards the hotel door I heard him call after me, "Are you sure you're not from Xinjiang? Because you can't stay there if you are."

Sitting on my hotel bed minutes later I felt jittery. After backpacker-friendly Southeast Asia, China felt freshly alien and not for the first time I wondered, *"What the hell am I doing here?"*

I briefly considered holing up in my hotel until my nerves settled. But instead, I channeled the ghost of Bruce Chatwin whose professed religion was the God of Walkers, venturing outside in an attempt to stroll off the blues. It proved a wise decision as Jianshui seduced me in ways I could not have prepared for, reminding me travel in China is always about the Good, the Bad and the Ugly, and not necessarily in that order.

The chief urban attraction was the magnificent Chaoyang Lou, a Ming-era gate that was thirty-one years older than Tiananmen in Beijing, according to everyone I spoke with. Yet unlike the heavily guarded Beijing equivalent, Jianshui's imperial gate was crowded by locals who were walking with their caged birds, sucking tobacco from bamboo pipes, or waging war with chess pieces. The scene was such a typecast vision of China it was a wonder images of the Chaoyang Lou didn't adorn guidebook covers.

But it was in the backstreets that I really began to lose myself in a Coleridge-esque dream of ancient Cathay, ambling by bamboo mats coated in sun-drying chili peppers in cobbled courtyards where kids ran feral while elders watched the days pass by in slow motion. Half-collapsed temples and overgrown pagodas peered over lost lanes populated by dogs, there was a sacred well containing special water used to make magic tofu and so many artisan shops. Everyone was sewing, thatching, banging, molding or shaping some kind of material into life. It was a China Paul Theroux would have recognized when he wrote, "The Chinese are the last people in the world still manufacturing spittoons, chamber-pots, treadle sewing-machines, bed-warmers, claw-hammers, 'quill' pens (steel nibs, dunk-and-write), wooden yokes for oxen, iron ploughs, sit-up-and-beg bicycles, and steam engines."

———∾∾∾———

In the cool light of the morning, when Jianshui still smelled of steamed buns and hot coals, I followed Xiongtao's directions to the first of his recommended French railway destinations, the Gebishi branch line. Construction of the line had began just three years after the Kunming-Haiphong line was completed, reaching Jianshui in 1928.

I walked inside the made-to-look-old Lin'an Station, with its ornamental wall clock embossed with the word 'Paris', and displaying a European-style wooden timetable, a retrofitted interior aimed at conjuring a romantic vision of Franco-Sino amity. All historic wrath reserved for France's imperialist incursions in Yunnan had been put aside in the name of tourism.

A diesel locomotive soon pulled into view, painted yellow in the colonial French color scheme, it coupled with three wooden carriages that we were instructed to board.

Progress was measured with modest speed as we lurched through the backend of Jianshui into a land parceled into duck ponds and fields striped with every edible green imaginable. It was a superb vista, China at its most bucolic, where sun-wrinkled farmers tended to the earth beneath the gaze of exotic birds looking on like supervisors from dangling telephone lines.

The first stop, some ten minutes down the line, was Shuanglong Bridge Station, named after the Double Dragon Bridge crossing a nearby river, a stunning, seventeen-arch stone viaduct crested with three ornate pavilions dating back to the Qing Dynasty.

On the far bank I sought out a good location to photograph it by balancing on a river boulder.

"Oh, mon Dieu, se tenir sur ce rocher est dangereux..." I overheard, and noticed a European family standing by the bank looking at me as though I might soon require rescuing.

"Êtes-vous français?" I called back.

"Oui, et vous?" said the elegantly dressed family matriarch.

"Non, I'm British, nice to meet you," I said, stumbling up the bank, muddy and unkempt, to make acquaintances with three well-to-do Parisians. The son was studying engineering in Hangzhou, or 'Angzhou', as he called it, and his parents had joined him for a tour of China.

"What are you doing here?" they asked.

"Je suis écrivain de voyage," I explained, adding, "with a bit of an interest in Chinese trains".

We reboarded the carriage together but after a few minutes chatting, we were instructed to alight at the second scheduled stop, the Xianghui Bridge Station, which also named after an ancient river crossing, a stone and wood beauty built in 1814.

The final leg of the journey took us to Tuanshan, a hillside village in a pastoral domain surrounded by dried-out corn stalks. I joined the French family as de facto translator, their scientifically minded son having learned virtually no Chinese at university. Mao-era Cultural Revolution slogans still adorned the walls of collapsing Qing-era villas fronted by ornate gardens and temples populated with the colorful monsters of the Daoist pantheon. I garnered from a tourist sign that Tuanshan was founded by the Zhang clan, which settled here during the Ming Dynasty. They prospered from the tin mining boom and the money from the mines had been splashed out on fancy houses and temples. It was tin that later lured the French railway men here from Vietnam, although nowadays, only a twice-daily tourist train brought in any money, tourist dollars spent on trinkets and food.

We lunched on the terrace of a *Nong Jia Le,* or Peasant Family Restaurant, and I chatted with the Parisians about affairs of distant Europe I knew little about.

Then we walked off the rice and spiced vegetables we'd just eaten in the village backstreets where we encountered a lady with a baby harnessed to her back washing clothes in the well, rinsing each item by hand before laying them on sunbaked rocks to dry.

"This in the country that manufactures most of the world's washing machines," the pragmatic French boy said, directing me to ask the woman why she hadn't bought a *machine à laver*?

"Washing machines are no good," she told me while beating a shirt on a rock. "This way is cheaper and the clothes get *really* clean."

IV

"Hello, Xiongtao."

"Hey, Xiao Fei, where are you now?"

"I'm still in Jianshui."

"Did you ride the train?"

"Yes, thank you for the tip, it was a great experience. The countryside is gorgeous and the old bridges are amazing."

"Where will you go next?"

"I think I'll go to Mengzi to take in the sites Master Fu spoke of."

Xiongtao promised to send me directions to a few old railway locations and help book me a room at his friend's hotel in Mengzi.

"One more thing, Master Fu might have people he takes photographing, so you might catch him in Mengzi."

"All right, I'll text him when I arrive."

"Take care, my British friend…"

"You too, Xiongtao."

Click.

Following Xiontao's sage travel advice, I bused to Gejiu. First impressions were of a Chinese any-old-where, although, according to Xiongtao, this had been a regional administrative center, and was thus the first station on the branch line to be connected with the trunk in 1918.

After a few wrong turns, I found the 100-year-old Gejiu Station behind a market in a heterogeneous borough. In front was a tiled pond and some laundry swinging from the telephone wires splaying out like flies caught in a spider's web. According to a nurse I spoke with, it housed a clinic specializing in bone aliments.

A taxi ride away, Jijie Station, by contrast, was in very

different company, a French-built station house that had been unceremoniously converted into a shop selling caged birds and potted bonsai trees. It was positioned trackside in a market town mostly populated by women in hijabs and bearded men in long white thawbs.

After checking out the train depot and old railway work unit building, I made an unplanned diversion, following a rickshaw driver's advice to see "the largest mosque in the region".

"Is everyone here a Hui person?" I asked as we bounced along the asphalt, half convinced I'd fallen through a wormhole and wound up in some Yemeni backwater.

"Mostly, but I'm Han and a Buddhist," he yelled back.

He pulled up opposite a plaza bearing propaganda signs like "China Dream" and "Love the Party." Their positioning wasn't unusual — every public space in China was being decorated with some form of political advertising in the Xi-era. But what these Party dictums confronted was a significant competitor to its claim to being the highest authority in the land, an enormous, white, Taj Mahal-like mosque flanked by four symmetrical minarets.

A small sign explained The Great Mosque of Shadian had been established in the Hongzhi years of the Ming Dynasty (1488-1505), although it had been destroyed more than once — testament to China's uneasy accommodation of Islam — the last time being 1975 at the tail end of the Cultural Revolution. What stood before me was a reconstruction, though it had the aura of somewhere far older.

"Let's go inside," my rickshaw driver said, leading the way.

"It's fine," he said, beckoning me forward, though I was a bit hesitant.

We walked up to the steps and removed our shoes. Men were filing into the main hall in huge numbers to pray on neat rows of cushions before an imam leading the congregation with a microphone. A security guard asked me some questions but offered no serious opposition to my snooping around. I had to pinch myself to make sure I was awake, so surreal and unexpected was the scene before me.

After prayers, the faithful left as swiftly as they'd arrived, most passing by me as if I were a ghost as they hurried down the stairs to get their shoes and restart their phones. But one man sporting a greying goatee beard confronted me.

"Where are you from?" he asked in a moderately friendly tone.

"I'm British," I told him.

"Are there Muslims in your country?"

"Some, of course."

"What about you?"

"No, I'm not really anything…"

"Christian?"

"Well no, I suppose culturally, you could say, lapsed Protestant… Are you of the Hui nationality?"

"That's what the Chinese call us, but we are simply Muslims. In this world there are only two kinds of people, Muslims and non-Muslims. You should study Islam."

How bizarre. In Jianshui I'd be accused of being a closeted Muslim, whereas in Jijie, I was made an unwitting candidate for conversion.

"Listen to me and repeat." He said something in Arabic and I tried to repeat him.

"Incorrect, try again."

I made another attempt at curling my tongue around the foreign syllables.

"You see, you are now speaking the sacred word, the words of Allah Almighty."

"Thanks," I replied, not sure what else to say about this

impromptu class on the steps of a mighty mosque in communist China.

The rickshaw driver pointed to his watch so I shyly asserted we must go, saying "I need to get to the station."

"Don't be like the Chinese," the man said, while I laced up my shoes. "They have no god."

V

I walked cautiously across a glass floor beneath which lay railway tracks and sleepers. The walls on either side of the entrance hall were festooned with images of the railway in Yunnan, including the Renzi Bridge.

"Hi there," said a girl at a front desk.

"Is this the Dianyue Station?" I asked.

"Correct."

"Then my friend Xiongtao should have made a booking for me."

"Let me just check," the girl said, staring at a computer screen. Meanwhile, I briefly scanned a lobby packed with enough railway paraphernalia to comfortably fill a wing of the national museum in Beijing. Even the tea house in the corner had been decked out to resemble Gejiu Station.

"Yes, Thomas, please hand me your passport."

I was given a vintage train ticket, "Your voucher to spend at the restaurant next door on breakfast," she said, then directed me to my bedroom, which was down a corridor decked out like an imitation green train passenger carriage. My room was not numbered but named 'Nanxi' after one of the stations on the old French line.

"Dianyue Station is confirmation that in a world of bizarre and kitschy themed-hotels, the Chinese are unmatched, even by the Americans," I jotted in my notebook before bed.

The following morning, I bused to another of Xiongtao's recommendations, Bise Station, which was on the original Kunming-Haiphong railway line and bisected by the Tropic of Cancer. It was historically significant, a village that had been home to only a dozen or so people until 1910 when it became "an extremely busy transit station and trade center fair". Telecommunications and post offices were established there as well as several foreign firms, particularly after 1936 when the Gebishi branch line became fully operational.

Most intriguingly, during World War II, some of Beijing's top universities fled to Yunnan where they forged the National Southwestern University with some of the faculties installed in a lakeside French customs house in Mengzi. Many of China's finest minds travelled south via train, alighting here at Bise.

But like Jianshui's made-to-look-old station, Bise had been given an over-enthusiastic tourist makeover. The end result was more fantasy France than reality. And unlike Jianshui, there was no means of travelling back to the grand stone bridges of Qing China as there was only a model steam engine where tourists posed for selfies in cosplay costumes.

I was glad to see Master Fu wander down the tracks.

"There you are, Xiao Fei," he called. He was with two photography enthusiasts dragging Nikons weighed down with lenses long enough to snap life on Mars. They quickly got to work photographing the station buildings while Fu sat down for a bottle of tamarind juice and a chat at a trackside café.

"Well, what do you think of the Dianyue Railway so far?" he asked, patting me on the back like comrades reunited after a long war.

"The scenery had been stunning. But in Vietnam, I saw some well-conserved buildings, whereas in China, I've either found tacky tourist stations like this one or rundown old buildings falling into disrepair. Nowhere looks like the pictures you and Cui Xiongtao showed me back in Kunming."

He stroked his mutton chops for a few moments and then declared, "Zhicun!"

"What is Zhicun?"

"It's a place. Not far from here."

Master Fu informed his clients we were going to Zhicun. "More authentic," I caught him saying and with the obedience of puppies, they followed Fu towards his car.

We were soon cruising into the high hills that surrounded Mengzi, losing visibility as we pierced the cloud line. The drive took less than an hour but the scene was very different, as if with each mile we hopped back a century. Fu pulled up and gestured for us to alight from the vehicle and follow him down some railway tracks. It was cooler at this altitude and scented with pungent farm smells.

"Here it is," Fu said proudly.

Sure enough, a superb, yellow station house that looked as if it had been airlifted from provincial France, stood trackside with the characters Zhicun Railway Station written from right to left in traditional Chinese script. It was neither touristy nor derelict.

"Pretty nice, huh?" Fu half asked, half asserted, putting his hands on his hips.

The scene came alive when a lady in fantastic traditional dress strolled down the track oblivious to our photography group. Her bonnet was pink, her stockings a range of purples. She was followed shortly afterwards by an older woman in a gypsy head scarf with green stockings carrying a bamboo backpack brimming with turnips. Her dress was not unlike that of the woman Richard He and I stayed with in the mountains of Lijiang.

"This is a Miao village," explained Master Fu. The Miao,

known as the Hmong in Vietnam, are dotted across upland South China and Southeast Asia. Originally from Hunan Province, they had long resisted assimilation into mainstream society, preferring instead, to band together in remote mountain locales like this one.

"Where are they all coming from?"

Fu pointed to a lane. "There's a market back there."

I followed his directions and soon found myself intruding on a Miao mountain bazaar par excellence. There was a plethora of medicinal fungi and wild herbs, most varieties unknowable to my untrained eyes. Makeshift stalls sold cheap cassette players, analogue wristwatches, shell-case mobile phones and other technological commodities long obsolete elsewhere. There were blocks of honeycomb swarmed by bees and huge bunches of dried tobacco leaves piled high on tables. Street-side tailors fixed fantastic dresses as if they were old socks; cobblers repaired shoes; soothsayers and traditional healers traded in advice, and most alarmingly, dentistry was conducted in the open air with only the most rudimentary of tools. I'd stumbled upon a world within a world, a lost kingdom hidden in the clouds.

I spent a good hour photographing the captivating Miao women, with their hooped earrings, radiant headscarves and brilliantly weathered faces. Nobody seemed to notice me or be the slightest bit bothered by my curiosity, which was strange, as the Han Chinese made a point of staring at foreigners. Market affairs, that's what mattered to the Miao of Zhicun, I realized.

It came as a surprise when a familiar voice accosted me, "Ah, here you are, foreign friend."

"Cui Xiongtao! What are you doing here?"

"I was bored in Kunming. I decided to drive down to Mengzi and then Master Fu told me you were up here. Come on, let's get lunch, everyone's waiting for you, you haven't been answering your phone."

Fu, the two photographers and a friend of Xiongtao were lunching in a wooden rice-noodle shack. The Miao men were all drinking baijiu with their meal, red-faced and laughing. It looked to me like a Miao version of ye olde inn. Just opposite, one of the buildings was a wooden dwelling adorned with a brass plaque.

"What does that say?" I asked Xiongtao.

"That's where Ho Chi Minh stayed in the 1920s," he replied, casually stirring his broth. "It says he came here to study revolutionary tactics."

VI

Mengzi turned electric after nightfall, transforming a docile prefecture capital into the regional karaoke mecca. Spas advertised foot massages with neon flashing feet while clapping girls lured diners to rowdy restaurants serving the city's signature dish, 'crossing-the-bridge' rice noodles, which derived its name from the story of a scholar who'd studied for the imperial exam on a lake island in a park on the edge of town, his wife crossing the bridge each day to deliver his lunch.

After dinner, we retired to the rooftop bar at Dianyue Station to analyze the photos of the day over bottles of beer. Fu was holding court, plotting aloud where we should visit in the morning. It was at this point I told Xiongtao, "I won't feel I've seen the Dianyue Railway until I've been to Renzi Bridge", with the hope that my earnest demeanor and quiet request would pull on the heartstrings of my hosts. I knew it was a long way, even from Mengzi, but the image of the *Viaduct de Faux Namti* had haunted me since I'd first cast eyes on it at the railway museum in Kunming. To get so close and not see it would be a train traveler's travesty. Xiongtao took my point seriously and went to work on Fu and company, drip-feeding the idea via the largely incomprehensible Kunming dialect before throwing me a reassuring nod.

The following morning, we divided into two groups. I rode with Xiongtao who drove fast, smoking cigarettes and singing boisterously along to songs in Chinese, English and even Italian as we ploughed southwards into the deep hills of Pingbian county. This was Miao country, defined by wooden mountain villages virtually hanging off cliff faces as if gravity wasn't a thing. Their primitive dwellings appeared in stark contrast to the Miao women's spectacular garments. Evidently fashion topped homemaking on the local priority list. The only traffic we encountered were open-top trucks brimming with tropical fruit: mangoes, pineapples and bananas, invariably heading north to Kunming. Otherwise, the road was ours, a snake of tarmac following the contours of the good earth. Only occasionally did man's ungracious hand reveal itself whenever we passed beneath an elevated expressway that was being driven ruthlessly through the landscape.

"When that's finished, it will be easy to get to the Renzi Bridge," Xiongtao said. "Just a couple of hours from Kunming, that's all it will take."

"Why would they build an expressway down here?" I asked. "There's not much of an economy beyond fruit plantations by the looks of things."

"For trade with Vietnam. Or war, if need be."

His last comment landed like a grenade in my lap. China hasn't been at war with anyone for decades but it always seemed to be preparing for armed conflict, as though sooner or later, Taiwan, Japan or Vietnam was going to warrant a rematch.

After some hours, we rounded a bend and began a magnificent descent into a valley shadowed by steep forested hills. The land was all oranges and reds, a blend of warm sunshine and rich claret earth.

"You can see the Dianyue Railway down there," Xiongtao explained, pointing to what looked like a contour line on a map. Only via my camera lens could I see what he was talking about, a lonely railway track following a lower lip of the hill until it disappeared inside a tunnel.

"This is the Sichua River Valley," Xiongtao said. "It's a tributary of the Nanxi that flows into the Red River at Hekou. The railway had to follow the path of least resistance; that's why the track does a loop through the ravine," he explained.

Three hours after leaving Mengzi, we pulled into a driveway in Wujia Village as if arriving at an old friend's house. Some Miao peasant women in full regalia looked through the glass at me as though I was a zoo animal.

"Relax, they know me, I've been here before," Xiongtao said.

While Xiongtao talked to the locals, I surveyed the scene: Wujia was a village of just five or so households stepped into the hillside. Trees weighed down with bulbous mangoes flanked us on all sides.

Water had carved the rocks into a natural gorge so pretty it could have been used for a billboard advertisement for a pricey brand of French mineral water. But it was the object binding the image together that was the pièce de resistance, two trusses lowered together like a drawbridge between vertical cliff faces that harmoniously bonded the natural world and the world of man. After days tracing this obscure railway, it was immensely satisfying to actually see the *Viaduct de Faux Namti*, or Renzi Bridge, in such a spectacular setting.

Xiongtao and I walked along the river following a narrow stone path, occasionally hopping from stone to stone across the water. The path zigzagged uphill and eventually enabled us to climb onto the railway track itself.

"Are you sure this is allowed?" I asked as we entered a cave with bats roosting upside down, like a scene from an Indiana Jones film. The smell of bat shit was eye-watering.

"It's fine," Xiongtao said, using his phone as a torch. "Trust me, the farmers around here use the railway as a road."

After a minute, we re-emerged into the sunlight, standing on the Renzi Bridge itself. There was a small guardhouse and bird cage but no man or pet in residence. A discreet plaque on the wall commemorated its completion in 1907. The bridge seemed smaller than I'd imagined but the view was a mighty one and we reveled in the vista of the lost valley before us.

By the time we got back to Wujia Village, Master Fu had arrived and was busy checking everyone into the village inn. While Xiongtao took a siesta and Fu led his clients on a photoshoot of the bridge, I changed into the beach shorts I bought in Vietnam and went for a swim. Meditating on the viaduct from the water below, it struck me that there was something primordial and sensual about it, its shape somewhat vaginal, the river flowing like the current from a mother's womb.

There were no streetlights in Wujia and after nightfall, the stars appeared in all their cosmic glory. We dined in a moon-lit courtyard on locally grown rice and vegetables, washed down with plenty of rice wine.

I felt rare state of contentment in Wujia, a sense that nowhere on earth was better than that remote village. The seemingly arbitrary quest to find an old French bridge had led me to the most beautiful, if far-flung places, imaginable, distracting me entirely from all my petite concerns about romance or work or whatever — travel serving as a potent remedy to the absurd worries that pervade the day-to-day. There, I was without yearning. Though village dogs howled at the moon, my 'black dog' had vanished entirely, left behind somewhere along that winding mountain road.

My belly full, I excused myself, planning to write up my notes before lethargy consumed me after such a long and wonderful day. But there was yet a surprise in stall.

"Hey, Xiao Fei, don't want to see the train?" Fu asked while chomping on fried spinach.

"Which train?"

"They still use the Dianyue Railway for freight. I called my train driver friend; it should be passing through around 9:45 p.m."

And so we grabbed our cameras and walked back up the river, this time in total darkness, settling on some boulders in the middle of the stream like hunters camped out for the night. The sound of the rushing water, the scent of the earth and the chill of the valley, all became amplified when blind. Invisible insects and birds hooted and sniggered. Our stake-out lasted unknowable minutes. Then, from down the valley, a horn blew and the shunting sound of a train bounced across the hillside.

"It's coming," Master Fu said, readying his camera like a sniper.

When the train disappeared into the tunnel the noise was amplified ten-fold, a sudden roar from the belly of the beast. Then it appeared on the bridge, *clappity-clap, clappity-clap,* cameras flashed rescuing the valley from darkness like strobe lights at a disco. I half expected the old thing to collapse, so sudden was the drama. But she held steady, an owl hooted and the train passed into the night.

THE NOT-SO-EXPRESS TRAIN TO WENZHOU

I

Due to the cuddly *guobao,* or 'national treasures' — as the Chinese call their pandas — easygoing Chengdu was on most tourists' itinerary. But this was nothing new. Notwithstanding some marked episodes of discontent over the centuries, Sichuan Province's capital had been embraced to the imperial bosom long before eco-tourism was a thing, lauded with praise since the Han Dynasty as one of China's finest cities.

As I transferred from station to hotel, my attention was lured heavenwards by the near-purple haze enveloping gargantuan malls. It was only as the taxi stalled in soul-wrenching traffic that I was able to contemplate the modern metropolis' lingering aura of Han China — flat and carved into right angles, its original plan an imitation of the imperial capital Chang'an, so I'd read on the train from Kunming.

Hip and fashionable, Chengdu served as the west China's de facto capital, a major economic and transport hub as Beijing looked back down the Silk Road to rekindle past glories. Yet the province wasn't the quintessentially Chinese place it was often made out to be. A few kilometres beyond the city's western limits, the pastoral lands of the sedentary Han submitted to vertical terrain far better suited to a wandering nomad in the company of a large dog. Four great Yangtze tributaries cascade down from the mountains, making eastern Sichuan a basin in a very literal sense of the word.

This meeting of the civilizational tides was conspicuous just outside my guesthouse where I was greeted to the provincial capital by a gang of burly Tibetans thumping the roofs of their minibuses while calling out distinctly un-Chinese destinations names like Gser Thar and Dar Mdo Grong Khyer.

I was lodging in Little Lhasa, a grubby borough that was home to an estimated 60,000 Tibetans, who, by the looks of things, principally made a living peddling animal hides, Buddha effigies and beady necklaces. The pervasive odour of yak milk and the odd glimpse of robed monks buying barley bread from handsomely dressed Tibetan women was a surreal scene in such a large, homogenous Chinese city, a rare glimpse of the exotic, and one I loved.

I soon felt the call of wild and contemplated heading west towards the Qinghai frontier. But it was a call that went unheeded due to the borderline sadistic hospitality of the Chengduers who would not let me go gentle into that good night without an unreasonable amount of Sichuan peppercorns and red-hot chilli peppers burning in my belly.

Along with sister city Chongqing—which was sliced off Sichuan to be made a municipality in 1997—Chengdu was the cradle of *chuancai*, often anglicized as Szechwan Cooking, a bold and complex gastronomic tradition typified by hot and spicy hot pot, a steaming broth so pungent it could cook you from the inside out. Hot pot was, of course, delicious, why else would anyone bother? But it was conversely devilish, for what excites the pallet can tear apart the lining of the lower intestines the following morning, and leave you dancing around the bathroom with a wet wipe squashed between your bum cheeks. Those unaccustomed to Sichuan food should consume it like strong liquor, in moderation. The Sichuanese, whose diaspora covers all corners of China, were just about the kindest people you were likely to meet in the Middle Kingdom. And on hearing I'd rolled into town, a queue of old acquaintances quickly formed, all vying for a frontline position for the honour of watching a poor travel writer eat himself to death on their account.

A series of long evenings burping through kung fu tea performances and *bian lian* — an ancient dramatic art of face changing — ensued, in the company of old colleagues and comrades. My body's bold efforts to digest the chilli-coated fodder mandated afternoons spent sprawled across my hotel bed watching Korean soap operas while farting.

This cycle of excess was only scheduled to end when a teahouse was agreed upon as the venue for a date with a local girl I'd been liaising with on WeChat.

Rattling beneath Chengdu on the metro, I found myself ahead of time, so I disembarked one station early at Tianfu Square.

Above ground, I encountered the city's famous Mao Zedong statue saluting a busy road like a giant traffic warden. Messianic, porcelain-white, the Chairman was flanked by two heavily armed SWAT teams. It was an unnerving display of power, although the weekend shoppers appeared oblivious to these imperial guardsmen who were scouring the crowd as if their Gucci handbags might conceal hand grenades.

The fashion set was clearly out in force for the weekend. Had I arrived from Mars, I could easily be convinced that a jockey named Ralph Lauren was sponsoring an event. I'd read that the denizens of China's sixth largest city had made it the country's third largest luxury brand market. But seeing was believing. One could only speculate why. Perhaps, this flaunt-it-all mentality was a by-product of the disasters that periodically rocked

HARMONY EXPRESS

Tianfu, 'the Heavenly Land' most recently in Jiuzhaigou, which was struck by a 7.0 magnitude earthquake in August 2017, just ahead of my arrival. Whatever the reason, for one who was so recently hiking amidst the ethnic minorities of southern Yunnan, acclimating to this globalist tribe required some adjustment.

I headed down the road to People's Park. Amongst the yellowing ginkgo trees, I found a public space trying its level best to be all things to all men, melding classical elements like Song-style moon bridges and scenic orchards with modern leisure facilities like pedal-boat hire and ice-cream stalls. Whether it succeeded was debatable, although it certainly was noisy and crowded, which for the Chinese meant fun.

The masses had gathered in their numbers to hammer through discordant renditions of dewy pop ballads such as *I Love You Like Mice Love Rice*. There were pensioners in silk pyjamas practising tai-chi and children running feral amongst the bamboo groves while their parents played *jianzi* — a game that involved kicking a feathered shuttlecock around on the heel of one's boot. A congregation of languid weekenders occupied the park's famous open-air teahouses, discussing the news of day with the 'ol' and 'lo' sounds that distinguished Sichuanese from Mandarin the way peppercorns and chillies distinguished Sichuan soup from northern broth. And everyone, it appeared, was determined to get between me and the patriotic monument without which no park in China could be considered complete.

I somehow managed to forge a worm-like passage to the foot of a stone obelisk, centrepiece of the Xinhai Railway Square. Large Chinese characters written on each side of the quadrilateral pillar expressed that the site commemorated the "Martyrs who died protecting the railway". Aesthetically, it was not dissimilar to monuments dotted throughout China. But the Railway Protection Movement that cost the thirty-three lives in 1911 had been no picnic in the park. In fact, this monument marked the stage where the death spiral of the 269-year-old Qing Dynasty began, bringing down the curtain on a system of governance that had endured for more than two millennia.

The lead-up to the Xinhai Revolution was closely aligned with the industrial revolution and the transport revolution that followed it, epitomized by the railways snaking their way around the globe. Except, that is, in China, where the tracks developed at the speed of a slothful panda after a bamboo banquet. The reasons for this were manifold, although historians usually cited the sense of haughty superiority maintained by the Manchu elite, and their foremost disdain for 'barbarian manufactures'. The opinion of many Chinese commoners aligned with their rulers, fearing smoke-belching iron horses charging through one's back garden would disturb a deep rooted Daoist sense of cosmic harmony. It was not until the Sino-Japanese War of 1894-1895, when Japan whipped China with its arsenal of Western-style weapons — in doing so triggering the scramble for concessions among other imperial powers — that attitudes toward railways became more favourable.

Throughout the first decade of the 20th Century, complex financial agreements were reached among investors, both local and foreign. But when the Imperial Court performed an about-face, nationalizing all the main railway lines, including the Sichuan-Hankou and Hankou-Guangzhou railways, the investors were understandably annoyed, especially when they learned they'd be compensated for just two-thirds of their investments. The Railway Protection League was established in Sichuan Province to contest this palace railway coup, but it soon assumed a patriotic tone, attracting 10,000 supporters to Chengdu in support of strikes and a tax boycott against a Manchu monopoly of the railway.

HARMONY EXPRESS

Beijing ordered the New Army garrison from Wuchang (in present-day Wuhan) to deploy troops to Sichuan to defuse the simmering tensions. But Wuhan at the time was a hotbed of revolutionary activity and at least one third of the 16,000-man-strong New Army belonged to underground groups, some with links to arch agitator in exile, Dr Sun Yat-sen and his revolutionary alliance, the *Tongmenghui*. Fearing the deployment would compromise their own plans for a revolution, a hasty rebellion was plotted. But their scheme would be overtaken by events when a bomb exploded in a kitchen in the Russian Concession. Their cover blown, the rebels had no choice but to rise up. Months of mutinies, pitched battles and strained negotiations ensued, concluding with the founding of a Republic on January 1, 1912, in Nanjing, with the election of Sun as Provisional President.

I wandered around pondering the convoluted collapse of the Dragon Throne. Chinese dynasties were usually brought down by epic wars, horrific famines and epidemics—not some provincial complaints about public transport. I couldn't help but wonder if the House of Windsor ever got edgy whenever the privatization issue flared up in the British newspapers.

A tap on the shoulder awakened me from my thoughts.

"Is that for me?" Gua asked sanguinely.

"Hey, you," I said, giving her a hug. "Yes, of course..." I handed over the balloon I'd purchased from a park vendor beside the Railway Protection Monument. "I hope you like Ultraman?"

"Oh yes, he's my favourite," she said, chuckling.

Heading over to a teahouse, it took some time before we were able to capture two seats from a departing couple.

"Finally somewhere to rest my knees," I said, releasing a long groan as I sat down.

But Gua was too kind to make a slippers and pipe joke. "It's so good to see you again," she said, while settling into her creaky bamboo chair in a far more elegant fashion.

"Isn't it busy here?"

"It's a Chengdu-thing, to come to People's Park on the weekend for afternoon tea. Especially for old people, the real Chengduers."

"Well they named the place accurately. A peoples' park this truly is."

"Yes, China's population is, well, how to say, *mafan*?"

"Troublesome."

"Right. But it's a nice park, not to mention, free."

"I can see why people would gravitate here," I said, casting my eyes to the leafy environs that sheltered us from the worst of the city smog. "I just would have thought some of them might do something else, like, I don't know, visit the panda sanctuary or something like that."

"That's for tourists, Silly," Gua said, evidently amused by my unease amid the masses. I'd often felt the Chinese found comfort in crowds, like a school of sardines, they instinctively perceived safety in numbers, the polar opposite of privacy-obsessed Brits who'd colonise a space in a park with some deckchairs and towels. Yet unlike my complaining compatriots, they were generally gracious, as Gua proved when she asserted, "You should be grateful to have found a seat. If we'd come on Sunday, we'd probably be drinking tea in one of those pedalos on the lake."

"Then I'm lucky I have allocated tomorrow for a serious procrastination session. Chengdu is, after all, the city of leisure, right?"

"So they say," Gua replied, before asking me, "When did you arrive in Chengdu anyway?"

"A few days ago. I came from Kunming. I was doing a bit of guidebook work, a few magazine assignments. Mostly bumbling around in the hills. I found an old French railway, which was pretty interesting if you like that sort of thing."

"Did you fly here?" Gua, asked earnestly.

"No, not me, I took the train," I said, proud of my travel stripes.

"What?" she half asked, half declared. "You're a fool. It's a really long way and flying is cheap these days," she said, firing up her phone to show me the price of an air ticket on a travel app.

"It's not about the cost, I like train travel, you know, the rhythm of the wheels, the view of the landscape gently passing by. And it was a fantastic trip, riding a green train all the way here."

It had been a fantastic trip, a full 1,000 kilometres from the high Yunnan plateau to the low Sichuan basin on a railway constructed through some of the wildest topography I'd ever seen in China. I told Gua of the great canyons carved by the waters of the Jinsha section of the Yangtze I'd seen, where I'd witnessed first-hand why Tang poet Li Bai believed it easier to get into heaven than to Sichuan.

Construction of the Chengkun trunk line had begun in 1958 with the onset of Chairman Mao's Great Leap Forward. The terrain proved so hostile that it cost thousands of workers' lives, evidenced by trackside martyrs' monuments that lined the route like milestones. But Beijing had political motives in getting the south western frontier zone wired to the grid. Yunnan was long considered a bit of a wildcard, like Tibet and Xinjiang. The province even went to war with Sichuan during the warlord period, when, after the death of wannabe emperor Yuan Shikai in 1916, China collapsed into several competing fiefdoms. So the twelve-year construction odyssey paid off in state-building terms. The Party was so proud of this feat of engineering, an ivory model of one of the Chengkun's finest railway bridges was commissioned and duly presented to the UN in New York in 1975. It remained there until 2013, when changing attitudes to artifacts made from dead elephants required its relocation.

"You didn't even take a high-speed train?" was all Gua could say of my epic and historical means of getting to People's Park.

"My friend Xiongtao told me parts of the Chengkun will be demolished soon, so I wanted to take it before high-speed rail supplants it. Such a pity. China moves too fast."

"Which tea would you like?" a hurried waiter asked, brandishing a teapot with a long spout like a medieval weapon.

I hadn't even thought about it, so grabbing the menu I picked the first tea to catch my eye. "I'll have the Snow Lake green jasmine tea," I said.

"And I'll take the Mengding Mountain sweet dew green tea," Gua said.

"When did you dye your hair?" I asked her, catching a purple-hued streak in the light of the afternoon sun, quite an act of rebellion in a pretty conservative country.

"My classmate did it, university is so boring in China, you need to do something to pass the time."

"Where is your university?" I asked, wondering privately if it was the leafy downtown campus I'd noticed earlier that day.

"It's out of town, in Meishan," she said, before adding thoughtfully, "It's a shithole."

"Why didn't you enrol in Fudan or Peking University?"

"I didn't get the grades; you know in China it's all about the *gaokao*."

Given how intelligent Gua was just confirmed my contention that exams are a flawed measure of human intelligence, particularly in a country where critical essays are more like painting by numbers.

"Didn't Su Dongpo come from Meishan?" I asked.

"Wow, you really know your history," she replied, complimenting me, as all Chinese do whenever you exude a whiff of knowledge about their culture.

"China makes a historian out of you," I retorted.

"Well, to answer your question, yes, he did. There's a statue of him in the Ancestral Temple next to the Dongpo Restaurant, which serves some delicious pork knuckles, you should go there for dinner."

"Pity, I'm a vegetarian."

"Anyway, you have esteemed alumni," I added. Su was one of history's lyrical masters, a celebrated Northern Song statesman and unparalleled creative force, even if he ate parts of the pig that should probably be thrown to the dogs.

"I suppose so," she said. "But I prefer hip-hop to old poetry. Have you heard of Sichuan rap?"

Curiously, given my abiding disdain for urban music, I had, after *Made in China* by the Higher Brothers—a group of four rappers named after the Hai'er brand of air conditioner and appliances—brought Sichuan rap onto my sonic radar. Though I was no connoisseur, the tune seemed far less derivative than Chinese rap, which usually blended the plastic aesthetics of a manufactured Boy Band with a sanitized version of street dance. The lyrics were funny and provocative, even if they presented affluent Chinese as ghettoised global minorities, a common Han conceit, and one that has always baffled me.

"Yes, I've heard a bit," I told Gua, "Who is your favourite artist?"

"I like Ty. He's very handsome. Have you heard his song *Hooked on Drugs*?"

"No, I haven't. But I have heard of Fat Shady."

If the Higher Brothers were vaguely jingoistic, Shady had

pushed the patriotism pedal full throttle with a song that ridiculed a widespread (if unrecognized) minority in China, namely, the ubiquitous English Teacher. His track *Gua Laowai*, Sichuanese for *Fucking Foreigners*, was an unabashed lyrical assault on trashy expats working in the Middle Kingdom. It had proved so risqué even the censors in Beijing had banned it, though not before it did the rounds on social media.

Evidently, Gua didn't associate *Fucking Foreigners* with me, a fucking foreigner.

"He's really awesome. He performed in Chengdu last weekend but I couldn't go, my uncle wouldn't let me."

"Well, at least you could stay in and revise some classical poetry," I quipped, trying to make light of the moment.

"How did you learn about Su Dongpo anyhow? Is he popular in the UK?"

"He should be. Actually, when I first came to China I worked in Huizhou in Guangdong Province, where Su had been banished for several years. He wrote a lot of poems there, you know, the usual stuff, waxing lyrical about the local women and wine. There's a statue of him by the lake."

"Are the women and wine particularly special in Huizhou?" Gua asked, sounding slightly jealous of an 11th Century bard.

"Not particularly".

"Then why did you take a job in Guangdong? Everybody knows the beautiful girls are from Sichuan," she said, laughing immodestly.

"This knowledge was acquired later," I replied, unable to disagree, having fallen in love twice since leaving my hotel, as well as feeling a bit smitten with young Gua.

The waiter returned with our tea, filling porcelain cups and leaving us a plastic flask of boiling water to refill as necessary.

"Enjoy," he said, before spinning away to serve somebody else.

"So where is your girlfriend?" Gua asked.

"I haven't really dated anyone since the Hunan girl who broke my heart in Shenzhen a few years ago," I explained. "I've been traveling too much."

"Yes, I've seen you on WeChat, you are never in the same place twice," she replied. "No wonder your Chinese name is Xiao Fei." Fei is the verb to fly. "You fly here, there and everywhere," she said, waving her hands like wings.

I'd met Gua working in her cousin's café in Shenzhen one summer. A pretty young thing bored by the tedium of her summer job and curious about the *laowai* trying to dry his shirt beneath an air conditioner, we'd hit it off. Her English competency had impressed me. But it had been her wide eyes that had drawn me in, dark wells of curiosity in an age of blinkered acceptance. It helped, of course, that she had some alternative tendencies evidenced in her black denim jeans, aviator shades hung from the neck of her t-shirt and faux Doc Martin boots, the latter purchased in Shenzhen's prime knock-off bazaar, Dongmen.

"So what will you do in Chengdu? Go to the panda sanctuary?" Gua quipped, while sipping her tea.

"No, I've been there before."

"Sichuan has lots of interesting places nearby like the Giant Buddha statue in Leshan."

"I've been there too," I said.

"Then what are you doing here?"

"I came to have tea with you."

"Ha, ha, you're a liar."

"Well I'm actually on my way to Zhejiang, I've been asked by a curator friend to write about a photo festival there. As I had some time, I thought I'd break up the journey. I had hoped to visit those beautiful lakes in Jiuzhaigou but the earthquake has quashed that plan."

"Do you have any other plans?" she asked, taking a loud slurp of her tea.

"Well there's an old steam train somewhere near the Big Buddha my friend Master Fu told me about."

"You and trains, you're such a train spotter these days."

"I hope not, I honestly don't know much about them. I just like to view China as a passenger; plus rail seems to me the best way to get around this country, especially when compared with cramped and polluting cars, the traffic in Chengdu is just awful."

"Cars are more convenient," she said, interrupting my flow by miming a steering wheel and beeping an invisible horn. "When I graduate I'm going to buy a British car, a *lao si lai si* (Rolls Royce)."

After we'd drunk enough tea to drown a Giant Panda, Gua took me by the hand and led me through the streets of Chengdu. Like so much of China, the city had changed radically since I'd last cast my eyes across it, with gaudy shopping centres in place of old brick neighborhoods and luxury vehicles clogging roads that were so recently the province of bicycles and motorbikes. But despite its superficial transformation, once we veered off the main drag, I found myself wandering down memory lane, passing rows of grey Mao-era tenements and oily backdoor eateries that resurrected a China largely painted over on the East Coast.

Eventually Gua settled on a *mala tang* (hot and spicy soup) restaurant that looked the same as the thousand we had passed saying, " This place is the best."

"I'll take your word for it."

The English translation 'Chinese fondue' made me chuckle even if the air within was so polluted with cigarette smoke and chilli mist, I was more inclined to cry.

"You can eat spicy food, right?" Gua asked.

I said 'yes' but it was a face-saving response given the blood-red broth into which she was soon dipping skewers of tofu and root vegetable.

"Shame you don't eat meat, the mutton here is famous."

"I'll live with it, as long as you order me a beer," I replied, fanning my tongue with a serviette.

I couldn't help but notice the place was jammed with youngsters, many sporting baggy rapper jeans and peaked caps, some, like Gua, having coloured their hair. It was a glimpse of renegade youth culture I hadn't seen in a while, reminding me of Beijing rock at its apogee in the mid-2000s.

"There are a lot of young people here," I said.

"We're near the university," Gua replied, chewing on some hyper-spiced spinach as if it were bubble gum.

I'm on my second beer by my third mouthful, already high from a noxious blend of cheap booze and endorphins triggered by the chillies.

"Do you have a tattoo?" she asked.

"No, I don't."

"I want to get one but it will have to be somewhere hard to see, you know Chinese parents…"

"The rappers don't seem too worried about what their parents think. Doesn't Fat Shady have a tattoo on his head?"

"Yes, I wish I had parents like his."

"What kind of tattoo will you get?"

"I don't know, any suggestions?"

"What about a chilli pepper on your bum? You are a Sichuan spice girl after all. And down there, your family won't see it, at least I hope they won't."

Gua threw her head back in laughter, her mouth so wide I could see her tonsils quivering as in a Tom and Jerry cartoon.

"I'll have to think about it," she managed to say.

After our meal, I tried to persuade Gua to accompany

me on a spontaneous mission to find a hip-hop gig. But she looked nervous and gestured to her watch. It was easy to forget university students are not considered fully fledged adults in China. Gua had an uncle waiting up for her, there would be no sneaking in through the kitchen window at one in the morning as I did at her age. And tomorrow morning, she'd be put on a bus back to her dorm room in Meishan for another week, diligently studying her English vocab by rote.

"Sorry, I must go," she said, looking forlorn.
"Not at all. We can't have you turn into a pumpkin."
"What?"
"Never mind. Thank you so much for tea and dinner. That fondue place was excellent. We'll have to catch a Ty show next time I'm in town."

I patted the invisible dog roadside until a passing cab pulled over. Then, opening the backdoor like a chauffeur, I waited for Gua to get in.

She suddenly embraced me, a long, tender squeeze. I could feel her heart racing against her chest. She smelled like angel dust; I imagine I smelled like a Tsingtao beer towel. But she didn't let go and I had to prise her from my shoulders like a koala cub.

"Come on," I said. "Uncle will be angry."
"Oh, fuck Uncle. You know traditional Chinese culture, it's so, *mafan*."

II

Following Master Fu's instructions, which included the words 'easy' and 'no time at all', I made an unscheduled diversion south, travelling two hundred kilometres via rail and road by late afternoon I'd made it to Jiayang, a charmless township clinging to the contours of a hill like weeds tracing the cracks in a broken pavement. The place appeared filled, uniquely, of mahjong parlors and everyone was sucking on a poor man's Cuban, the cigar smoke giving Jiayang a heavy, old-fashioned air.

Half anticipating a tumbleweed would roll by, I wandered to a memorial plaza where a band of women were practicing a traditional dance involving imperial drums and colorful folding fans. The plaza was flanked by a few historical billboards recalling the good old days of coal, forged since the Jurassic period and excavated since the late Qing Dynasty, I read.

Abutting the plaza was a smart station house-cum-visitor center that was evidently constructed with tourists in mind. Inside, however, the ticket vendors gossiping behind a desk were bonded by a mutual contempt for the "*Jiayang Huanying Nin* – Jiayang Welcomes You" big character slogan written down the side of a block of flats.

"Good afternoon," I said in my cheeriest Chinese, winning various looks of indignation. "Are tickets for sale?"

"Sorry, no sightseer trains today, only on weekends and holidays," the group matriarch said.

"I see," I replied, as the prospect of spending a night in Jiayang hit me like a dagger in a prison latrine. "But isn't there a regular train service to Bajiaogou?"

"Um, yes, last one's at 4:45 p.m." She looked at her colleagues who nodded like obedient puppies.

"That's what I'm looking for. One ticket please."

"Do you want a return ticket?"

"Is there a return service tonight?"

"No. But you could come back on the same train."

"Why would I do that?"

"I don't know."

"What about tomorrow?"

"That's hard to say."

"Why?"

"There's been some damage to the tracks. There may be maintenance work tomorrow."

"You don't know?"

"I don't know."

Resolving that whatever Bajiaogou was like, it couldn't be any worse than Jiayang, I asked for a return ticket before inquiring, "Are there are any hotels there, in case I decide to stay the night?"

"*Yexu*," she replied bluntly, maybe, then resumed conversation before I'd unwittingly disturbed cosmic harmony.

Confusingly, the name of the station outside was not Jiayang (as would be typical) but Yuejin, meaning Great Leap after The Great Leap Forward. In the late-1950s Chairman Mao tried to catapult agrarian China into the industrial age with a massive nationwide mobilization program. It succeeded like one of those pedal-powered airplanes launched from a cliff in black and white films. Hysteria gripped a country trying to realize unattainable goals set by an increasingly dictatorial leader with only an abstract grasp of reality. Few, if any, recalled the time of backyard furnaces and People's Communes with much fondness. The Great Leap's principal legacy was death, estimated to be thirty million, mostly from hunger, making Yuejin a baleful designation.

After a few minutes, a tiny steam engine reversed into view along the narrow-gauge track, belching smoke like Jiayang's ubiquitous smokers. I'd half anticipated it to be painted gaudy colors like the train in Yunnan but as this assembly of nuts, bolts and filth heaved into view, I realized the tourist yuan was yet to corrupt the authenticity of the experience.

Standing beside me was a wrinkled man in a blue Mao hat and worker's jacket who looked to have been frozen in time since 1958 and only recently thawed out. He moved slowly, twitching to suck at a cigar and appeared slightly nervous in the presence of a foreigner armed with a camera and a notepad.

A uniformed man communicated with the driver by whistling until all four wooden carriages were coupled to the steam engine. He then ordered the old man, me, and a gaggle of vegetable-burdened peasant women, to board.

With some disconcerting shunts we began our journey, soon forging a route through muddy rice and cabbage fields. I struggled to get acquainted with the wooden chair, although the bucolic environs more than made up for the discomfort of the carriage.

We shunted into Honeybee Crag twenty minutes down the line, a railway graveyard littered with rusty train engines and abandoned gondolas, relics of a time before China's 21st Century great leaps. A villager boarded, clutching chickens, one under each arm, which squirmed and squawked as the train engine noisily decoupled and skirted around us — making a switch back — reconnecting at the rear to push us up a steep mountain ridge.

We were soon rolling through thick vegetation, wild forests blanketing a deep gorge called *Xianren Xiagu*, Canyon of the Immortals.

"Where are you from, foreign friend?" the man in the Mao hat asked, having overcome his initial shyness.

"The UK," I called over the clunking carriages and chicken chatter.

"*Hao difang*," he said giving me a thumbs-up, meaning "a good place."

"It has its charms, I suppose."

He paused for a while, then said, "It was you Brits that made this railway famous. They started to come here again about ten years back, photographing everything and asking all sorts of questions."

"Really?"

"Oh yes, just a few of them at first, then more and more until the government decided to make this into a scenic spot and open it up to tourism."

"Why did you say *again*?"

"Because you people came here before. A long time ago"

"Really?"

"You'll see what I mean in Bajiaogou."

We pull into Rapeseed Flower Dam, where the man alighted just ahead of the highest point on the railway, Eagle Beak, a perilous ridge we traced at half speed. I couldn't help but imagine the train tripping into the river below, our untimely end commemorated with a Hollywood-style explosion. But our premature end comes at Jiao Dam instead, commemorated by an unhealthy wheeze of the boiler, one stop before our destination.

"The tracks are damaged up ahead," the conductor said, unapologetically, adding, "We stop here."

I followed the peasant women onto a minuscule platform and they promptly dispersed into the villages, leaving me alone for some confused minutes, stricken in deepest Sichuan.

Eventually, a villager sporting Wellington boots called at me from a trackside field, "Where you going, *Laowai*?"

"Bajiaogou." I replied.

"Need a ride?"

"Sure."

"Five yuan?" he asked.

"Great," I said, knowing I would have paid 100.

"In China, there is always a way," I managed to scribble in my diary seconds before he arrived on his Yamaha, a cigar butt dangling from his lip as if it had been glued there years ago.

For half a mile at least we coasted along the ballast, until, just before a tunnel, he swerved from the tracks onto a narrow mountain road. Our route then traced a path with more turns in it than a snake hugging a hosepipe until we stopped at a vintage hillside settlement half submerged in vegetation.

"This is Baijiaogou Industrial Township," he explained, applying its full name before pointing to the town square. "You can find somewhere to stay over there."

Hoisting my backpack onto my shoulders, I paid him and made for the square, The East is Red Plaza, suggesting the handiwork of an enthusiastic local tourist bureau. Yet this was no romantic piece of branding. The plaza itself boasted an enormous outdoor theatre topped by a portrait of the youthful Great Helmsman and a big character sign that read: "Mao Zedong Thought Grand Stage." The scale of the square was extraordinary when compared with its surroundings, evoking a time when this place mattered, or mattered a lot more than it did when I arrived. Though the square was empty bar a few aunties exercising to the beat of a Taiwanese pop song, my imagination couldn't help but populate it with fanatical Red Guards, a landlord on stage wearing a dunce hat and confessing his class crimes, a standard form of humiliation during those ideological times.

In the People's Canteen opposite the stage, I encountered some old-timers sucking on long tobacco pipes and sipping tea. None could speak Mandarin with any fluency, so I followed my nose down a side street to a restaurant dishing up Sichuanese staples like Pockmarked Granny's Bean Curd and accosted the restaurateur, "Excuse me, Boss, know of anywhere I might stay for the night?"

"Follow me," she replied, promptly removing her apron and marching me down the road like a child late for school.

I was led to the end of a hillside street and, effectively, into somebody's house, then abandoned in the courtyard while she walked street side to call someone on her vintage Nokia. Bats were already whizzing about overhead, daylight fading.

Eventually, a man wrinkled like an old sock arrived with a set of keys as big as a school janitor's. Opening the door, he led me into a room equipped with all the mod cons you might expect in a place where *March of the Revolutionary Youth* was still top of the pops, including an ensuite squat toilet and complimentary hose, a rust-colored roof fan and an enormous Sanyo television set manufactured circa 1983.

"I'm assuming the honeymoon suite is already occupied?" I quipped.

"*Shenme?*"

"Never mind, how much is it?"

"Thirty yuan."

"I'll take it."

"Here's the key. It doesn't work very well so just leave the door open when you go out, okay?"

"Is it safe?"

The man and woman burst into laughter. "Is it safe?" he repeated, and they wandered away without checking my passport or asking for a deposit.

Despite my rustic and somewhat bizarre environs, it felt good to have secured a roof for the night. I dropped my bag, pulled out my diary and tried to take stock of the day. China's all-encompassing public transport network had moved me from a city of electric brand logos to a township of Cultural Revolution slogans, "a shift in time and place only possible in a country as big and lopsided as this one," I wrote.

I consoled myself with the prospect of the dawn, concluding my diary entry thus: "Tomorrow will shed light on everything." Then closing my Moleskine, I triumphantly fell onto the bed, which collapsed, rolling me head first onto the floor like an armadillo.

HARMONY EXPRESS

Morning did illuminate everything. Waking up to a perspective-shaping view of some vast limestone pillars overshadowing the town was worthy recompense for one who slept at a forty-five degree angle. Despite a faint aftertaste of coal, the petrichor was magnificent.

Lured by the comforting sound of running water, I settled beside the mountain stream that bisected Bajiaogou, an ideal setting to breakfast on steamed buns in the company of some ducks. The water was flanked by Cyathea plants, which have been around since the age of dinosaurs, providing a 'land that time forgot' backdrop to the town China forgot.

Just downstream, I came upon Zhongfu Street, a lively, if somewhat shabby strip where an ad hoc wet market had made it the only point of serious human activity. Apparently the buildings here dated back to the 1940s, when, according to a wall sign this had been "the business and trade center of Bajiaogou, where smoking houses, gambling houses and brothels were in service before 1949". Sounded like a happening place. But there was little vestige of vice left, sadly, just a cobbler, a seamstress and several cabbage vendors.

Beyond the market hubbub, I finally encountered what the man on the train had been talking about when he'd insisted the Brits had been here before, an Anglo presence evidenced in some collapsing cottages, what the tourist bureau has rosily dubbed a "British Style Residential Community". It was the least expected of sights to confront deep in Panda country, and spookily familiar for one who grew up in a Victorian town, prompting a visit to the Party and Mass Workers Office — nowadays a small museum, where I hoped to figure out what English country houses had to do with a 1950s railway line and relics from China's not-so-swinging '60s.

While surveying display cabinets packed with random knickknacks like a songbook of Hong Kong boy band Beyond, a miner's tin hat and a collection of 1980s ghetto blasters, I struggled to ascertain what the museum was trying to say. Even the wall placards told a fragmented story that bounced from the heroic defense of the Motherland to the railway's commanding role in the transportation revolution that began with James Watts' "first practical steam engine in 1776" and stretched right through to 2013 when "the narrow-gauge Jiayang Steam Train continues the history of industrialized civilization."

What I managed to discern was that it was the Japanese invasion that triggered the industrial colonization of this otherwise obscure corner of China: "In 1937, the War of Resistance against Japan broke out. Zhongfu Coal Mine Company, a Sino-British joint venture in Jiaozhou, Henan, was in danger." Fearing that their precious mining equipment might be captured by the invading forces, hero-of-the-day General Manager Sun Yueqi declared, "Japan is friendly to England, but an enemy of China. We shall not allow our enemy to fight us with this equipment, we must dismantle it."

The mining equipment was duly moved to deepest Sichuan and reassembled. After 1949, the pits came under state control. The narrow-gauge railway, which was constructed by hand, was completed in 1959, delivering coal to the river barges moored at Shixi that fed the Great Leap smelting plants in Chengdu and Chongqing.

Curiously, there was no mention of Mao's decree that China's steel production should exceed that of Great Britain's within fifteen years that provoked such furor. Nor was there any detail of the nationwide tragedy during the Cultural Revolution that laid the foundations for the contemporary Maoist theme park outside. As so often was the case in China, there was propaganda by erasure.

On leaving the museum, I briefly quizzed the doorman on what happened to Bajiaogou.

"I was sent here to mine in the '60s, we had no choice. Back then, this was a bustling place. There were four mines. It was dangerous work, of course, and lots of people died. The hills around here are full of bodies. The mines began to close when Comrade Deng Xiaoping came to power. The young people all went elsewhere. But some of us were too old to leave so we stayed on."

I asked him why they kept the train running after the mines closed.

"As a means of transport for villagers, of course. There was no mountain road until a few years back."

"But the train is still running."

"It's convenient, especially for village elders who don't have a motorbike. It also brings sightseers like you from time to time."

He recommended I visit a nearby pit located down the road at Huangcun, which periodically opened to tourists. But it was closed, so I walked back to my guesthouse, packed up my things and got ready to depart on the afternoon train.

"You should have come here in spring when the rapeseed flowers are in bloom," said the restaurateur when I returned my hotel key. "We get plenty of tourists then, this place is packed with photographers and train buffs."

"I'm happy to have visited in the off-season," I told her. "I've had the place to myself."

"You shouldn't travel alone, it's meaningless," she said, accusingly.

"Perhaps," I said, privately believing the contrary to be true.

I asked her how to get to Jiao Dam in time for the 2:10 p.m. train.

"Just walk along the tracks, that's the easiest way."

"Oh yes?"

Yes, that's what we villagers do. It's not far, twenty minutes or so. Just be careful."

Climbing onto a mossy railway bridge, I took one last look at Bajiaogou, more an old people's home than a model industrial township. Given China's rate of progress, the place appeared more antiquated than it actually was, a coal age Angkor Wat, now largely the domain of cats, its semi-abandoned homes pitted in a losing battle with the native plant life.

Turning my nose towards the tracks, I set off on my own Long March back to the 21st Century following the bamboo flanked railway as it arced into a tunnel. It was a rare and glorious thing to be alone in China and I only passed one individual, a grandma skirting a basket of sweet potatoes along the rail brace.

I trod on for perhaps a kilometer or more until I reached a red sign warning of construction work, so I followed a stone staircase into a hillside hamlet where more miners' cottages had been oriented back to agriculture, a subsistence from which modern industry was supposed to have liberated locals. Firewood was stacked high, cobs of corn dangled before the barn doors and the entire place smelled of pig shit. There were a few old-timers playing cards and smoking but they did their level best to ignore me.

Finding the tracks again, it was not much longer before I arrived back at Jia Dam Station where I dropped off my bag, leaned back and enjoyed the scenery while patiently awaiting the steam train.

But it didn't materialize, long after it was due.

"Is the train delayed?" I asked a passing farmer, two buckets swinging from a stick of bamboo hung across his shoulders.

"Sometimes," he replied, monosyllabically

"Is it ever cancelled?"

"Sometimes," he repeated, pointing to a piece of paper taped to a post warning of disruption due to track repair.

"Shit!" was my immediate reaction, blurted out in English to the bemusement of the man. But as I digested reality, a sense of relief sunk in. It was a glorious day, the light shafts beaming through the tree canopy turning the track into an impressionistic painting. I had no pressing need to be anywhere and the Sichuan countryside awaited.

"*Xiexie*," I said as I passed the farmer, "thank you." Then, aligning myself with the steel corridor on the floor, I stepped forth onto a wooden sleeper and carried on down the line.

III

I'd arrived in Sichuan via forty-year-old Chengdu South but I departed from its junior colleague Chengdu East. Although scarcely a decade old, the station nodded to history, or indeed prehistory, with some decorative features of the Bronze Age Shu culture that modern Sichuan had largely cemented over. Notwithstanding the architect's best efforts at distinguishing the place, it was very much a 21st Century Chinese rail depot, airy, languid and sustained by fast-food franchises. It was not much of a launch pad for an eastbound railway odyssey that would accompany the Yangtze River by degrees all the way to the East China Sea. But once I'd found my bunk I couldn't help but award the station symbolic status as the start point of a journey that follows the great Chinese metaphor for life, *cong shan dao hai*, "from the mountains to the sea".

The Chinese called the Yangtze *Changjiang*, the Long River or sometimes simply *Jiang*, the River. At 6,300 kilometers, this was not an overly generous name. The Thames, by contrast, flowed just 346 kilometers from source to sea. History's largest naval battles were fought on the Yangtze's waters, its wild gorges had inspired the greatest of poems while its floodplains sustained over one third of China's population (one in thirteen humans). Despite the introduction of the railway in the late 19th Century and the miles of tarmac tattooing China, the river was no less significant today, generating an estimated twenty percent of China's GDP. So when the K1258 creaked into motion, its wheels sang with anticipation.

The famous Victorian travel writer Isabella Bird, whom I greatly admire (not least for her surname) sailed up the Yangtze in 1896 when researching *The Yangtze Valley and Beyond* at the prodigious age of 64. She described Sichuan as "The empire province [...] with the great navigable tributaries of the Yangtze, by which goods are conveyed at small cost to countless towns and villages..." She wrote gushingly of "a superb climate" and "rich soil" that "under careful cultivation, yields three and even four crops annually" and waxed lyrical of "forests of grand timber" and "the most valuable and extensive coal-fields in the world".

There was not a great deal of the Empire Province to see as we rolled through a dense plume of autumnal humidity, however. What was clear beyond the water-doused windows was that a century of exploitation separated Isabella Bird's view from that of Thomas Bird's. Though the Sichuan basin was still considered a breadbasket, or rice bowl, the patchwork fields look tired to me, like an old boxer who was too poor to retire. The trees had been cut like regulation army crewcuts to the very fringes of the hills by struggling farmers inhabiting rammed-earth abodes centuries removed from the metallic world of electricity pylons encroaching on their muddy lots like invading robots. Occasionally, we passed the elevated high-speed line along which bullet trains shuttled between Chengdu and Chongqing in four hours flat, inequality writ large in transport technology.

HARMONY EXPRESS

Our caravan found the Jialing River sometime before noon and followed it into Nanchong, a 'city of fruit' the train's inboard speaker informed us. The pause afforded me a moment to douse the pot noodle I'd bought with boiling water from the water dispenser and then scan the vista, one devoid of fruit trees. I dined alone. Nobody in the carriage was able to muster more than a few words of conversation with the weird foreigner who had gate-crashed their pajama-party-on-wheels. One peasant even asked me why I hadn't travelled high-speed as he presumed a rich foreigner would. Down the corridor there were several factory girls bound for Wenzhou where they told me "there's work sewing" but they fell unconscious in their high heels within an hour of our departure, apparently desperate to catch some shut-eye while they could.

In the adjacent booth, a ragtag audience had formed around a provincial patriot ranting about American "dogs" and those "little" Japanese and it was a welcome relief when a valiant China Railway employee interrupted the man's monologue to hawk a product so exemplary of China's manufacturing overcapacity, I felt compelled to listen.

"This marvel of the technological age will change your life!" he declared before grabbing a cucumber to give a live demonstration. "Just look how thin this device slices..." he said, parading up and down the carriage, showing off a perfectly shaved cucumber peel. "Here, have a taste," he said to one of the factory girls. "Pretty good, right?" he asked a man in a dusty suit. "The cucumber peeler brings convenience and happiness to any kitchen. Just look at that, wafer thin!" he exclaimed, while sticking neat circles of cucumber flesh onto a child's forehead, much to the amusement of the crowd. "We Chinese have long understood food must look good as well as taste good, right?"

"Right," echoed the carriage occupants like a game show

audience.

"Well, with this device you can cut the cucumber into different shapes to perfectly suit whichever dish you're preparing, cold spicy salad, stir-fried cucumber with pork, shredded cucumber and black fungi..."

I didn't know what fascinated me more, the man or the product. He looked as though he was assembled from leftover body parts at a hospital morgue. His face was long and stretched, as if he'd met with the wrong end of a vacuum cleaner at some point in the past. His enormous limbs were totally out of proportion with his body, although he used them to good effect, the wide spread of his legs supporting him like camera stand while the carriage lurched and jolted, his extended arms able to reach around the bed bunks to force slices of cucumber on unsuspecting travelers.

"Here, try that," he said to the girl humming along to headphones on a bed bunk.

Of course, no advertisement in China could afford to neglect a given product's medicinal benefits. "Cucumber is essential for good *qi*. But did you know putting cucumber on your skin can even turn you white?"

I had never once imagined that a peeler unique to a vine fruit could in any way be of service to mankind but I clearly stood on the wrong side of history because business was booming. By the time we were tickling the fringes of Dazhou county, the vendor had shifted a dozen of the gadgets, departing with a kick in his step to cajole the occupants of the next carriage.

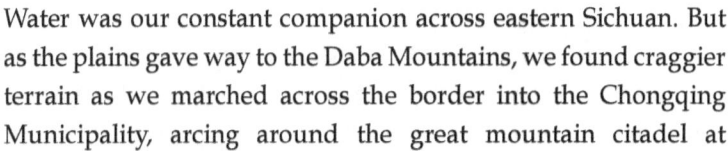

Water was our constant companion across eastern Sichuan. But as the plains gave way to the Daba Mountains, we found craggier terrain as we marched across the border into the Chongqing Municipality, arcing around the great mountain citadel at

Liangping, and only finding the Yangtze again as the sun began to dim.

We approached the city of Wanzhou in a wash of orange light. Located at the upper reaches of Three Gorges, Wanzhou famously lost its old town beneath the reservoir of the Three Gorges Dam. The mega-project had first been envisioned by Sun Yat-sen in 1919 although it wasn't until 2006, when I was still a China newbie, that the cement began to dry. It took a further six years to fill the world's biggest bathtub, in doing so submerging the homes of over a million people. The list of concerns associated with the dam were manifold, not least that an earthquake could crack the thing, washing 400 million lowland farmers into the East China Sea before they could scream, 'A'ya'.

But it was at the Pingyao International Photography Festival the previous year where I chanced upon an exhibition by the photographer Yan Changjiang (whose name appropriately means Long River) that I grasped what had been lost. Yan documented ancient stone Buddhas slowly drowning like condemned men as the waters rose, the sacred past submitting once again to the new religion of technological progress.

Despite the controversy surrounding the mega project, this part of the Yangtze valley was defined by vast jade peaks and cascading gullies — the majestic Three Gorges, emblematic of geography on a truly Chinese scale. This scenery had lured poets and travel scribes for centuries, from Li Bai to Isabella Bird. Thus it was with an air of irony that the railway timetable mandated we were to miss the most picturesque part of the journey, the last embers of sunlight extinguished between the river ports of Enshi and Yichang.

I wandered languidly into the dining carriage for some fried rice, washed it down with a can of Tsingtao, then retired to my bed early. But it was a restless slumber, disturbed by strange dreams, the snoring of my neighbors and the miasma of sweaty socks. By the time we were crawling into Wuchang I was wide awake, perched window-side, just as the big hand ticked four, a Chinese homonym for death.

The witching hour was truly upon us. Everyone in the carriage was out for the count except for a couple who shared a middle bunk at the end of carriage, their soft groans suggesting the might have even been involved in a romantic act.

Beyond the metal cocoon, Wuchang's steel mills that earned the tri-city Wuhan its 'China's Chicago' moniker, churned and growled breathing bursts of fire into the dark.

Before the city limits, the river revealed herself in all her naked enormity. All appeared calm, although this was a stretch of the river where Yangtze's banks burst but a few months before. The official number of those affected was almost fifteen million, a typically huge Chinese statistic, but it was the home videos friends had shown me of their villages in Hunan and Hubei consumed by a brown tsunami that illustrated just how temperamental, and indeed terrifying, the Long River could be, her scale matched only by her propensity for destruction.

When writing about the Yangtze it was the river's length that most people fixated on. But when you gazed upon it, the river's breadth is her most striking quality. No wonder Chairman Mao swam across it, not once, but twice, in 1956 and again 1966, symbolically expressing his enduring power. Even at high noon one could seldom see to the other side. Marco Polo said it was "more like a Sea than a River" and claimed to count no fewer than 15,000 vessels docked outside a single city. Despite seven centuries of travel advances since Polo's day, mighty iron barges—the modern-day successors to huge wooden trading junks—are still evident by their wake, their baritone horns groaning like the mating calls of great river beasts.

HARMONY EXPRESS

Although I was passing through one of the most densely populated corridors on our human planet, there was intense solitude, a loneliness Tang poets ascribed to the shimmering moon reflected in the Yangtze's waters, a potent allegory for the melancholy flooding my veins at that juncture. Despite the ghostly allure of the River, I somehow succumbed to my demons, and dreamed of someone to hold through the long night. I fixated on all the way's CC's and my relationship might have worked out, if only I'd tried harder. I thought of Gua and wondered why I hadn't picked her up, spun around and ask her to marry me in People's Park, like a scene from a 90s rom-com. Eight hours behind me and five thousand miles away, my parents would be catching the last of the evening news in suburban South Wales, flicking off the box and putting the cat out for the night. In the restless night, with only myself for company, my insatiable wanderlust succumbed to an intense hankering for home, family, routine and familiarity.

———∽∽———

Sunrise on the Yangtze revealed the main thrust of the River bending north while the railway veered south. The train speakers burst into life with a sentimental Mandopop love song. My carriage grew animate, through a ritual of yawns, head scratching and Chinese throat clearing, the familiar refrain *"jidan, mixian, baozi, dounai"* accompanied by clunking trolleys and the crinkle of polystyrene, all adding timbre to the discord.

Morning light did little to exorcise my mood. I was still many miles from where my heart was, afflicted with the abiding sense that this itinerant railway life was becoming more of a retreat than a quest. I tumbled into a routine of fitful naps and snacking with intermittent bouts of exercise, much to the amusement of my fellow carriage occupants who gawked at me doing jumping jacks in the carriage corridor like a circus monkey. But I hated being the source of their amusement. They talked about me but never to me. It was as if all I'd ever be was a *guilao*, a foreign ghost. My reputation wasn't buoyed by the frequency with which I visited the toilet. My body was in the process of offloading a week's worth of Sichuan fare, forcing me to repeatedly shuffle past the smokers who crowded the bathroom area in order to raise my buttocks above the bare railway tracks flowing continuously beneath the squat latrine.

The first few pages of a novel I pinched from the hostel in Chengdu absorbed an hour but my mind was busy, my thoughts stranded on some distant platform way back down the line. The railway towns of northern Jiangxi were mutually rundown, half old, half new—construction sites that made me wonder if New China would ever be finished.

Although the approach to Lishui steered us into a lush, hilly province awash with autumnal colors, it was with some relief to disembark after over 35 hours in captivity. I stumbled onto Lishui Station's platform like a lowly Welsh merchant arriving at the dock in colonial Shanghai, after being at sea far, far too long.

IV

"Ah, Xiao Fei, you've arrived!" announced the renowned curator and critic Teacher Bao, having caught me trying to suck all the caffeine out of a cup of stewed black tea. "I didn't see you on the plane from Beijing. When did you touch down?"

"I took the train from Chengdu and got in last night."

"High-speed?"

"No, I took a green train. All the high-speed tickets had sold out, plus I would have had to have changed at Nanchang."

"That's a long way!"

"Tell me about it," I said, sensing the stiffness in my limbs.

My railway blues had followed me to the Xierdun International's buffet restaurant, which, in tandem with the hotel's faux-Western branding, served such 'international' delicacies as French fries and birthday cake for breakfast. But the impassioned conversations of festival attendees buoyed my mood. "Can there even be postmodernism in a communist society?" I overheard a young shutterbug inquire. "Chinese photography cannot escape Jameson's national allegory trap," complained a crabby critic in French-lilted English.

"I missed the opening ceremony. Do you think the organizers will be annoyed?" I asked Bao earnestly.

"Oh, I never fucking go to those things. Some mayor standing there talking about cultural development and all that shit. Those speeches are nonsense, what do those cadres know about contemporary art? And then there's a song and a dance, some fireworks, I ask you?"

"Perhaps you're right," I told Teacher Bao. "But I am here to cover an event."

"They say it's the biggest photography festival in China with five thousand artists exhibited," he continued, already sporting his critic's cap like a battle helmet. "Artists indeed! Most of them are goons. It's total shit. This fucking country just does things to scale, size trumps quality every time. Make sure you don't write about any of *their* crap."

———∽∾∽———

I'd began to take a serious interest in Chinese photography after my friend LZD invited me to Lianzhou Foto, another art photography festival held in a remote mountain town in Guangdong Province where his series *The New Chinese* was exhibited. While I scoured the repurposed factory walls displaying some of the most potent images I'd ever seen, it dawned on me that I should start moonlighting as an art writer. After all, Chinese artists were, I rationalized, best placed to tell the most significant story of the age, namely, China's convoluted rise. The realization proved prescient.

As I'd spent more and more time in the company of Chinese photographers, I found them to be a closely knit community working tirelessly to get their work seen in a country intensely suspicious of its creative classes. They were a wonderfully eccentric bunch, far less tribal than musicians or authors, an eclecticism that was reflected in their work.

I'd gotten to know some of the movers and shakers on the scene, including Teacher Bao, a standard-bearer for serious photographic art since the early days of reform and one of the few individuals still able to breathe air into the torn sails of China's art industry. Inevitably, he commanded a lot of respect, even if he left a fair bit of fear and loathing in his wake as he stalked around galleries like a velociraptor with a splinter in his toe.

As I finished off my fries and birthday cake, Bao dropped a casual tip: "Head to the oil-pumping facility on the hill, Xiao Fei, that's where the good stuff is. And make sure you check out Walter Wang, the kid was born in the '90s, he photographs trains, which you seem to like writing about these days…"

Along Lishui's riverfront, the cicadas sang from the trees between a moss-covered imperial gatehouse and the spruced up ancient observatory, a three-story classical tower from where Lishui folk once searched heaven for answers. The city's main boulevards were prosaic but the newly erected condominiums shielded from view an inner city redolent of a textured past, a place of flaking temples and crumbling old houses wired together by cobblestone alleyways. No wonder Chinese friends soon began echoing the "*tai shufu le* — so comfortable" refrain, while planning their early retirement there. And when one of the festival organizers confessed to me the photography biennale was part of a broader effort to shake off the low-end manufacturing image American author and journalist Peter Hessler's writing had helped disseminate a decade ago, I couldn't help but see reason in the scheme, especially when he explained that the high-speed railway had brought Lishui into the orbit of Yangtze Delta denizens. "We can get to Shanghai in two and half hours now, Hangzhou is even closer, under an hour away…"

But some habits die hard and there was an assembly-line efficiency with which media guests were channeled through warehouse-sized galleries like traders shopping for MP3 players at the Canton Fair.

I hatched a prison break, following Teacher Bao's directions to the oil pumping facility instead, a Mao-era industrial complex lodged on a hillside that wouldn't have looked out of place along the Jiayang Railway back in Sichuan.

Stepping inside was like hopping a fast train to the Chinese underground. The avant-garde crowd had encircled Teacher Bao, who, microphone in hand, was in the midst of giving a rousing lecture before some quixotic images taken by Duzi, a Beijing-based artist who has documented the soiled and savaged landscapes of China's industrial wastelands.

After soaking up Duzi's exhibition, I journeyed deeper into the oil-pumping facility in the hope of finding less depressing work. An image of a young child sporting a puffy winter coat standing before a level crossing on a railway, stopped me in my tracks. The image was composed of two photographs, the childhood snap framed within a photograph of the same stretch of railway today, the latter colored black and white thus subverting the flow of time.

"Dat is'ah mee," said a brawny twenty-something wearing an official Chinese railway cap.

"Are you Walter Wang?" I asked. "Teacher Bao said I should look out for you."

"Fuck, your Chinese isn't bad, comrade," he replied, in the curse-laden-Chinese typical to a native Beijinger. After exchanging some pleasantries and submitting a brief explanation of my interest in wandering Chinese train travel, Wang willingly waded into my river of questions.

"I grew-up beside the railway in Xizhimen," he told me, his youth spent in the part of Beijing where the old West Gate had been before they pulled down the city walls in the 1950s. "There was a railway station there at that time and my primary school was located trackside. Sometimes we walked home along the tracks. I got hold of a family camera when I was about eleven years old and started photographing the railway, mostly just for fun. After I finished primary school, I went to Beijing No 19 Middle School, which, coincidentally, was where Zhan Tianyou was buried before he was exhumed and moved to Qinglongqiao in 1982."

I'd visited Zhan Tianyou's ancestral home in Guangzhou when I was a magazine editor in the South. He was one of the first Chinese to be sent abroad during the late-Qing period, in his case, Yale. A brilliant student and engineer, he has been posthumously crowned 'Father of the Chinese Railway' principally for his role as chief engineer of the Beijing to Zhangjiakou (Jingzhang) Railway, China's first to be constructed without foreign assistance.

Wang showed me two pictures of Qinglongqiao, an antique station near the Badaling section of the Great Wall. The first image was a black and white archive photo of passengers awaiting a train, the second a color image from the exact same angle with present day railway employees assuming the same formation of the passengers in the original image, a Walter Wang trope, I was learning.

"One day when I was about fifteen, I learnt they were going to tear down a beautiful water tower beside the tracks. They didn't need to; it was simply marked for demolition. It was built in 1918! I was a Middle School student but I had to do something, so I got in touch with *Beijing Youth Daily*. They reported on it and some people from the China Railway Museum saw the story. They intervened to save it and it is now conserved in the 798 Art District in Chaoyang district."

"I've spent a lot of time in the galleries out that way," I told him. "I've seen it there. I'm amazed it was there because of you."

Wang explained how his initial success inspired him to become an independent photojournalist, a career to finance his efforts to document and conserve railway heritage. He'd travelled far and wide on the Chinese network, hawking stories and images to the likes of *China Geographic*. But he always returned to his first love, the Jingzhang Railway, documenting every meter of the fabled iron road. His obsession led to a publishing deal, a series of beautifully illustrated books he produced for China Railway Publishing House. His cross-disciplinary approach — including cartography, illustration, photographs, and text — was reinterpreted as the exhibition that surrounded us, titled *My Jingzhang Railway*.

As we talked, it grew evident Wang seriously resented the wrecking ball mentality aggressively reshaping China. "In the West, you look after old buildings, but these bastards haven't got a clue. All they think about is money."

Notwithstanding his grievances, Wang had figured out ways to play the game, filing proposals with the district cultural heritage department, getting journo friends to report on significant and jeopardized buildings and blogging aggressively on social media.

"This is a picture of Qinghe Station," he said, pointing to a lonely old stationhouse surrounded by a construction site like a desert island. "I got this marked with a cultural relic plaque, and this one in Qinghuayuan as well," he added, pointing to a boxy, low-rise building in a residential community somewhere in Beijing.

Wang told me he had managed to get four buildings officially preserved for posterity in the Beijing area alone, and he was campaigning for many more, although he also lost some battles.

We wandered around taking a closer look at some railway photography, much of which was taken with a drone from the air, a technology China had pioneered.

"Zhan Tianyou studied in the US he had a lot to do with you Brits. He apprenticed under Claude Kinder on the Beijing to Shenyang line even before he built the Jingzhang Railway…"

"I'd like to go to Shenyang," I told him. "I've only been to the Northeast once but didn't see much…"

"I see you two idiots have found each other," interjected Teacher Bao, passing through the factory with his disciples. "Everyone, take a moment to check out Walter Wang's exhibition for a minute, this kid's got real balls."

Amongst the entourage I saw Dawei, a curator friend from Beijing.

"Hi there. Xiao Fei, long time no see."

"It's good to see you, Dawei."

"We're going to the Nanming Restaurant tonight on Liberation Road if you want to come along, that's where some friends will be hanging out."

The dinner proved to be a classic, round table banquet, hosted in a grimy backroom cloaked in near-impenetrable cigarette smoke. Friends from all corners of China got reacquainted over a baijiu bottle toasted between long laments regarding censorship and commercialization, the principal grievances amongst

Chinese artists. It was a conversation that went back and forth like a shuttlecock in a rally where there could be no winner, until everyone was too drunk to play and the conversation descended into banter and small talk.

The following day played out like day one, boozy meals punctuating the long hours stalking the galleries. By day three, sensing I'd seen everything worthy of note, I awoke with a strong urge to breach the city limits.

"Have you any idea which bus goes somewhere nice and rural?" I asked one of the festival staff.

"What do you mean *somewhere rural*?"

"You know, some rolling hills, a river perhaps?"

"Listen, if you hurry to the Feida International Hotel there's a coach leaving for a country tour at 11:00 a.m. It's a photographers' trip but I don't see any problem in your tagging along."

"Sounds great, I'll head on over."

Sure enough, a brightly colored coach was filling up with foreigners flowing from the revolving hotel door. I waved my festival media pass at a driver who, distracted by some issue with his trouser fly, just ushered me on.

After some minutes of commotion, we rolled out of town. A glimpse of the Ming-era hilltop Shahe Pagoda signaled we were leaving Lishui's city district behind. The road tracked south keeping company with the River Ou before lurching north at the township of Dagantou from where we rolled into a pastoral scene dominated by oblong fields overseen by pretty white-washed farmhouses.

We passed a riverside temple in Songyang county, eliciting gasps from my fellow passengers, all of whom appear to be China novices. Yet I couldn't help but share their felicity, scarcely able to believe my luck at having scored this free trip bound for wherever we were heading.

My trance was only disturbed by a sour-looking woman holding a clipboard who asked me my name.

I waved my media pass at her. "I was invited by some curator friends in Beijing to cover the festival in Lishui."

"You weren't invited on this trip, though."

"The girl at the festival office, I think her surname is Chen, she said it would be fine to tag along."

The woman scowled and marched off to consult with her colleague, a balding man with thick-framed glasses who exuded a general air of fatigue.

I overheard 'foreign' and 'writer' applied like swear words, which in certain circles, they very much were.

But his replies were more restrained, *"mei wenti,"* I catch, no problem, and *"fangsong",* which roughly translates as, will you relax?

"Vot iz 'appening?" asked a man in the kind of Slavic English prerequisite to a role as a Bond villain.

"Oh, nothing," I reassured him. "Chinese red tape".

"Ah, vee ave zat eelot in Rrrrrussia," he said, his tongue rolling like an adder's.

"You're Russian?"

"Ukrainian, actually I come from Crimea. It complicated. I teaching art at Rrrrrussian university."

It turned out he was not the only one to hail from the former Soviet Union. The coach's lingua franca was Russian, and I eventually learned the bulk of the group worked for universities scattered throughout the Stans and Eastern Europe. The one exception were the two Spanish speakers sitting behind me, who hailed from Cuba.

Conversation subsided as we steered onto a precipitously

steep road climbing into vertiginous hills dancing with bamboo. We pulled over at a hilltop village sign-posted Pingtian.

Before us were some rammed-earth structures linked by worn stone staircases. It was a quaint place, and the photographers quickly went to work finding angles to shoot Chinese serfs presenting their country bumpkin ways for the digital record of Albania or Azerbaijan. I caught one photographer sporting a heavy mullet who humiliated himself beyond the remit of his hairstyle when he tumbled knee deep into a paddy field while trying to picture a farm girl holding a chicken like a pet rabbit.

I was less excitable. My suspicion that the village had been given a major makeover was substantiated when I peered into a hillside home to be met with a handicraft exhibition. Another house had been converted into a café complete with a coffee machine serving cappuccinos. There was a sense of order and polish one never met on a remote hillside in China. Where were the farm tools, the cigarette butts and discarded plastic cartons, the dull living rooms where only a fading Mao poster offered any color, the kitchens blackened by years of wok oil?

It slowly dawned on me this was something of Potemkin Village, an idealized hamlet curated to please visitors, in this case, a group of photographers and academics sourced from countries where China probably wanted to build railways.

The Cubans saw through the charade, too. "Kind of fake isn't it?"

"You're telling me."

When I got back to Lishui to recount my misadventure, my photographer friends found the entire ordeal hilarious.

"Xiao Fei was duped!"

"Probably the China Photography Association, they're government-affiliated."

"I hear you're writing about Red tourism these days? Some

travel writer!"

The cool crowd were congregated in the leafy grounds outside the oil pumping facility with curators from New York and critics from Paris, drinking craft beer and talking art.

"Come on, Xiao Fei, cheer up, have a drink," said Dawei, kindly offering me a bottle of Master Gao's IPA beer. "There's going to be an award ceremony soon and then we can all go for dinner and drinks, fancy the Nanming Restaurant again?"

V

I concluded my journey to the coast at high-speed along the Jinliwen railway line. Wenzhou was under an hour away from Lishui yet almost half the journey was cloaked in the darkness of tunnels. The noise of such a powerful machine burrowing through mountains at over 200km per hour proved an unnerving experience, particularly as Wenzhou was the scene of China's only major high-speed rail accident.

I remember the day it happened vividly. It was a little after Christmas 2011 and I was in Guangzhou putting the finishing touches to the January edition of the magazine I worked for, when the managing editor marched into the office ranting about official corruption.

The day before, two trains had collided on the viaduct just outside of Wenzhou city proper, costing the lives of forty people and injuring 191. But what turned Weibo (China's answer to Twitter) into a seething forum of dissent was not so much the accident as the bungled response, after it became widely known the Railway Ministry had called off the search for survivors after just eight hours and turned their attention to clearing the wreckage so rail traffic could resume. Workers even dug a pit and buried one carriage before investigators could show up to analyze the cause of the disaster. Incriminating pictures went viral and the Party lost face, big time. In the wake of a public outcry, several high-profile arrests and sackings were made, construction of high-speed rail lines in China was temporarily suspended and speed limits on major high-speed railways were reduced. But to many, a lightning-strike that had caused signaling equipment failure also illuminated systemic problems that transcended the management of railways; namely the human cost of New China's slavish devotion to the Money God invariably paid.

Outside Wenzhou Station, I flagged a taxi that followed an elevated expressway through an acrid haze of neon-hued smog. Rows of monstrous high-rise blocks lined the route into town, organized with terrifying uniformity, the antithesis of the geomancy which informed Chinese architecture for centuries, the kind of dystopian cityscape the sci-fi writer Philip K. Dick might have dreamt up after a heavy amphetamine binge.

In the light of the morning I rented a bike and cycled through the drizzle to see if I could find anything of interest. Snaking my way through horrific traffic, I traced roads that linked new condominiums with dilapidated factories and their associated dormitories, the cramped collective homes of Wenzhou's migrant classes, numbering thirty percent of city's population. Businesses visibly catered to the dual-strata society, fine diners abutting slop shops, boutiques beside discount stores.

Wenzhou was known by its nickname, 'Chinese Jerusalem', on account of its large Christian population and I passed several headless churches, their crosses having been removed in a recent campaign of urban 'safety' and 'beauty' that riled human rights activists abroad and briefly bounced Wenzhou into the global headlines. But there were just as many Buddhist and Daoist temples, the like and quantity of which I hadn't seen since I rolled through the Chaoshan region in search of folk songs. Religion was evidently important in this godforsaken Chinese metropolis.

Every street seemed to resurrect one of the images of the *Lens on Wenzhou* exhibition I'd caught in Lishui days before: Zhu Yongchun's *Wetland Villages* came to life when I cycled along the remaining canals that had made an oriental Venice of the city until they were concreted over; open-front sweatshops evoked Zheng Gangfeng's series *Wenzhou Private Enterprise* series documenting small-scale, family-run manufacturing that was still predominant. I even encountered a temple converted into a fruit shop, recalling Chen Jianrong's photo series *The Ancestral Temples* — images depicting how village shrines were being incorporated into modern buildings like schools or supermarkets. Indeed, by the time I'd met the muddy banks of the mighty River Ou, I felt as if I'd just passed through an installation work that had taken photos from Lishui's gallery walls and made a three-dimensional movie out of them.

———∞———

Teacher Bao connected me with Mr Chen, the chief curator of *Lens on Wenzhou*, who invited me to lunch with some artists at a modish art gallery located in the freshly landscaped Bailuzhou Park. It was the kind of setting, the tourist bureau would to brandish a Wenzhou city exhibition.

"We didn't want to produce a postcard collection," he explained. "Instead we asked the photographers to capture their city, their family, essentially the world around them. You know many Chinese photographers want to run off to Tibet and take pictures of snow leopards. They forget about what's on their doorstep. Contemporary art is not necessarily about form or technique, rather, it should be about maintaining a connection with the experiences we have and the times we live in. That's what *contemporary* means."

I noted these "times we live in" were chaotic.

"Wenzhou used to be a beautiful place full of canals. You'll notice that many of the street names end with *qiao* [the Chinese character for bridge]. I think Zhu Yongchu has captured the last vestiges of this way of life with his images *Wetland Village* depicting the people who still live in the marshes, which are now being filled in and redeveloped."

"I remember those pictures," I said, thinking of one of Zhu's photos in particular that captured an elderly lady in her slippers watching chickens feed, while just across the waterway behind her, ancient houses had been reduced to rubble.

"Then there's the economic downturn. Wenzhou hasn't fully recovered from the ripple effects of the recession in the West, so you see migrants struggling to find work in Liu Feng's photographs."

Loss, it seemed, was an overriding theme of the collection, as the photographers, who were all middle-aged men, attempted to capture the last vestiges of the Wenzhou where they grew up before they disappeared.

"Zheng Yonghui's work is interesting in respect to loss," Chen said of the series titled *Fireworks*. "He has photographed elderly people who live by themselves in primitive rural areas. They're a world apart from the Wenzhou of today. Things change so fast even I struggle to keep up."

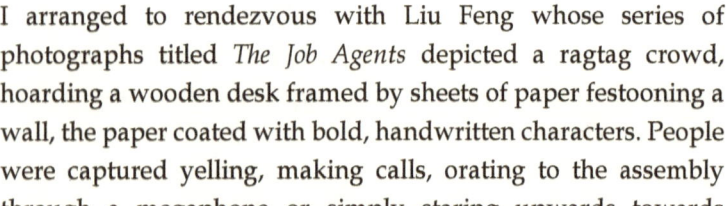

I arranged to rendezvous with Liu Feng whose series of photographs titled *The Job Agents* depicted a ragtag crowd, hoarding a wooden desk framed by sheets of paper festooning a wall, the paper coated with bold, handwritten characters. People were captured yelling, making calls, orating to the assembly through a megaphone or simply staring upwards towards something desirable located beyond the frame. It looked like a struggle session from Mao's China but Liu had told me, "They're simply looking for work," before explaining how rural migrants didn't know how use computers to search for jobs and hustled employment in this rudimentary fashion instead.

Rui'an, where Liu lived, was about an hour's south of Wenzhou city district. I hopped a taxi, which deposited me next to a pile of rubble—what had been a downtown plaza until developers set in. The place looked like a warzone, the broken Buddha statues photographed by Zheng Xiaochang for *Lens on Wenzhou* scattered across a side road wasteland like the aftermath of a Red Guard raid during the Cultural Revolution.

Liu picked me up and we drove towards the city center. There were factories everywhere, one even in the middle of the road, the tarmac looping it like a moat.

"That factory owner has connections, he didn't want to move," he explained.

Beneath some tarpaulin, we saw women dishing up cheap meals to hungry migrant workers. The only respectable building in sight was a church, albeit, minus its rooftop cross.

We went inside for a quick look around. Passing a Christmas tree and a Santa Claus in the lobby, we ran into the vicar in the main hall.

"We have three packed congregations every Sunday, two for the locals and one for outsiders," he told me proudly. "People who come to work here often convert quickly."

"I can kind of see why," I said, peering through the stained-glass windows at the hellscape beyond.

After lunch in the school canteen where Liu worked, Liu took me to the recruitment agency that he photographed for the exhibition in Lishui. But the shutters were pulled down, and only few men were hanging around outside smoking, looking at the graffiti on corrugated iron as if *Tianfu*, the heavenly land, was located on the other side.

One of the men took a liking to Liu's camera that he sported around his neck like a medallion wherever he went.

"Do you like photography?" Liu asked, exhibiting the sympathetic character of a professional teacher.

"Oh yes, very much, I take pictures all the time," said the young migrant worker in a thick but familiar accent, before revealing a knockoff smartphone. The screen was cracked but we could still just make out his pictures.

"I take pictures of my home in rural Sichuan; people say the countryside is poor but I think it's beautiful."

"I was in rural Sichuan not long ago," I said.

"Really," he said. "Then you'll recognize this kind of landscape."

He flicked through a series of images depicting muddy rice fields, duck ponds, bamboo groves and brown dirt paths bisecting fading hills. "This is my home," he said, as the photographs transported us inland, far from the factories and broken gods that framed us here in Wenzhou, right back to Isabella Bird's 'Empire Province'.

GHOST TRAINS TO TIANJIN

I

Orientation in China was seldom intuitive. After following several contradictory signs, and asking umpteen bystanders for directions, misunderstanding and mis-turns finally got me out of Pudong Airport and headed in the direction of the ticket counter.

In the queue ahead of me, some out-of-towners — identifiable by oversized sun hats and brightly colored wheelie suitcases — crowded one another with the intimacy of kittens, the *yin* to the teller's *yang*, who vended tickets with the verve of a robot.

Inside the spartan waiting room, a pair of Ming vases, a model train in a Perspex case and some illustrated wall plaques furnished the only points of interest beyond selfie-stick portraiture. On the wall, under the heading 'Maglev Superiorities' I read how the machine I was about to climb aboard compared with other popular modes of transport. "Car 160km/h, F1 350km/h, Rapid Train 300km/h, Metro 80km/h, Maglev 430km/h." Following those impressive stats, the subheading 'Safe' antedated the promise, "During running, the vehicle wraps around the guideway (eliminating the possibility of derailment)", a relief, as the prospect of being hurled into the Huangpu River wasn't quite what I had in mind when I conspired to arrive in Shanghai in style.

Settling window-side, I noticed the train was scarcely half full. But we were not about to wait around, as with surprisingly little fanfare, the Shanghai Maglev took off, quite literally levitating above the track, the carriages held in place by opposing magnets. We whistled along at 100, 200, then 300 kilometers an hour, banking around the first bend like a super bike at the Macau Grand Prix. When we reached the top speed of 431 kilometers an hour, the engine rumbled in concert with the spattering of passengers cheering like children on a roller coaster that was about to go loop- de-loop. Outside, factories, parks and multi-level expressways blended into a surrealist dreamscape. Inside, all eyes were trained on the speedometers strategically positioned above the carriage doorways.

Moments after we reached this exhilarating pitch, however, the train decelerated and we soon arrived at Longyang Road Station, a terminus devoid of interest or distraction. I descended to ground level where the oily odor of Chinese fast food coalesced with smog; my first proper lungful of Shanghai air, dank and heavy.

While haplessly looking around for a signpost to somewhere, I couldn't shake the lingering sense that the eight-minute dash probably wasn't worth the fifty yuan ticket fee, which is why the Shanghainese largely shunned the Maglev in favor of the metro, rendering the world's fastest commercial train a tourist novelty.

───∞∞───

The Maglev was not the only mode of rail transport to be trialed in Shanghai. In fact, China's pre-eminent metropolis could lay claim to the nation's first commercial railway, the fate of which was somewhat allegoric of the confusion and mistrust that permeated the interactions of East and West in the 19th Century.

The two faced off across the Huangpu River.

A platoon of sightseers had gathered on the river banks to memorialize themselves saying 'yeah' and flashing V-fingers before the skyscrapers of Pudong. Two freight ships sailed past, as if choreographed to create the perfect frame for a *Time* cover article about the 'Rise of the Dragon'. Yet it was not the gilded glass towers of New China, but the superb row of colonial-era art deco and neoclassical buildings on the west bank that spoke of Shanghai's heady ascent from obscurity to becoming East Asia's principle entrepôt.

There had, of course, been a Shanghai long before any Europeans showed up prospecting on the lower lip of the Yangtze's mouth for somewhere to buy tea. But Shanghai mark one had only ever been a marginal player in the grand Chinese drama. The story only really got going when some British merchants strolled into town in November 1843 and evidently saw what they were after, namely, a coastal city with access to the riches of China via its chief trading highway, the Yangtze. By 1865, almost 3,000 foreigners were calling Shanghai home. These Shanghailanders — the British and Americans who forged the International Settlement in 1863 when their concessions merged — as well as the French, whose concession remained distinct — would come to forge a new city in old China, one that rose like a hot air balloon while the rest of the country progressed like a kite caught in a blustery storm.

Interest in building a railway had been gaining traction for some years amongst the Shanghailanders, but it wasn't until 1872 that anybody actually had a go. American O. B. Bradford, the US vice-consul at Shanghai at the time, had the initiative, leasing land to construct a carriage road for horses (although he conspired to build a railway). His designs were hampered by the view that American involvement violated the Burlingame Treaty of 1868, which had established friendly relations between China and the US, so the American interest was sold.

Enter the archdukes of Far East imperialism: Jardine, Matheson and Company (the forerunner to Hong Kong multinational Jardine Matheson that survives today) to take up where the Americans left off. Co-founder Scotsman William Jardine had been resident in Guangzhou from 1820 to 1839 when he made a fortune pedaling opium. On his return to England, he'd been one of the chief lobbyists for the Opium War that ultimately blew open China via places like Shanghai. As you might expect, a company built on such moral foundations wouldn't be too concerned by, say, illegally building a railway on foreign ground and the Woosung Tramway Company was born.

Rails and rolling stock began arriving from England in 1875 and on July the following year, the line was inaugurated. Nobody seemed to mind until five months down the line when a Chinese national was run over, provoking serious legal wrangling between the Brits and the local Mandarin, Shen Baozhen. It was eventually agreed the Chinese would buy the Woosung Road for the sum of 285,000 taels (around £64,000) to be paid in three installments over one year. On the delivery of the last payment, the Chinese would assume responsibility for the railway.

The agreement was met on October 20 the following year and Shen duly took over the line. But to the bemusement of the Shanghailanders, he dismantled it and shipped it to Taiwan where it was left on a storm-ravaged beach to rust, the inglorious end to China's very first railway.

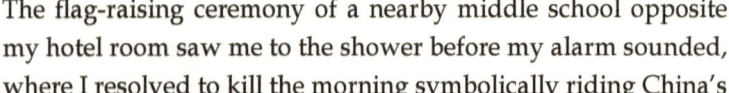

The flag-raising ceremony of a nearby middle school opposite my hotel room saw me to the shower before my alarm sounded, where I resolved to kill the morning symbolically riding China's first railway, just to see where I ended up.

It turned out to be a good day for it. A sea breeze had blown the worst of the smog inland revealing the azure skies that had been hiding behind the collective exhaust fumes of 26 million Shanghainese. Locals were busy hanging out their laundry on bamboo poles, metal window rods and anything else that would support an auspicious red blanket bearing the character 'Fu' or 'poop pants' — tiny trousers with holes at the rear allowed infants to relieve themselves on the go. I even caught an old lady hanging some green vegetables out to dry.

Lining the route to West Yan'an Road, cartoons of crustaceans informed the world that the annual wonder, the hairy crab season, had begun. But I was not in the market for an exotic breakfast. Ascending to the platform, as Line 3 runs on an elevated track, I found myself hemmed in by white-collar commuters flooding the world's busiest metro network. Few, if anyone, was likely aware the train we were crammed into traced the old route of the Woosung Tramway.

High-rise Pudong was just visible on the horizon, while low-rise Puxi nestled in the fore. It captured the gaze, a maze of leafy lanes fronting whitewashed houses that set Shanghai apart from other Chinese cities just as the Shanghainese cosmopolitan culture distinguished them from the billion or so residents of *Shanxiang* — the 'Mountain Village' as they disparagingly dubbed the rest of China.

We passed through Jiangwan Town, the midpoint on the Woosung Road's nine-mile run, before entering into the more industrial realm. Factories, warehouses and vast docklands were cluttered with metal freight containers marked CHINA SHIPPING, COSCO, MAERSK.

I alighted in a charmless suburb dominated by somber apartment blocks and greasy ground-floor restaurants serving food from Sichuan, Harbin and other places where migrant labor was typically sourced. I eventually found my way onto the only discernible point of interest, Paotaiwan National Wetland Park, a former slagheap turned public garden sandwiched between the Huangpu and Wusong (now channeled into one estuary) and the mouth of the mighty Yangtze itself.

HARMONY EXPRESS

Passing a socialist-realist sculpture of a steam locomotive and some cartoonish soldiers at the gate of the park, the sweet olive aroma of the Osmanthus flowers that bloom in the region during autumn pervaded my nostrils. Inevitably, a patriotic monument was the park's centerpiece, a mound decorated with artillery guns alluding to the park's name, *paotai* meaning battery and *wan* meaning bay. A large stone plaque explained Wusong had been attacked by the British in the 19th Century and the Japanese in the 20th Century, the bookends of the 'century of humiliation', the 'liberation' from which the Communist Party sourced its mandate to rule.

I followed a boardwalk across a muddy stream to the water's edge. Great rusty freight ships were sailing in and out of the river mouth like krill washing around the mouth of a giant feeding whale. Everything was somehow miniaturized by the vastness of the scene.

Confucius saw rivers as metaphors for time, "What passes away is, perhaps, like this. Day and night it never lets up," and there was something quite unremitting about the Yangtze's journey from the mountains to the sea. I'd half expected some kind of natural theatre to commemorate the close of its grand odyssey but as it had grown old, so it had matured and there was little of the spectacle of the rushing Jinsha section of the river I'd witnessed in the southwest. Within its great mouth there were islands forged by the 500 million tons of alluvial silt the river carried from its Central Asian genesis to the sea each year, a motherlode that helped push the coastline a kilometer east every 70 years, turning ancient ports like Suzhou and Hangzhou into inland cities today. Even Shanghai was no longer really 'Upon the Sea', as its name translated, and I privately wondered if the poop I had taken at Tiger Leaping Gorge had made it this far, my small contribution to the building of China.

Beyond the park, I followed Wusongkou Road along the coast until I got to Linjiang Park where I found an enchanting patch of woodland. A moss-greened plaque beside an earthen mound read Baoshan City Wall and I wondered if this is what remained of the Qing fortress captured by the British in the Battle of Wusong, or the ruins of something far older.

Pursuing the contours of the wall led me to an antique bridge and a spherical sluice gate, suggesting some settlement had stood here before British canons, Japanese bombs and communist town planners had all but razed the past.

These ruins were a prelude, it turned out, to a gorgeous classical building hidden in the woods like the residence of a Kungfu Master in an old Hong Kong movie. I thought it had been a Confucian temple and sure enough, I soon caught sight of the characters *Dacheng Dian* — the Hall of Great Achievement, suggesting it probably was. It would have been here people sought the wisdom of China's great sage, conducting rituals or making offerings. Many probably studied here too, as most Confucian temples doubled as colleges, versing aspirational civil servants in the classics, a system that remained in place for one and a thousand years, right up until 1905.

I walked up the stairs and bowed to the wise one, awarding the temple honorary status as the terminus of the Woosung Road Railway. Then, satisfied I'd been taken somewhere far more worthwhile than the Maglev had managed, I set off in search of a comparatively worthy brunch.

II

A decade on from the Woosung Road fiasco, the Chinese were more eager to get their railway network up to speed. In 1895, the Guangxu Emperor approved the construction of the Huning

(Shanghai to Nanjing) Railway and in 1899 permission to build the Jinpu Railway was won by an Anglo–German joint venture, connecting the political cities to the north with the economic powerhouses along the lower Yangtze valley. As modern Chinese trains still trace the transportation corridors roughed out by Europeans, I decided to travel to the Shanghai of the North, as Tianjin was known, at high-speed, making some detours along the way.

The first diversion was Wuxi, forty minutes west of Shanghai as the crow flies. The G7010 purred out of the Shanghai Station right on time.

I put the seat back and began to scroll through some of the finest Chinese railway pictures I'd ever laid eyes on, while the lower Yangtze Delta whizzed by in real-time beyond the windowpane.

Qian Haifeng's work depicted a starkly different world from the affluent and much lauded 'land of fish and rice' we were racing through. Beginning in 2008, he spent all his spare time budget-travelling through Chinese backwaters, enabling him to create a photo collection of astonishing breadth and quality. I meditated on his intimate portraits of third-class rail passengers for some long minutes: A striking image of two men sharing a blanket like a double-headed worm while the train trekked through frigid Heilongjiang Province; a villager climbing haphazardly aboard a train with a television set strapped to his back in rural Sichuan; a cast of Yunnan's minority people sitting in a carriage crowded by wicker baskets overflowing with market-bound legumes; a woman traveling with a full pig's head planted on the table. The minute detail in each frame was extraordinary, a rare, almost confidential peek into that other China, the one that, like Ah Lan's home in Jiangxi, didn't make it onto billboard propaganda posters.

Qian's lens was adept at "capturing souls not smiles", as

the photographer Dragan Tapshanov surmised what good photography should be about. But he didn't neglect the big picture either, one that was so often defined by that great Chinese malady, the crowd. He'd shot provincial stations brimming with desperate migrants, the militant train guards poised to manage the multitude with batons if need be; he'd captured carriages overflowing with black hair, heads pressed awkwardly against windows, legs stacked upon loved ones, limbs flailing like a thousand-armed Buddha; and he showed us how people endured these arduous odysseys: a card game played on the top bunk; toasting *baijiu* in the third-class aisle or simply suffering silently, as the Chinese are schooled to do from birth.

Qian gave the photo series an understated title, *Lüpi Huochi* or Green Train, bundling the bottom three classifications of Chinese trains into one color-coded document of national inequality. The term soon entered the popular vernacular when the series unexpectedly won the grand prize at Lianzhou Foto in 2015. I had since heard of urban hipsters who, inspired by Qian's work, went out and re-explored China via her peripheral railways. Guangdong-based Wu Tiao Ren even made a Green Train-themed album, the supporting tour for which had the group travel exclusively by rail.

However, for one like me, who'd traveled so much and so far on Chinese trains, his work had special resonance. I felt as if I could smell again the hot and smoky carriages I'd taken to Hunan as a China newbie. I could feel the bitter wind blowing beneath the door as I sat on the floor beside a toilet while chugging through Inner Mongolia after a Chinese New Year spent in the desert province of Ningxia. I could hear babies crying and the whispers of courting lovers, the echo of horns through tunnels, a pop song playing from a cheap mobile phone, the rattle of the food cart, the aching holler of the steamed bun vendor. And it made me think about everyone I'd ever met on Chinese trains, and wonder to which station fate had delivered them since we'd briefly shared hot tea on a second-class bunk.

The Wuxi Grand Hotel was flanked by two stone lions between which photographer Qian Haifeng was standing stoically, sharing the guardian's stony expression. He was wearing beige overalls and large black boots, a walkie-talkie in hand, he looked like a plastic action-figure.

"Where have you been? I thought British people were punctual, or is that the Germans?"

"I'm sorry, Haifeng," I said, "I got a bit lost on the way over, I've never been to Wuxi before."

"*Mei guanxi*" he yelled, a habit symptomatic of one whose hearing was deteriorating, "not to worry". Then putting a hand on my shoulder with the warmth I'd come to expect from Chinese artists, he guided me through the glass door into the hotel foyer.

Glazed red floor tiles reflected the dull lights of a ceiling. To our right there was a group of chain-smoking cadres bunched on a sofa in the Lobby Lounge. An ornamental porcelain bowl had been strategically placed to remind us this was an ancient part of China. And the whole place was perfumed with some kind of acidic chemical detergent.

Qian soon got busy introducing me to his colleagues, "This, this, this is Xiao Fei, who is here to interview me," he stammered at a passing maid. "He's a British writer," he went on to tell a row of pretty, if bemused girls behind the front desk.

I took a picture of him posing with a fellow electrician and we shook hands with a manager before making it to the lift.

"The Grand Hotel was the tallest building in Wuxi when I came to work here in 1988," Qian explained as he pressed the button for the 20th floor.

We were delivered to a Chinese approximation of Japan, replete with ornamental screens and plastic cherry blossoms, and promptly seated beside the window by waitresses in pink geisha dresses. This penthouse sushi joint, I speculated, was established to cater to visitors from across the East China Sea who had been key investors when China reopened to the world three and half decades before.

I told Qian he needn't have booked such a fancy place.

"Not, not, at all. I usually eat in cheap noodle shops on the street," he said, referring to a strip of rustic eateries below. "But I'm not allowed to leave the hotel grounds while on duty and I'm trying to do as many hours as possible. At least up here you can get a good view of Wuxi. Look that's the Grand Canal," he said, causally referring to the world's longest man-made waterway—its terminus lying on the outskirts of Beijing—as if it were a piddly stream. Since its construction in the 6th Century, it has been periodically repaired and expanded, but it remained China's main north-south transport corridor right up until 1912 when the Tianjin-Nanjing Railway was completed.

I cast my eyes past the canal to some dour Mao-era tenement blocks beyond which stood some glassy skyscrapers of the new Central Business District. I felt glad to be dining in this retro-licious relic of the 1980s, imbued with fading good intentions, instead of one of the monstrous glass beacons that were now colonizing Chinese cityscapes.

Food soon started arriving but before tucking in, Qian cleared his nose and throat behind a serviette "Sorry, I have to do this," he said, "ever since my cancer operation my sinuses are not right, I can't eat spicy food and have trouble swallowing."

Qian had been diagnosed in 2002, when he was thirty-one.

"I was trained on the job. This was a prestigious place to work back in the 1990s. I remember my salary was 1,000 yuan when the average was just 400. In 1995 my daughter was born and I was rich enough to buy a camera so I could photograph her growing up. I've owned cameras ever since."

"What do you do here?"

"I'm basically on call, if there's an electrical problem, a TV broken or light that needs fitting, I go and attend to it. We also do general maintenance but to be honest much of the day is spent waiting around. This was the first hotel in Wuxi to permit foreigners to stay and it was granted special license to receive foreign television channels like BBC, CNN and NHK. I used to watch foreign documentaries to pass the time so I have a pretty good idea of what the outside world is really like.

When I got the all-clear from the doctor in 2006, I suddenly felt reborn. There was this intense urge to see the world I'd seen on TV. I worried I hadn't been anywhere and wanted to experience as much as possible. You know for Chinese people it's not as easy to travel the world as it is for you *laowai*. I didn't have much money. My salary had plateaued at 2,000 yuan a month and medical bills had been costly."

"So what did you do?"

"Working here at the Wuxi Grand Hotel, I only have to fulfil a quota of hours each month. If I work several double shifts in a row, beginning in the early morning and finishing late at night, I can easily free up days or even weeks to go travelling. I decided to ride around China and visit small places that haven't been opened-up to tourism."

We were served a seaweed salad and some cucumber rolls. Qian grew serious and leaned forward. Despite a mild stammer, a strong Wuxi accent, compounded by difficulties swallowing and hearing, he clearly enjoyed telling his story.

"Let me tell you, Xiao Fei, I'd go anywhere, sleep in youth

hostels and on people's sofas. The cheapest place I ever stayed cost me five yuan a night. That was in Inner Mongolia."

"I see. But when did you start to document your travels?"

"That was 2008 when I saw an exhibition of Wang Fuchun's photos."

"I know Wang," I told Qian, "we've met a couple of times in Beijing." Wang was China's original railway photographer, who, since the late 1970s had documented 'Chinese on Trains', a series that had been exhibited and won accolades globally.

"I'd only photographed mundane things before. But when I saw Wang's work, I thought to myself, I can do that. This changed my whole approach. I remembered the documentaries I liked to watch in the hotel rooms on quiet days. They all told human stories. I followed their example."

"But 2008 was the same year China introduced its first high-speed railway service," I said. "Didn't you want to move with the times?"

"No, I went the other way," explained Qian, "treading the opposite path from the direction the nation was heading, on the slow, obscure services, the cheap old trains—the green trains!"

Though Qian admitted his photography was originally intended just to document his post-recovery nomadism, when he posted images on a local website, his sympathetic portrayal of China's neglected migrant classes caught the eye of a photography luminary who introduced the work to Teacher Bao.

"It was Teacher Bao who really discovered me. He liked my photos and exhibited them at Lianzhou in 2015. That's the year I won the grand prize."

Qian, a hotel electrician from a city better known for producing bike parts than contemporary art, appeared from nowhere and promptly topped the photographic charts. His win rocked the Chinese art world. But few could argue with his down-to-earth authenticity, coupled with the scope of his work, qualities combined that more than justified the accolade.

I chewed down some radish sushi, while Qian attempted to slurp on a bowl of noodles.

"Do you remember that I mentioned on the phone it would be a good idea if we took a green train journey together?" I asked. Qian nodded. "Well, I was wondering where we could go?" I said.

I privately considered some of the regional highlights, the Tang trade city of Yangzhou or Zhenjiang perhaps, where American author Pearl Buck had lived.

"Yes, I've thought about it. Actually, I need to take a train tomorrow. I have to go to the French consulate to get a visa as I'm having an exhibition in Europe. We can book a green train if you'd like?"

"Oh yes, and where is that?"

"It's in Shanghai."

"But I just came from there!"

"Don't worry, Xiao Fei, it's hairy crab season. We can have dinner together."

The following day, it was Qian's turn to be late. I noticed him across the railway station forecourt before he saw me, recognizable by his unshakable deadpan expression and crucible haircut, features which somehow matched. He was taller than the average southerner and surveyed the scene like a meerkat until his gaze locked on me standing beside a tree near the main entrance.

"I, I, I'm sorry, Xiao Fei," Qian said while wiping his mouth of excess saliva. "I had to help my mother with some chores. You know, it's Chinese tradition to look after your parents. I'm in my forties and I still live with mine."

I can't say I was entirely surprised given his innate boyishness but asked instead, "Did you book the tickets?"

"Yes, third class aboard the K781, leaves at 9:31 a.m. and it takes two hours to get to Shanghai."

We negotiated layers of security checks and found our way into a sizable waiting hall. Qian could get a ticket from a machine but as a foreigner I had to queue up to show my passport to a teller.

Once I had my ticket, I found Qian standing outside yet another bag scanning device. "What the hell is this? Chinese railway security is getting ridiculous!"

"Yes, it's a pain," he agreed. "The green trains can only be accessed via this waiting room, the other platforms are exclusively for high-speed trains. As people who take green trains are generally poorer, you know, there needs to be more security I suppose."

Tickets, ID cards and bags were checked once again before we're permitted entrance into the secondary waiting area. Inside, grungy workers sat on sacks bundled together with string. There weren't nearly enough chairs and many were seated around on bamboo mats, as one might do beside a paddy field or construction site, playing cards.

"The high-speed train is really expensive," said Qian. "Nobody thinks about it. But consider the price today. Business class from Wuxi to Shanghai costs 182.5 yuan whereas third class on the green trains costs 19.5. And that's more than a *real* green train."

"What do you mean *real* green train?"

"During Chinese New Year, old trains are rolled out to move all the workers from the factories to the villages, they don't have air-conditioners or heaters. The cost is even lower, it would be around nine yuan to get to Shanghai from here."

"So high-speed can be more than 20 times the cost?" I asked, while attempting some basic arithmetic on my fingers."

"Something like that."

With nowhere to sit, we waited around people-watching, as well as inviting people to watch us — the great Chinese sport of staring.

The sign above the gate informed us the train was ten minutes late.

"The green trains are often delayed," observed Qian. "High-speed travel is more punctual."

While we lingered, Qian cleaned his camera lens and quizzed me about my afternoon in Wuxi. "Did you visit the Qingming Ancient Canal Scenic Area I told you about?"

"Yes, I did. The moon bridge is beautiful but the white-washed cottages looked a bit too pearly for my taste."

"*Jia de!*" was all Qian said, applying China's all-purpose term for "fake".

"Yes, it was kind of synthetic. But beyond the scenic area Wuxi is far more interesting. It hasn't all been gentrified. There are some cobbled lanes lined by old dwellings on one side and canals on the other, really evocative areas to stroll through."

I showed him some photos on my camera of men sitting in doorways chain smoking, chickens stalking the courtyards of communal 'work unit' residences and the bright-eyed girl holding a red balloon I'd enjoyed brief conversation with before a cyclist nearly knocked me into the canal.

"All of Wuxi was like that when I was growing-up," said Qian, "I don't know what happened to it."

"I went to Li Yuan to watch the sunset too," I told him of a classical garden I'd visited. To be honest, it was no heaven on earth but I got to see Lake Li, a sheltered part of Lake Tai." This was China's third largest body of water and the source of the hairy crabs currently being consumed all over Shanghai.

"Come on, Xiao Fei, the train's here," called Qian, already pushing himself into line, driven to hurry as all Chinese were, when faced with a crowd.

Prior to Wuxi, the K781 had already been rolling for over 16 hours from Yingtan in eastern Jiangxi Province, a distance expressed in the mounds of bird seeds and egg shells we found on carriage tables. Despite the lingering funk of pork broth and the dancing light of the morning sun, some commuters were stubbornly trying to sleep, their heads propped awkwardly against windows, a towel or t-shirt acting as some kind of pillow.

As we rolled southeast back towards Suzhou, Qian quickly befriended some of the passengers, asking them where they were heading and where they were coming from. A humble electrician, he didn't threaten anyone; he quickly grew intimate with strangers.

"You, you, you have to be friendly, Xiao Fei. Talk to people. Never say you're a writer because Chinese people are shy, especially country folk. You have to show them some care. Then they open up, like a flower."

He wandered down the carriage, talking to people and taking pictures then returned to show me his fresh shots. His photography technique, he explained, essentially boiled down to getting as close to the action as possible.

"I bought this Nikon D750 second-hand. It's my fourth second-hand Nikon. You can see I've dropped it a few times." He showed me some scratched plastic. "I don't use long lenses or flashy equipment. It's all about proximity. The photographers you see at festivals with telescopic lenses and fancy toys are not professionals, they're almost certainly amateurs."

Qian began photographing a man seated a few rows down from us who was sporting a large pair of women's sunglasses and an old military jacket. He was the kind of eccentric you might miss in China as you hustled your way aboard a train but once Qian starts photographing him he proves a striking subject. Like most people from the countryside he was tiny, his bones bound together in leathery skin. But he was blessed with a Cheshire-cat smile and raucous smoker's laugh, one that rattled the chest.

"Hahaha, why do you want to photograph me?" he asked.

"Just relax, you look handsome, older brother," Qian said, "we Chinese look good on trains…"

"Qian's genius was locating the remarkable in the everyday, the beauty in indignation," I jotted down in my notepad, while he chatted with the man, showing him images on the camera screen and praising his 'good looks'.

He might have good people skills but as we crawled through Kunshan, Qian confessed that his art has landed him in trouble a few times. "I've been arrested on several occasions, even spent time in a cell. The last time I was arrested was in the Northeast. I was taking a picture of a girl outside a train when three men approached, they said they were police officers and took me in for questioning. My equipment was checked and I was warned that I was in a sensitive border region."

I asked him what he thought of the photography at festivals he'd attended since his prominence in 2015.

"I, I, I believe you're friends with LZD, right? Well I love his series *The New Chinese* because he shoots people, although his focus is different from mine as he's more concerned with consumer culture. But I don't like a lot of the work I've seen, especially if it's too abstract and doesn't say anything about society. Many young photographers are concerned with conceptual art these days but that's not my cup of tea. I think they lack attitude. I'm interested in Old Hundred Names and the places you've never heard of, that's where you get a real picture of China."

III

Having been Shanghaied back to Shanghai, I was forced to kill another day in the great metropolis before getting back on track. As a guidebook author periodically stuck in Asian cities, I usually seek out an ancient temple to explore. But this being Shanghai, the key attractions pertained to the celebrity inhabitants of its golden age when it had been an oriental jazz town brimming with political factions, writers' salons, Chinese elites and foreign scoundrels, the great and ghastly all living under cover of a city 'belonging to no country', as Peter Fleming, brother of 007 creator Ian Fleming, put it in his travelogue *One's Company*.

Anyone who was anyone spent time in Shanghai, including one Dr Sun Yat-sen, whose former residence in the French Quarter I decided to visit. Little known to the West, Sun was a towering figure in the consciousness of most Chinese, his name commemorated everywhere on both sides of the Taiwan Strait.

Born in obscurity in the South, Sun spent sixteen years overseas masterminding doomed-to-fail uprisings against the Manchu Qing. When revolution finally followed the Railway Protest Movement, Sun was raising money in Colorado. He didn't get back to China until on Christmas Day 1911, when he sailed into Shanghai to be resoundingly met by no one.

The revolutionary delegates were all in Nanjing haggling over who should assume the leadership of the provisional government, pending proper elections. Not everyone was happy about the man from Xiangshan turning up late for the party. But Sun had friends in low places, namely Chen Qimei, the godfather of Shanghai's infamous Green Gang, who helped see off serious opposition. The deadlock ended, and Sun was nominated for the leadership.

The Republic of China came into being on New Year's Day 1912 with Sun as provisional president. He had prepared for this role for his entire life, but would play it for just six weeks before being forced aside by Yuan Shikai, a powerful northern general ambitious to become emperor.

The last fourteen years of Sun's life were as ungrounded as his revolutionary years abroad although foreign-controlled Shanghai offered some sanctuary. After marrying his friend Charlie Soong's daughter, Soong Chingling, Soong and Sun lived for time in the heart of Shanghai's French Concession, while Sun plotted his political comeback.

On the former Rue Molière, I entered Sun's western-style villa. Beside the house was a rather dry exhibition of Sun-related artifacts, although a sepia-hued photo of Sun facing a crowd outside a steam engine at Zhangjiakou Station caught my eye. Sun had been a keen advocate of a national network. As he had drifted around the world as an itinerant wannabe revolutionary, he had advocated scientific modernity, including railways, which he perceived an engine to drive China forward and thread its disparate regions together as a united whole, a concept being fully-realized in the high-speed era.

A few months after losing the presidency, he petitioned Yuan Shikai to give him the authority to build railways. His Australian adviser William Donald later reported Sun said he wanted to build "two hundred thousand li (100,000kilometers) of railway over ten years," conjuring mileage from his imagination and applying tracks to a map of China like a cubist painter obsessed with lines.

Sun was eventually given some authority to plan a national railway network. He visited the Northern provinces to promote his vision of China crisscrossed by iron, which is probably when this picture was taken. It would take the assassination of Song Jiaoren at the ticket bar at Shanghai Railway Station the following year to derail Sun's brief career as a public transport tsar. Song was the founder of the Nationalist Party of which Sun was the titular head. The blame was firmly put at Yuan's door and Sun declared war against his northern nemesis. What followed was years of infighting, factionalism and rebellion, but Sun would not live to see the end of the strife.

I ended-up ghosting Sun's passage to Nanjing in 1911 aboard a special train, taking something of a 'special' train myself, the Fuxing Express — Xi Jinping's signature 'Rejuvenation Express', high-speed trains (named after his goal of national rejuvenation) connecting Beijing and Shanghai. With top speeds of 350km per hour, these were effectively China's fastest trains, at least on main lines, covering a distance equivalent of that from Chicago to New York in fewer than five hours, a journey that took nineteen hours on Amtrak in the US.

Like the Maglev, people were keen to get photographed outside this iconic train. Unlike the Maglev, it was completely full, although the only discernible difference from this imperial service and the regular Harmony high-speed trains were plastic flowers strategically placed on tables and an unfortunate beige-colored interior.

Once we got going, I was relieved. Like Isabella Bird whose "chief wish on arriving at a foreign settlement or treaty port in the East is to get out of it as soon as possible", I'd never really enjoyed lingering in Shanghai.

The previous evening had been spent watching an American-Filipino trio bash through a bog-standard set of jazz standards in a trendy bar while I tended to an overpriced pint. The venue had been chiefly populated by modern-day Shanghailanders, mostly balding white men in the company of Shanghainese women. I'd caught snippets of conversations about sports and start-ups. Nothing endeared me to this congress of polo shirts and I'd left before the band had finished the second verse of *I Don't Stand a Ghost of a Chance with You*.

Nanjing, I hoped, would be easier to get in step with. After all, in addition to the many historic wonders associated with the 'southern capital', the city that birthed post-punk outfit P.K.14 and Master Gao's craft beer must have something to offer a failed musician with a penchant for quality booze.

The most immediate of Nanjing attractions are the city walls. I rented a bike and cycled to an entrance gate with the goal of circumnavigating the city.

Nanjing's walls took 20 years to build and are said to be the longest city walls anywhere in the world, covering thirty-five kilometers, so I may be forgiven for not completing the entire circuit. Although they'd been restored in places, these battlements still expressed the legacy of Zhu Yuanzhang, a peasant from rural Anhui who went on to become the Hongwu Emperor, founder of the Ming Dynasty, it's capital proclaimed in Nanjing in 1368.

Zhu was laid to rest just outside his signature city, in the shadow of the Purple Mountain, coral-hued with autumnal leaves when I arrived. I followed the 'sacred way' that led to the hauntingly beautiful and opulent Ming Filial Mausoleum fronted by a vermillion gate adorned by weighty green tiles.

The site appeared more citadel than crypt, a conceit endorsed when I found my way into the Square City Pavilion to be confronted by a tortoise supporting a dragon-crowned stele listing the "Godly Merit" and "Saintly Virtue" of the deceased in several classical scripts. But notwithstanding the extravagance, I couldn't help but be seduced by the ghostly grandeur of it all. Ancestor worship has been an integral part of Chinese culture long before the followers of Confucius made it gospel, so it stands to reason the Son of Heaven would earmark a nice plot for future generations to venerate him.

Sun Yat-sen came here to pay homage just after founding the new republic in 1912. "How could we have attained this measure of victory had not your Majesty's soul in Heaven bestowed upon us your protecting influence?" he was reported to have said.

Eighteen years after Sun's first visit to Nanjing, he too, was laid to rest on this woody hillside. Like Zhu, who emerged from the ashes of the Mongol Yuan Dynasty, Sun was credited with wresting China back from foreign rulers, an achievement Sun's Nationalist successors were keen to underline. They spent four years building an elaborate mausoleum for their Party's patriarch, perched on the hilltop, crowned by a blue roof and colored white—the colors of the Kuomintang—it was accessed by 392 marble steps that almost killed the unwitting Welsh travel scribe attempting to ascend them. At the summit stood a five-meter high marble statue of Sun enjoying an unrivalled vista of Nanjing's cityscape.

Sun styled himself as a man of the people and his three principals Nationalism (Minzu), Democracy (Minquan) and Well-being (Minsheng) still adorned the walls of the mausoleum. He had favored Western suits and was a Christian convert, who died penniless, having devoted all his money to the national cause. But when Sun's coffin rolled in on a train from Beijing, his body was dressed in Confucian robes, planes flew overhead and bands marched through town. What the distinguished diplomats witnessed that day was history, in the grand Chinese tradition, being rewritten, for the man who famously said, "All under heaven belongs to the people" who was given a funeral fit for an Emperor.

HARMONY EXPRESS

Nanjing's position on the Yangtze someway between Wuhan and the Grand Canal cities of the lower Yangtze valley made it a natural transport hub. The railway age consolidated Nanjing's southern gateway status when two lines, the Huning and the Jingpu met in the auspicious first year of the Republic in 1912, making it a nexus for the industrial age.

I cycled over to Nanjing West Railway Station. Opened in 1908 and renovated in the 1940s, this marked the spot where generations of commuters from Shanghai arrived. I'd read online there were plans to turn it into a museum but all I found was a lemon-colored period building boarded up in places and apparently being used as an office.

The station's significance declined from 1968 after the opening of the centrally located main station, which enabled Shanghai commuters to continue North via the Nanjing Yangtze River Bridge, which was completed the same year.

This enormous double-decker road-rail truss bridge was an icon of Mao-era engineering. I watched a green locomotive drag a long cargo of carriages across the lower deck while a parallel world of automobiles zipped along the upper deck. Beneath this overpass, great freight barges were steaming through bridge's arches, a dizzying frame of motion and activity only China could curate.

In the 1980s, Paul Theroux wrote, "The bridge over the river is a famous landmark, because halfway through its construction the Russians pulled out, believing the Chinese could not possibly finish it themselves; but they did and it remains one of the few modern engineering feats in China that is actually pleasing to the eye."

To cross the river, pedestrians had to go downstream to the Zhongshan Wharf. Parking my bike outside, I walked in to pay the two-yuan ticket fee. I needn't have bothered to abandon my vehicle, it turned out, as everyone else seems happy to cycle, motorbike or motor-trike straight through the waiting room.

It took just a few minutes to reach the muddy north bank. Great machines of industry hung over the plastic waste floating in the misty water like frozen androids. The neighborhood was downtrodden and broken. Yet, in stark contrast with its shithole surroundings, Nanjing North Railway Station, just a hundred meters inland, appeared through the mist like a movie set.

Pukou Station, as it was also known, had been slapped with a 'protected cultural relic' plaque as "a major historical and cultural site", the terminus of the Tientsin-Pukow Railway that had been designed by the British and completed in 1914 in "the English-style".

The stationhouse was not quite Saint Pancras but there were touchingly familiar architectural elements, including the green metal pillars supporting platform porticos you still see in Victorian stations throughout England. I peered through a window but could only distinguish an abandoned room sewn together by cobwebs and dust.

Around the back, there was a large rusty gate that was unlocked so I slipped inside. The train platforms were aligned in neat rows as if obediently awaiting passengers. Flecked in a riot of yellow and copper brown there was a strange air imbuing the place that recalled the aura of the Ming Mausoleum. The place was so redolent of the past, I couldn't help but fantasize director Wong Kar-wai coming here to shoot a period drama. Zhang Ziyi would be sobbing as she ran down the platform in slow motion as Tony Leung rolled off to fight the Japanese, his concubine Fan Bingbing looking on jealously from the sidelines, all to the accompaniment of cellist Yo-Yo Ma's soundtrack.

There would have to be some photo-shopping of course.

Some boob had parked their car on one of the platforms while cabbages had been planted amidst the rail ballast.

"Hey you! What are you doing here?" shouted an angry voice. I turned around to confront a man puffing on a blue-filtered Nanking cigarette. "This is government property, you're trespassing."

"But the gate was open."

"Do you walk through every open gate you see?"

"Sometimes."

"Get out or I'll call the police."

"You'd best leave," said a smartly dressed man whom I'd previously noticed on the ferry with his wife standing behind the gate. He spoke English but switched to Chinese to address the cadre, "He's just a lost tourist."

I walked around the railway building before I dared say anything. "Thanks for that."

"Not at all, but be careful, you can't just go anywhere you like in China."

"Understood."

"My name is Mr Wang by the way and this is my wife Mrs Liu."

"Nice to meet you, my name's Thomas but you can call me Xiao Fei if you like."

His wife bowed her head modestly and said, "Nihao, Xiao Fei."

"Her English is just so-so," explained Mr Wang.

"But your English is excellent."

"Thanks, I work in a university in Beijing."

"I can tell by your accent."

"Oh really? But I'm not actually a Northerner, my family came from the South although I've been in Beijing most of my life. My grandfather used to work the crane lifting trains onto boats."

"Is that why I saw you near the old ferry terminal?"

"That's it, we noticed you, too."

The couple were so elegant they appeared to have come in period costume, Mr Wang in a sharply fitting suit and overcoat, Mrs Liu in a floral dress, her hair tied in a bun and held in place by a chopstick.

We walked around exploring the neighborhood and chatting. Gone were Nanjing's Toyota-cluttered boulevards. Potholed roads were the domain of e-bikes in old Pukou. The area was rundown and half boarded-up, the battered homes of stoic migrants. Some renovation had stalled. Torn 'China Dream' banners flapped in the wind but no signs indicated what would become of these beautiful, if broken-down period houses.

Eventually, Mr Wang suggested we lunch together.

"Good idea," I said, "although I imagine options are limited."

But this being China, we still managed to find a single-room eatery where a box-shaped auntie dished up gluttonous bowls of noodles while we chatted under the watchful gaze of a Chairman Mao poster.

"My wife and I went to England before, but we didn't visit Wales."

"That's okay, most people skip it."

"But I remember the tour fondly, it's a very nice country. We traveled by bus for two whole weeks."

"You must have seen a lot." I replied, refraining from mentioning that I'd been travelling China by train for years. "When did you both meet?"

"In university in the 1970s."

"But, um, wasn't education largely halted during the Cultural Revolution?"

There was a sigh and a momentary silence. Mao's Great Proletarian Revolution was still quite a taboo topic, especially amongst the older generation.

"Those were special times," Mr Wang said, eventually. "But we were lucky as the first year able to go back and study in 1978."

I didn't doubt him. As Deng Xiaoping began to imagine a modern China of televisions and fast trains, he knew he'd need a class of educated people to get the country back on track. In 1977, a year when only a few thousand people attended university, Deng organized an education conference in the Great Hall of the People. University exams were duly reinstated and millions applied.

Judging by the look on Mr Wang's face, however, politics was not welcome terrain for our conversation, so I remarked instead, "It's good this railway station is protected isn't it? Sometimes the government bulldozes foreign-built buildings."

"I don't think it is protected because it is British, you know, a very famous revolutionary martyr from the May Fourth era set an influential story here."

The May Fourth movement grew out of student frustration with China's treatment at the Treaty of Versailles, in particular, the award to Japan of the German territory of Shandong, the home province of Confucius. It provoked protests and unrest but also inspired debate, nurturing a generation of some of the finest writers to emerge from China before or since, many of whom based themselves in Shanghai.

"Oh really? I read Chinese literature at university. Which writer was it?"

"Zhu Zhiqing, he wrote a story called, *Beiying*, I'm not sure how to say it in English. Maybe *View From Behind* or something like that."

"What is it about?"

"It's about family relationships in that difficult period. It's quite philosophical. You know fathers and sons are somewhat special in traditional Chinese culture."

"Because of Confucianism, right?"

"Right. But this was all being questioned at the time. In the story, Zhu needs to go to Beijing to study. His father accompanies him across the river here to Pukou and buys him fruit for the journey. Old and fat, he struggles to get back on the platform. Zhu notices his father from behind and sees him from a different perspective. That's it really, not much happens. It's just about looking at people in a different way."

"Perhaps that's all it needs to be about," I replied, before asking, "Have they've made a film about it yet? They could use the station as a set."

Mr Wang just laughed and said, "I don't think young people would enjoy this kind of story."

That evening, I was swigging a bottle of Master Gao's IPA in the made-to-look-old touristic bar street 1912 Block, when my mission to Tianjin was side-tracked further after I remarked to the barman, "Cheers, *Pengyou*! Your Ming capital is a fine city, indeed."

"I'm from the real Ming capital," he said, with a hint of knowing.

"What do you mean, Beijing? Didn't Beijing become the Ming capital later on?"

"It's in Fengyang county over the border in Anhui Province. That's where the Hongwu Emperor was born."

It was going to be called *Zhongdu*," he said, showing a picture on his phone of an incredible Ming-style tower.

"The Middle Capital of the Middle Kingdom, aye?"

"Exactly.

"My ancestors came from there. There was a big famine

during Mao's time and they all fled here."

"What happened to it?"

"They never finished it."

"Sounds like half of China."

"Hahaha, you're cheeky for a *laowai*. Want another beer?"

I nodded and he handed me a bottle.

"Does the train go there?"

"No."

"But the train goes everywhere in China."

"The nearest stations are Chuzhou and Bengbu."

"Write it down," I said, handing him a serviette.

He obligingly wrote down two characters, 'phoenix' (feng) and 'sun' (yang) and the following morning I made an unscripted detour to the Ming capital that nobody had ever heard of.

The two-and-half-hour, two hundred kilometers of rail and road proved to be pure time travel as Fengyang had more akin with Mao's China than modern China. Phones lines tied lampposts with houses in an unfathomably complex overhead web, beneath which, people were out and about shopping for groceries in their pajamas. The local pharmacy proudly exhibited dead sea turtles, the body parts of which were advertised to cure a variety of ailments. Birds sang from cages suspended outside open-front shops where belt-driven machines stirred sesame oil. Chunks of lamb dangled from metal hooks near the local mosque, spilling blood across the pavement, which simply added to the rich pallet of Fengyang street odors.

"It's a land before KFC," I jotted in my diary, "the China of the Iron Rooster."

I soon came upon the Drum Tower the barman had shown me on his phone. The triple-layered classical roof towered above the tumbledown buildings and pervasive anarchy of the street below like something otherworldly. The main body of the building was wrapped in green scaffolding netting but I could still distinguish the big character sign which boldly proclaims this to be *wanshi genben*, "The Source of All Things."

I was guided to Ming Huanggucheng National Archaeological Site Park, where the Hongwu Emperor, who'd worried Nanjing was too far away from the central plain to be an effective administrative center, had ordered a palace to be built. Construction had begun in the 1370 but was marred by worker unrest. It wasn't until 1397 that the 'middle capital' was completed, a year before the emperor died. When the third Ming Emperor Yonghe muscled his way into power four years later, he favored Beijing as his seat of power and set about moving the Ming north. Zhongdu gradually fell into disuse. Peasant wars and the looting of bricks led to the gradual destruction of the great capital that never was.

Beyond the main gate of the Site Park, there was a huge field dotted with stone ruins and grass-covered knolls, all that was left of the southern Forbidden City. The centerpiece was the Meridian Gate "built in 1370 and destroyed in the Cultural Revolution", a sign read. There were not many other visitors but I noticed a lot of young couples here whispering sweet nothings on 700-year-old battlements or holding hands amid the flower gardens that looked recently planted to give some tourist-appeal to this otherwise barren place.

Tracing the mounds of earth that constituted palace walls, I reached the East Gate beyond which there was a stream used to irrigate vegetable plots. Standing on the edge of this Ming-haunted meadow, I felt like the recipient of a warning from the past. Or perhaps I was glimpsing the future, a postcard from Beijing after the fall.

HARMONY EXPRESS

IV

By the time the train crossed the bridge over the River Huai, the character of the earth had changed. Gone were the muddy rice fields, the duck ponds, the cloying damp air. The hills were green, but of a darker shade, overspread by coal-tinged skies, the heavy scent conjuring the milieu of the North.

It was said that the first rule of China was geography, the second rule was history. But on the great plains of Shandong, space and time blended like spilled ink. The land was furrowed; traces of centuries-past etched into the soil like the wrinkles around a patriarch's eyes. Between the great smoking factories and forlorn brick farmsteads, traditional tombstones arched like waves across a grainy sea, intimating just how long the central plain had been inhabited.

According to the Sinologist Lloyd Eastman, when the Iron Horse first galloped into China, it distressed many laymen who feared, "the movement of the locomotives, and the stench of their engines would upset the balance of geomantic forces, with catastrophic consequences for both the living and the dead."

This posed a problem for the British and Germans prospecting the railway passage north as the gravesite of gravesites was located directly enroute. For centuries, the descendants of Master Kong, better known to the West as Confucius, had tended to the clan cemetery. But the original survey maps for the Jinpu Railway had tracks running just past the western wall of the Forest of Confucius, as the family cemetery was known. This was believed to violate the natural feng shui imbuing the woods and a complaint was lodged with the Guangxu Emperor in 1904, the Kong linage claiming that the railroad would "shake the tomb of the sage" and "stop the sage's very pulse," and "the spirits of the ancestors would not be able to rest in peace."

Under pressure from Beijing, engineers altered the original

route of the track to curve right around the cemetery forest and thus both of Qufu's railway stations, high-speed and standard, were located some way out of town.

I managed to flag a battered taxi. The driver steered us down a tree-lined country road towards the city, humming along to the Wang Feng song *I Fly Higher*.

"Where are you from?" I asked him.

"I'm local," he replied.

"Really. What's your name?"

"Mr Kong."

"So you're related to Confucius?"

"I'm the seventy-fifth generation, my father is seventy-fourth, my son is seventy-sixth."

"That's incredible!" I exclaimed.

"Not really. Almost half the people in Qufu are surnamed Kong."

"Still, it must be nice to have some famous blood," I said, even if school registers must have been a real confusion.

"*Hai Hao*," he said, with characteristic Confucian deference, "It's all right."

According to official histories, Master Kong was born in 551BC in the State of Lu, as this corner of Shandong was then known, during the Warring States Period. Yet Confucius was nostalgic for an epoch that existed 500 years before his own, which he idealized for the stability and virtuous government that was lacking in his time.

Though he considered himself a transmitter of past wisdom, his collection of sayings known as *The Analects* competes with *The Bible* to be the most influential book in history. Master Kong is easily the most significant figure in the mental landscape of East

HARMONY EXPRESS

Asia. As recently as 1912, China was officially a Confucian state, apparent in the Confucian temples like the one I found at the end of the Woosung Road Railway. As Sun Yat-sen's Mausoleum expressed too, the founders of the new Republic proved unable to shake off the trappings of a Confucian statecraft, a failure which would be equally conspicuous when Chairman Mao reprised the role of Emperor after the founding of the 'Red Dynasty'. Indeed, it is the unchanging political grammar of China that analysts ascribe to Confucius' rigid view of cosmic hierarchy, the so-called four relationships, "Let the ruler be a ruler, the subject a subject, the father a father, the son a son."

On the ground, Confucianism is often cited by people talking about the fundamental difference between the Chinese and the rest of the world—a popular dinnertime topic. The expression 'Confusedism'—was still uttered whenever foreigners confronted the submissiveness of colleagues who refused to question the edict of their boss, or the abiding systems of hierarchy and ritual that informed everything from business dealings to drinking culture.

As a traveler, I felt an affinity for a man who never made a pretty penny but became "a wanderer in many lands" for some fourteen years, coincidentally, the same number of years I'd been kicking around China when I arrived in Qufu. I admired, too, how self-effacing he was—"Real knowledge is to know the extent of one's ignorance"—and that his chief concerns were terrestrial, namely, how we should live, how we should organize society and how we can secure the well-being of those for whom we care for—universal questions universally unanswered, 2,500 years on.

Tourists had been coming to Qufu to pay their respects as early as 120 BC, making it one of the oldest tourist destinations in the world. During the Ming Dynasty, when Chinese domestic tourism seriously took off, the travel writer Zhang Dai dubbed Qufu a "tourist trap" and was annoyed by the entrance fee.

I'd mentally prepared for the worst: a Confucius Mall, The Sage Water Park or Analects Café perhaps.

Although a few hotel facades were evident through the coal haze, wandering around the following morning, I found myself amid ramshackle small businesses secreted into dusty alleyways inhabited by the kind of characters Qian Haifeng would like to photograph. Flying carpets — motorbikes fronted with windshielding fabrics — zipped among crowds of men in flat-caps and horse grandmas haggling over the price of leeks piled high on the backs of motor trikes. I'd imagined the first family under heaven might have exploited their unique position in the cosmic order of things but perhaps the Kong clan remained above the corrupting power of money.

At the main gate of the Confucius Temple, however, the inevitable tourist horde arrived, tracksuit-clad schoolchildren who soon began to shell me with salvos of "Hellooo ah!" while pointing, laughing and aiming smartphones, behavior their teachers did nothing to discourage.

It was a relief to get inside the temple grounds and veer away from the kids. Ambling amongst the steles and memorial arches was a stirring experience. But at every gate or sacred hall, I was forced to wait for another school group to pass through and take a mandatory group photo.

The opulent Confucius Mansion was located nearby, another superb complex of halls, gardens and ornate buildings. But I suffered similar waves of stares and "hellooos" when another platoon of schoolchildren was dispatched to ruin my outing.

By midday, feeling like a hounded celebrity, I retreated to my hostel for a bit of R&R. While writing in my diary, the house matron walked over and started-up a conversation.

"Your Latin characters are very pretty," she said, complimenting my scribble.

"Are you joking?" I replied, aware my handwriting was illegible to most mortals.

"My staff told me you could speak Chinese."

"You're the owner?"

"Yes."

"Nice place. It's very luxurious for a youth hostel."

"Thanks."

"Are you a Qufu local?"

"No, but I've been in Qufu for a long time."

"Has the city changed a lot over the years?"

"Actually Qufu hasn't really changed much at all."

"They've added a high-speed railway station," I remarked.

"Yes, that's true. But it hasn't really improved business."

"Why not?"

"I'm not sure. I opened this place for foreigners, for backpackers. It used to be like the United Nations here, packed with people from all over the world. Even though my English is a bit limited, I loved meeting people from different countries."

"So what happened?"

"I don't know. Somewhere along the line you foreigners just stopped coming. I hear it's hard to get a visa for China now."

"Yes, it's not easy."

She ordered a glass of hot water and sat down. "Last year I refurbished the place so it would be more attractive to Chinese customers. You have to rely on the domestic tourism market these days."

"It's a lovely place," I told her, which was true, clean, well-furnished, a fridge of international beers strategically placed behind the bar.

"Yes, but can I ask you what happened to the foreigners?" she pleaded.

"This I cannot tell you. There were probably many factors in play. I don't meet many foreigners whenever I travel beyond places like Shanghai either. I sometimes feel like the last of my kind. But it looks like plenty of people are still coming to Qufu," I said, gesturing to a window where two coach loads of schoolchildren had just rolled up. "Just look at all those kids."

China's middle school population was larger than the entire population of the United States and I was privately wondering if all three hundred million of them had decided to visit Qufu on this particular day. But the owner quickly qualified what was going on.

"Since President Xi Jinping quoted Confucius in a speech, schoolchildren have been coming here in huge numbers. Qufu has been marked as a patriotic education base."

"Really? I didn't know that." I was of course aware that Xi Jinping styled himself as a benevolent ruler, his nickname Xi Dada or Papa Xi lifted straight from Master Kong's vision of the state as an extension of the family, with the Emperor as its father.

"Anyway, they don't spend money like foreigners do, or used to."

"Don't worry, I'll pay my bill," I told her. "But first, tell me which way do I walk to get to the Cemetery of Confucius?"

"I made my way outside and strolled past rows of rickshaw drivers who hollered *"lai, lai, lai* city tour" at me until I found the cemetery fronted by a red ochre gate topped by glazed tiles. Beyond the elaborate entrance, however, it made good on its claim to be a 'forest' with some 10,000 trees shading the burial grounds of the Kong clan.

It was far less crowded than the temple or mansion had been with the exception of the Tomb of Confucius himself, which had inevitably drawn a lot pilgrims keen to glimpse the sage's final resting place. It was no Ming Mausoleum but a discreet earthen mound fronted by a stone tablet bearing an inscription in antiquated calligraphy. People were decorating it with flowers when I arrived, some even praying to the man who had little concern for the spiritual realm but who had nonetheless assumed god-like status since being canonized as the state philosopher.

I heard birdsong permeating the space between the junipers and whispering pines. It was a rare thing in a country so obsessed with balance that it even named its high-speed train fleet 'Harmony' to find yourself somewhere actually harmonious, but it struck me that the forest of headstones and the forest of trees composed a rare expression of an ideal realized.

The lovely surroundings only made the thought of the train loads of Red Guards arriving to desecrate the tombs a grizzly one. The Criticize Confucius campaign had been actually directed at Lin Biao, a onetime protégé of Chairman Mao's turned enemy-of-the-state. But the struggle trickled down to the layman. Even these hallowed grounds were not spared. Four decades on, however, Master Kong was back in vogue, the old sage having been "rehabilitated", as one might say in Party-speak, the Forest of the Kongs restored.

V

Hebei Province looked boreal; the grass appeared to have retreated underground leaving the last parcels of open ground earth-toned and cracked. A Beijing friend called this kind of cold 'Khan's revenge' as it blew right off the steppe. Exiting in Tianjin Railway Station, I felt the curse of Mongolia biting at my ears.

Thankfully, Tianjin's principal railway station was a rarity in this high-speed age as it was located in the city center. With the sun fast fading, I couldn't afford to shop around. I crossed the Hai River, pushed through some plastic drapes into a steamy Shanxi noodle joint, the owner taking my order while smoking next to a 'No Smoking' sign. After sucking up some egg and tomato soup noodles at a speed that must have constituted a world record, I ask this affable chimney where I might find some affordable lodgings.

"*Loushang*," he said, 'upstairs'.

Above the restaurant rose a multi-story business hotel like a stone pagoda stripped of all decorative features, the age of utility writ large in Chinese modern architecture.

The unsmiling staff offered me the penthouse suite for a 'bargain' 200 yuan.

"It's a deal," I said, slapping my passport on the desk.

It turned out 'suite' didn't quite translate into 'deal'. The room appeared to have been colored, and scented with tobacco, the towels had holes in them and the shower taps were ominously labelled 'Warm' and 'Gool'. The floor looked uneven, a theory I later tested by placing a coin on its edge, which rolled straight into a dusty corner. Beneath the window-side chair I found a condom (unused) and a can of Tsingtao (used), while several call girls' cards were strategically stuffed below the room door in case I needed some company in this prison cell.

Tianjin's central heating system was, like Beijing's, a relic of China's centrally planned economy of the 1950s. As we were already past *Gong Nuan Ri*, 'Public Heating Day' — when the government benevolently switched on the citywide heating system — the room was recording Finnish sauna degrees. It was so hot that I was forced to open the window to let some gool air in, which also helped dissipate the lingering funk.

The winter breeze carried the cacophony of car horns and intermittent rail squeal. I peered down at the lanes of tracks feeding the station like wires protruding from a socket. Tianjin was a major northern transport hub and this was just one of seven major railway stations to call the city home.

The skyline, however, alluded to little out of the ordinary, just concrete towers checkered with square lights within which the silhouettes of people going about their day-to-day lives like termites in a hive.

"I've arrived in the Shanghai of the North," I wrote in my diary, "But it might more aptly be considered a poor-man's Beijing..."

―――∽∾∽―――

The next morning, I put all the clothes in my bag on to offset the winter cold. Catching my reflection in a shop window I looked rather paunchy but so too did the Tianjiners, a noticeably rotund people, their physique possibly owing to their celebrated cuisine, the carb-rich *goubuli* steamed buns and cholesterol-doused *jianbing guozi,* a breakfast crepe made of mung bean flour and flavored with pickles, chilies, eggs and crispy fried crackers. The latter was invented in Shandong but perfected in Tianjin and was synonymous with the city. To eat one in Tianjin was equivalent to wolfing down a freshly baked *pain au chocolat* in Paris, a culinary must, unless you were watching your weight

The hotel lobby staff directed me past the clock tower and over the iconic Jiefang Bridge to the other side of the river where I duly ticked another 'must do' off my Chinese bucket list.

"Extra egg?" asks the vendor.
"Why not?"
"Coriander?"
"Please."
"Spicy?"
"Just a little."

My belly full and my soul fulfilled, I set off to see if the winter sun cast Tianjin in a better light. I was soon footslogging down streets of brick dwellings linked together by laundry lines and huge steaming pipes, the kind of housing that recalled Theroux's description of 1980s Shanghai as "an old brown city with the look of Brooklyn".

Tianjiners shared with the Brooklynese the habit of standing on doorsteps and chatting, and like native New Yorkers, they spoke with a strong accent that linked them indelibly to their hometown. There was a localized vibe imbuing the backstreets and it occurred to me that unlike Beijing or Shanghai, Tianjin had not been so diluted by migrants from the provinces, its unique urban identity pronounced in food and language and the buxom appearance of its pancake-loving denizens.

But it was along the river promenade that I learned of the Shanghai association when I came upon a bewildering collection of architectural styles ranging from Italian to Japanese to what's been dubbed Sino-European, recalling the age when this city had been a patchwork of eight foreign concessions. Some of these old abodes had been given the tourist treatment, particularly along the riverfront and around Jin Jie (Golden Street), a pedestrianized drag where international brands like Starbucks and Zara now occupied gorgeous period buildings.

Central Tianjin, like Shanghai, was easily negotiable on foot and I passed a full morning wandering around the downtown area purposefully lost. Notwithstanding the catalogue of fine churches, hotels and European villas I encountered, it was evident Tianjin had not enjoyed the renaissance Shanghai had. It was visibly less glitzy, its architectural heritage standing as evidence of a cosmopolitan heyday long passed. But I liked the place for its unimposing character and earthy tones, if nothing else.

Eventually, I encountered a point-of-interest, the Zhang Yuan building that lured me inside with the promise of central heating and a bit of local history.

The imposing European-style building had been built in 1915. With its arched windows and doorway, its sloping red roof and steeple, I initially thought it was a church. It had been the residence of a Northern bigwig named Zhang Biao. Occupied by the Japanese in 1935, it became the post-war garrison headquarters for the Kuomintang in 1947 until 1949 when it was made the first public office of the Tianjin Committee of the Communist Party of China. It would remain so until 1956.

Its association with the communist administration of Tianjin meant the entire ground floor was dedicated to an eye-watering exhibition of communist achievements, including 200 pictures and 100 cultural relics and a lot of Marx-speak.

I anticipated more reasons to yawn upstairs but somewhat bizarrely, and unexpectedly, I was reunited with the Last Emperor Pu Yi and First President Dr Sun Yat-sen. Apparently both men had lodged here in the 1920s.

Significantly less was made of the Last Emperor's four-year stint (from 1925 to 1929) than the Doctor's brief stay in 1924. Sun's old room had been made up, complete with a red wood desk, ink brushes, antique telephone and green lamp befitting a statesman of the day. On the wall, a plaque conveniently neglected Sun's democratic credo, emphasizing instead the profile of a patriotic patriarch that has been conjured posthumously, "a great national hero" whose "immortal spirit will encourage us to push the great renaissance of the Chinese people forward constantly in the new era."

LAST TRAIN TO THE DEEP NORTH

I

Walter Wang and I arrived in the capital of Heilongjiang Province exhausted, having spent the day exploring the frigid obscurity that was Gongzhuling so Wang could photograph some semi-derelict railway buildings of Japanese and Russian provenance. Then we rolled across the entire breadth of Jilin Province at high-speed, alighting at Harbin South Station after dark.

Our lodging proved to be foul and decrepit; a youth hostel run by a gang of students who were treating it as their own private hangout, it was tellingly devoid of guests. The hostel was in good company, for the neighborhood was a crooked one; every sign leaned, every step was cracked and every gate was bent out of shape. Even the trees struggled to stand up straight. While searching doggedly for somewhere to eat, we'd noticed someone had written the Chinese characters for 'fuck' and 'cunt' in a dusty window.

The decision to relocate downtown early the following morning transposed us to the gentrified heart of one of China's 'top tourism cities', although there was very little Chinese-ness about the place.

We licked frozen-in-Harbin lollipops while ambling along Zhongyuan Boulevard admiring the pastel-colored facades of Russian-style shopfronts. At a quaint bakery, a tall, blonde couple was stocking up on pastries. This picture-postcard of Slavic domesticity took us somewhat by surprise. Even though I knew there had been waves of Russians coming to Harbin since the railway arrived in 1896 — the white Russians in 1917, the Soviet army in 1945 — I'd imagined they'd be long gone. Yet Russians were not only conspicuous in number, their fingerprints were on everything: from the plethora of bakeries scattered across the downtown area to the skyline of bulbous onion domes and the ubiquity of Cyrillic script. Wang and I even found Vladimir Putin-brand chocolate bars on sale.

When the travel writer Peter Fleming rolled through in summer 1933, it was not only the season that contrasted with my view of Harbin. Fleming was traveling through Japanese Manchukuo and its new governing class had supplanted the Russians to become what he called "the masters of Harbin".

He went on, "Harbin has been called the Paris of the Far East, but not, I think, by anyone who has stayed there for any length of time. It is a place with a great deal of not easily definable character. In outward things, Russian influence is almost as strong as American influence is in Shanghai. But behind Harbin's hybrid façade it is today the Japanese, and the Japanese only, who count; this is true everywhere in Manchuria."

The city was embattled, although the war was not military but criminal, a reminder that Northeast China's struggle with graft was nothing new.

"In 1933, when I was there" Fleming wrote, "conditions were improving. Bandits still flourished, but the Japanese saw to it that they thrived, not on foreigners with sensitive governments behind them, but on the Chinese and the White Russians. Adequate protection was now available to all sympathizers with the new regime in Manchukuo."

When Paul Theroux arrived half a century later, he encountered a nominally poor provincial capital of "skinny frost-bitten faces" that shivered through daylight temperatures of minus 29 degrees. Although China was already on the road to reform, capitalism-sponsored wastefulness had yet to surpass socialist austerity and nobody heated their shops or hotels adequately. "They did not take their clothes off, even indoors — neither their hats nor coats, even when they ate. It was easy to see why. The heating was turned to an absolute minimum — the Maoist doctrine of saving fuel and regarding heating and lighting as luxuries except where they affected production of something like pig-iron or cotton cloth."

Three decades on, and those "skinny frost-bitten faces" were plump and red, fueled by Russian-style street snacks and hot coffee.

Every time we veered inside a shop, we stripped off layers of clothing, so pervasive was the city's central heating system. Ironically, it was the broader consequences of technological comfort that essentially trounced the reason anyone visited Harbin in winter.

"Have you read the news?" asked Wang. "Apparently Harbin's ice festival is melting and they have to close it early."

"What!"

"Yes, because of climate change, so the article says."

"But it's bloody cold!" I declared, glaring at heaven.

"Apparently not cold enough, our trip has coincided with an unseasonable warm spell that has pushed average daytime temperatures above zero," read Wang aloud from his phone, "forcing the famous Harbin Ice and Snow World to close down 10 days ahead of schedule, the earliest time it has ended in its history."

"Even Beijing winters aren't as cold as they were when I was a kid," said Wang, a millennial born five years after Theroux rolled across China by train, when Harbin had been twenty degrees colder.

We rendezvoused with Wang's friend Tian Cheng, an

adventurous Heilongjiang-born photographer, at the doors of St Sophia's Church, a Russian Orthodox cathedral built in 1907.

From the church steps, he guided us to some fantastic heritage buildings including the faded yellow Longmen Grand Hotel dating back to 1901, "The original hotel of the China Eastern Railway Management Bureau…" and a mini chateau-like building, "the former residence of the Chinese East Railway Authority."

He left us the following day, but our group soon expanded when we met up with Teacher Cui, a good friend from Beijing, and Manman, a South China-based indie filmmaker who spoke pretty good English and was keen to explore the Deep North. Sporting mirror shades and the winter attire a skier might wear when frequenting the café terraces in Chamonix, she made Wang and me look pretty shabby by comparison. But as we'd walked along the icy banks of the Songhua River, it grew evident that she was not just a pretty face, but a brave filmmaker to boot: "I've just made a film about Chinese migrant workers living in Europe," she told us of her international arthouse credentials.

Although she'd been successful, she was without the pretensions endemic to Western art circles, and bubbled instead with the effervescence for which the Hunanese are known. By the time we'd reached a Russian-style café at the foot of two mighty river bridges, we were getting along like old friends reunited.

"This is Songhua River Great Bridge of the Eastern Chinese Railway," interrupted Wang, ever keen to play tour guide.

"Built between May 1900 and October 1901, the longest single-span railway bridge in China of its time, as well as the first bridge to cross the Songhua. This bridge survived the Japanese, the Soviets, the Cultural Revolution."

"But not the consumer age," interjected Teacher Cui, pointing to the new bridge adjacent.

"Exactly. They didn't need a new one, they just wanted one."

Wang might not have been willing to give much credit to town planners for replacing the historic girder bridge but at least they hadn't demolished it. Instead, they'd converted the old overpass into a fantastic river walkway, which we duly crossed, despite the bitter wind whipping across the turquoise ice of the frozen river biting at our faces like winter bees.

The best preserved of all the Russian railway buildings in Harbin turned out to be Xiangfang Station, a flaxen-colored stationhouse that dated back to 1898 in the city's rundown eastern suburbs.

"It's still in use and it's a protected relic, let's hope the bastards don't knock this one down."

The building was yet more evidence that no large Chinese city owed as much to the railway as Harbin. The place had been an obscure riverside village until the Russians built the Chinese Eastern Railway — a shortcut for the Trans-Siberian Railway that cut through China, and later, the South Manchurian Railway that stretched all the way down to their colonial acquisitions on the Liaodong peninsula. When the tracks met in Harbin, it became a nexus point in a newly connected world.

This world ran all the way to Paris, hence, the Paris of the Far East epithet (it shares with umpteen other cities in Asia) because the trappings of the jazz age first made landfall here. The town's population had swelled to include an impressive 200,000 foreigners, not just Russian, although it was considered an exemplar of Tsarist Russian imperialism in Asia. Like Hong Kong or Shanghai, it struck me that this was not a city with a foreign quarter so much as a foreign city built on Chinese soil. But unlike those famous southern entrepôts, it was the iron road, not the trade winds that had brought the world to Harbin.

Steeped in the Russian atmosphere permeating central Harbin, we all headed to Tatoc, a subterranean brasserie opened by an American of Russian descent, a century back when Harbin had been a thriving cosmopolitan city. It proved to be a real time porthole. The waiters and waitress all dressed in black and white French aprons and carried silver treys at shoulder height. The place smelled of mashed potatoes and hummed to Tchaikovsky's 1812 Overture.

Over pickled gherkins and beetroot salad, Walter Wang and I regaled our newly acquired travel companions Teacher Cui and Manman with anecdotes about how we'd got to China's northernmost provincial capital from Beijing.

"Xiao Fei got accused of being a spook," said Wang, quaffing a glass of imported wine.

"And Walter almost got us arrested," I added. "And that's before we'd even met the North Koreans."

The passage north had been innocently conceived as way for Wang to photograph some railway heritage sites, while I escaped the capital funk I'd slipped into. I'd been home alone in Beijing over Chinese New Year, and was camping out until the chaos of the holiday season ended. It was a particularly bitter winter after a particularly tough year. China's trade war with the US was in full swing and anti-foreign sentiment was on the rise. Various government crackdowns were putting immense pressure on the domestic art and music scenes that I was closely connected to. As one foreigner put it to me, "The sliver of space between the state and society which we have all inhabited since the 1980s is slowly closing again." The man understood Chinese history well enough to see the future.

Though I had no inkling of a virus that would emerge in Wuhan twelve months later to turn the world upside down, I sensed my days travelling China would soon be coming to a close.

The golden era of Anglo-Sino relations and the optimism of the age that had illuminated the genesis of my grand railway project, already felt like history. The Party was tightening its grip on all sectors of society and toughening its stance abroad. The wider-world's curiosity about boom time Cathay was transmuting into suspicion and fear. I suspected these were the last of the fat years, a remarkable period of history, when closeted China so briefly, opened up to the world.

The grim suppression on Muslim minorities in Xinjiang was now headline news, globally. Mass surveillance in the province implied I could not ride the Iron Rooster through Chinese Turkistan, as I'd long dreamed. The Taklamakan Desert's name is said to translate as "you can go in but you won't come out" and I knew that the fate of any unwitting travel scribe bound for Kashgar would be just so. Yet despite the gathering storm clouds, I still had a few remaining points on the Chinese railway compass I could yet touch; China's most northerly point somewhere on the Heilongjiang frontier, as well as the world's highest altitude track, which ran across the Tibetan plateau all the way to Lhasa.

Walter Wang and I had become close friends since meeting at the Lishui Photography Festival, regularly meeting up to discuss our two preferred topics, train travel and rock music, usually blended with our third common interest, craft beer.

It was one such boozy night that we contrived to touch the crest of the dragon.

We'd departed from Beijing Railway Station, rolling against the tide of Chinese New Year returnees aboard the K1301 bound for Manzhouli, alighting just after lunch at Tangshan, an old mining city devastated by the 1976 earthquake. It was home to the China Railway Origin Museum, an only-in-China kind of place, the pit head of an old yet operational mine shaft towering behind an ostensibly modern museum complex, which chronicled British engineer Claude Kinder's imperial railway built through North China at the tail end of the 19th Century.

The line had begun in Tangshan as a humble miners' tramway, but the project soon expanded, spreading in two directions, overcoming geographical obstacles, climatic challenges and political obstructions as power ping-ponged between pro-railway reformers and traditionalists with a penchant for sedan chairs. Ultimately the railway won, connecting Tangshan to Beijing by way of Fengtai in 1897 and reaching distant Shenyang in 1903.

It was along a travel corridor forged by this little-known British engineer that we continued our journey north past the imperial garrison town Shanhaiguan located where the Great Wall meets the sea at Old Dragon Head.

"The locals dubbed Kinder's imperial railway line *Guanneiwai Tielu*, the railway within and beyond the Great Wall," Wang explained, before we alighted at Jinzhou, a provincial city that was home to impressive Japanese colonial buildings, as well as an ancient pagoda.

From Jinzhou, we traveled deeper into Liaoning Province, past hog farms ringed by log fences and Mongol yurts peppering black muddy fields blasted by snow.

We were having a great time until we rolled into Yixian, where we ran into some trouble. Although poor and rustic, the county town itself was not uninteresting, home to another pretty Japanese station house of 1930s vintage as well as some magnificent wooden Buddha statues carved in the 10th Century that were housed in a downtown temple.

"Then what happened?" asked Manman, slicing through a rump steak.

"We took a bus out into the countryside to visit the Ten Thousand Buddha Cave Temple," explained Wang. "We were checking out some ancient painted grottoes from over a thousand years back, when a dickhead of a security guard pushed us towards the exit gate, telling us we'd need to be outside by five p.m., even though it was only half past four. We were left sitting on a stone wall near the main gate waiting for a taxi to pick us up. It was there a woman came over with her daughter and called Xiao Fei an Old Russian."

"I told her I wasn't Russian," I said, "but she insisted I was, arguing that all foreigners in the Northeast were Russian. It was quite bizarre. I even showed them my British passport. That's when her daughter chimed in, saying, her teacher had told her if she saw a foreigner she should report him or her as a spy. Wang was so angry; it was so disrespectful. He shouted at them, asking how dare they accuse his friend of such things, but they wouldn't listen."

"Why on earth would a foreign spook visit a Northern Wei temple in Liaoning Province anyhow?" Wang asked rhetorically. "This was hardly the place where 007 could unearth any state fucking secrets!"

"But that wasn't the worst of it." I said. "We arrived in Yixian West Station ahead of the night train to Shenyang. We walked straight into an unpoliced waiting room and sat down among the other travelers. But then some security guards arrived — by the looks of things, after a long dinner — and ordered everyone to walk outside and back in again through the metal detector while feeding their bags through the bag scanner."

"It was ridiculous," said Wang. "We were already inside, if there was a terrorist amongst us they'd have already planted a bomb, this was just conforming to some stupid fucking regulations."

"Other travelers grumbled too, some even shouting at the station guards," I added.

"So what did you do?" asked Teacher Cui, topping up everyone's glass.

"Walter saw a hotline on a wall poster so he dialed the number to leave a complaint. Moments later, a uniformed man beckoned me into a side room. I followed him in and he began to interrogate me on why I had complained about Chinese railways. I said it wasn't me, so they dialed my number, but the ringing, of course, came from outside."

"So they hauled Walter in?" Teacher Cui guessed.

"Exactly. And he was in there for some time."

"*Sha bi* — stupid cunts," said Walter. "What's the point in a hotline if you can't complain? Honestly this country is completely back to front."

Despite Wang's lengthy shakedown by the transport cops, we made it to Shenyang, arriving in the wee hours, and feeling rather ruffled.

At least our environs were pleasant. We were staying in the Liaoning Hotel, which was constructed by the Japanese in 1927 and had been kept in the style of the 1920s, with a monochrome tiled floor, a grand piano in the lobby and an antique wooden staircase leading to a second-floor balcony. Peter Fleming had stayed there during a Japanese air attack, as had Mao Zedong, although to stay in the Chairman's suite would have cost us 888 yuan.

The hotel was part of the Zhongshan Road Historic District, an area comprised of several fine banks and administrative buildings built in the '20s and '30s when heavy Japanese investment attempted to create an international business enclave in the Northeast. Even the central railway station was built by the Japanese.

The colonial architecture also recalled the onset of World War II in Asia. The first major incident occurred when the 'Old Marshal' Zhang Zuolin, the chief warlord of Mukden, was assassinated trackside by the Japanese.

Walter Wang found the exact site of Zhang's death, forcing me to climb over a wall and up a hill while clinging to a barbed wire fence just to see a rail side plaque that marked the spot of the assassination.

But the death of Zhang didn't quite get the Japanese what they wanted, as his son, the 'Young Marshal' Zhang Xueliang proved a more than competent ruler, effectively controlling much of Manchuria until 1931 when China's nationalist government reasserted its control. This provoked two colonels from the Kwantung Army — a semi-independent force closely aligned with the South Manchurian Railway Company — to concoct a scheme to detonate a bomb on the railway and blame the Chinese. They did so on September 18 and by the 19th, the Kwantung Army had taken Shenyang. It would become known as the Mukden Incident as was commemorated at Shenyang's September 18 Historical Museum, which stood at the site location of the railway bombing. "No 46 Wenhua Nanjie, Dadong District, Shenyang, at the site where the earth-shattering September 18th incident broke out," read a plaque outside. The dramatic language was very much justified, as the Mukden Incident was a step towards war that, from 1937 onwards engulfed the region as the Empire of the Sun spread with ruthless efficiency across much of East Asia.

———〜〜〜———

"One afternoon we were checking out the Xita, one of four Tibetan-style stupas dotted around the city," I told Manman and Teacher Cui. "From there, we followed directions from a ticket vendor to a nearby food street. It turned out to be Northeast China's largest Koreatown. Many of the restaurants were run by Chinese-Koreans, but I noticed one decorated North Korean flags so we went over. The doors were pulled ajar by two porcelain-skinned girls in fur coats."

"They said *welcome* in Korean," interjected Wang. "We asked if they both spoke Chinese, which they did, of course. We then asked them where they came from and they said they came from Pyongyang, North Korea."

"I inquired if the restaurant was open to non-Koreans and they said of course, so we followed the girls up the stairs into a large dining room decked out with images of Kim Il Sung and soaring white cranes flying around sacred Mount Paektu. Korean karaoke was echoing down the hallway."

"The Pyongyang beer was great, as were the beef noodles," Wang recalled, licking his lips.

"Yes, it was probably the best meal we'd had since leaving Beijing. After dinner, we got chatting with the waitresses. They told us they were there to perfect their Chinese. When Walter asked for a photo with one of the girls, she was more than happy to oblige. We suddenly found ourselves in the midst of a North Korean selfie orgy, as a number of waitresses formed a line to pose for a picture with Walter and me. It was so funny!"

Teacher Cui was laughing. "Sounds like you had quite an adventure just getting to Harbin," he said.

"Yes we did. But we have a thousand kilometers to go if we're going to reach the frontier," noted Wang.

"Do you know, when Peter Fleming came to Harbin in the 1930s he went to an opium den," I told the table.

"Who was Peter Fleming?" asked Manman.

"He was a travel writer from England. His brother wrote 007."

"Oh, I thought you were the first British travel writer crazy enough to come to Harbin," joked Teacher Cui.

"No, a few other lunatics have strayed this way before. A famous American author named Paul Theroux wrote a book about trains in China in the 1980s. He found Harbin to be an austere place, noting that Parisian striptease and Dixieland jazz had been prevalent before the communist revolution."

"I noticed a bar near the Russian church," said Teacher Cui, who was a regular at Beijing live venues and always has a nose for a gig. "It was called Blues Bar in English and had a picture of BB King in the window. I wondered if it was a live house."

"Maybe we should check it out," suggested Wang, "especially if there's some opium or strippers."

We settled the bill and headed out and went down a side street to the Blues Bar.

Outside, it did appear to be a venue of sorts. But inside, it was not quite the smoky jazz lounge we'd hoped for but a dank, cabaret dive. Finding a stage side table, we settled amid an audience of cigarette-puffing hoodlums who looked like a cast of Chinese Goodfellas. Entertainers were rolled out one after another to keep the crowd amused—first a not-to-subtle lady boy who flirted with the predominantly male audience, invoking awkward laughter, hoots and finger pointing.

Then the music got going when a saxophonist emerged to play Black Magic Woman while dancing about nicking shots of beer from stage-side patrons. He invited everyone to dance and Manman heeded the call, leading us straight onto the stage for a boogie.

Falling back into our chairs after cutting a rug with Harbin's finest, laughing at the absurdity of it all, the main attraction was introduced by a game show-style host wearing a tuxedo. "Ladies and gentlemen, comrades and friends, the main attraction..."

Amid some artificial fog blasts and strobe lights, several stumpy Russian girls dressed in suggestive, if ill-fitting frocks, emerged to perform a very contrived dance. And the men in the bar went wild, staring and pointing as if they were in the

Moulin Rouge. None of the dancers appeared to be relishing the experience. I caught one girl half-yawning, while shaking her bottom at a troll-shaped man who was clapping and grinning like a child at a birthday party. The Russians, whose ancestors built this city, might not like it, but it was the Chinese who had the deep pockets. The tables had turned.

II

"Are you awake, Xiao Fei?" asked Teacher Cui, looking up at me from the carriage floor.

I gripped my blanket one last time, then kicked it off and wiggled worm-like to the end of the bunk.

"Barely," I replied.

"We've just passed Xinlin," he said.

"Is that anywhere near the beach?"

"Quite the opposite. But it is beautiful outside, you should take a look."

I'd somehow ended up with auspicious ticket number 10, 001 — carriage number ten, upper bunk number one — which was inauspiciously located at the other end of the carriage from Walter Wang, Teacher Cui and Manman. Cui, with the characteristic thoughtfulness of a cool uncle, had come over to give me a morning nudge. Apart from the lingering taste of spicy duck eggs still clinging to my tongue, I'd survived the night intact, and after a few more yawns I was able to shimmy down to the carriage floor to survey the scene.

It was a milky world outside; a raft of pallid trunks pressed between a pale heaven and an even whiter earth. The train wheels threw powder up like surf jettisoned from a jet ski. Only an occasional fleeting glimpse of an evergreen tree contrasted with an otherwise blanc vista.

"We've been traveling for over 12 hours," said Cui, as I glanced at my watch.

"How many more to go?"

"Still half a day yet. Walter Wang has booked us a driver at Mohe as that's as far as the train goes, so we'll need to rent some wheels if we're going to make it to the frontier."

"Good to know."

The gangway was splashed white with snow, as if some vandals had hurled some paint through the door when the train last stopped. Plastic sheeting had been tapped to the toilet windows, yet I still almost lost a buttock to frostbite when I hung over the squat toilet. Everywhere, and by whatever means, the cold was trying to break into our metal cocoon.

A steamed bun purchased from a passing vendor went some way to revive me. A pop song hissed into life, signaling we were rolling into Changpin Station, which served 30 houses and about a billion trees. Beyond these spartan homesteads, there was nothing of human provenance, just snow and rocks rolling by our window with repetitive certainty.

The last outpost we passed before reaching Mohe was Amur, demarked by a Ming-style pavilion dripping with blue icicles. Broken into Chinese characters 'A Mu Er' was the Russian name for the Heilongjiang from which the province sourced its evocative name meaning Black Dragon River. This watercourse, close to 3,000 kilometers long, defined much of the eastern border between these two Empire states until it spilled into the sea at the Strait of Tartary.

"Do you want a guide?" asked a stout lady wearing a pink puffer jacket, as we prepared to disembark.

"A guide to where?"

"To wherever you want to go?"

"Which is the most northerly point on the Chinese map?" I asked.

"Beihongcun is further north than Beijicun," she said.

"Isn't that a bit counter-intuitive?" I asked. Beihongcun means North Red village but Beijicun means North Pole village.

"North Pole village is open for tourism," she said, "it's more fun and there's plenty to do there."

"Then we should head to North Red village if that's true north, and less touristy."

"There's nothing much up there. I'm a guide, you should trust me."

"I do, but I believe we already have a guide," I said, looking at Walter Wang who nodded.

Sure enough, just beyond the frozen station gates, Mr Liu approached us clad in winter wear that only left his face exposed to the elements, like an old-school deep-sea diver.

"Nice to meet you," he said to Wang, "we spoke on the phone."

While they discussed our route and destination, I glanced back at the whitewashed station. Two feral dogs ran past, the canines better adapted to these Siberian conditions than their human overlords, which in Mohe consisted of a few men shuffling about in long coats and big fur hats. Yet this nowhere really was a somewhere—the unassuming pinnacle of the world's largest railway network. South of us extended 139,000 kilometers of iron road snaking through all the provinces to its southern periphery on the south side of Hainan Island.

Once we were packed into Mr Liu's car, we began tracing a strip of frozen blacktop through a primordial land of snow-quilted forest, while quizzing him about life on China's northern lip.

"Were you born here?"

"No, but I've been here thirty years, I'm forty-eight now."

"You don't look it."

"Where are you from originally?" asked Manman.

"I'm from Hebei Province."

"And that wasn't cold and backward enough for you?" quipped Wang.

"I was sent up here, you know in those days the state still found work for you. I was working in the forestry department. Then they banned hunting and forbade logging. There was nothing to do. Most people left. I decided to stay."

"Why?"

"*Xiguan le*," he said, meaning simply, "I got used to it."

Liu said the recent development of tourism had been a lifeline for a place depopulating like autumn leaves.

"There are a few tourist sites on the way if you'd like to visit them?"

"Sure," said Manman. "I could do with a walk after all that train travel."

We pulled over at a roadside cabin advertising snowmobile rides, operated by a member of the Evenki tribe, reindeer people who lived both sides of the Sino-Russian divide.

Mr Liu led us into the surrounding forest. There was a rope-swing suspended from a tree branch, some red lanterns and few other strategically curated selfie spots. Otherwise, the scene was albino — even the tree trunks had curiously pale bark.

"Look at this," said Mr Liu, kicking some snow off a stump. "This is what's left of a 200-year-old tree. In 1987, there was a great fire here. It lasted 28 days, spread quickly and killed over a hundred people. All this is regrowth. I arrived in 1989, not long after the disaster. Old-timers still talk about it, describing an entire mountain and valley ablaze. But it has made the government very serious about looking after these forests, which is a good thing." Casting his gloved hand towards the pale horizon, he added, "All this is protected land." Having seen white fluffy hares bouncing about and even some bear prints in the snow, there were signs that game was no longer game in the province of the Black Dragon.

Through the ankle-deep powder, Mr Liu took us to see a few trees that survived the inferno, stoic plants of Qing Dynasty vintage lost amid an ostensibly modern forest, reminding me of the temples one found isolated amid modern Chinese cities.

Back in the car, we crossed what Mr Liu said was, "the last bridge in China" below which a van was stuck in the frozen river. Otherwise, the scene was virgin, there were no other vehicles and I began to wonder that if we skidded like that unfortunate van driver, we'd probably topple from the edge of the world.

We found the limits of Chinese civilization half an hour later, a one-horse town in a very literal sense, a tiny settlement fronted by a pony pulling a sleigh down the only street of any significance.

"This is it," said Mr Liu. "Beihongcun — North Red village."

Beihongcun would have been a nowheresville par excellence were it not for the geopolitical lines humans draw — coordinates carved into a riverside plaque commemorated, "the most northerly point in China". Even the ramshackle convenience store was named The Most Northerly Supermarket and was aptly staffed by a giant Russian who spoke Chinese.

"I was born on this side of the river," he explained, or perhaps complained, when asked how he ended up a Chinese citizen.

After posing for pictures outside the shack houses that constitute China's John O'Groats, we intuitively walked onto the Black Dragon herself, a white serpent frozen hard enough to support our racket without awaking it from its hibernation.

"I wonder if we can make it to Russia," I said to Wang while eying the north bank. But before we got halfway across the river, a loud speaker warned us to turn around.

"What the fuck?" I complained.

"Look down there," said Wang, pointing.

Sure enough, a small watchtower stood guard over this forbidding borderland.

Unable to gate-crash Tsar Putin's realm, we climbed a nearby hill to get a good look at the backend of the Russian Federation, a satisfying panorama as enormous and empty as I'd ever imagined Mother Russia to be. The south-facing vista was little different. Yet I couldn't help but think that beyond the emptiness rested China, all of it, the grand stage of a 5,000-year drama — that cloying, crowded country of a billion plus souls all going about their daily business. It was like looking at the earth from the moon, you got the outsider's perspective.

III

Having touched China's most northerly point, and endured a night on a communal *kang* — a heated bed — in the company of three men, filmmaker Manman set off home. But Cui, Wang and I were still committed to the iron road, and determined not to go back the way we'd come.

Leaving North Red village, we hopped a minibus bound for Mangui, a township in neighboring Inner Mongolia that Wang assured us had "the first train station on the Yalin Line, China's most northerly track".

It was an arduous road trip, the minibus sliding on ice, each near-death collision reminding me of why I preferred rails to roads. We got stuck in the snow twice. But the driver seemed adept with a shovel and overcame such delays with some quick digging and strategic revving of the engine, while our fellow passengers sneaked into the woods for a roadside pee and a smoke.

Much of the day was lost to that forest road. The only discernible change came when signs started to appear in Mongolian script, signifying we were drawing on the world of steppe nomads.

Our destination, when we finally arrived, offered little reward for our efforts. Flanked by the frozen Jinhe River, Mangui was a low-rise, snow-dusted township of a few unpaved streets with more dogs than people.

China was generally a comradely place, its mind-blowing population density cultivating a village kind of intimacy amongst strangers, even in big cities. But the frontier folk of Mangui shuffled through the snow with suspicious eyes and the solitary composure of wild things. Presumably, this had been a logging town in its day, but now it was unclear what people could really do but keep each other company over steamed dumplings. The local karaoke joint looked like it was opened in the 1980s and closed down in the 1990s and this had been the only point of diversion.

Trudging through the snow in days-old clothes, I still managed to muster a fondness for Mangui, for its isolation if nothing else. Before human numbers ballooned to several billion, I imagine life was lived in this kind of place and travel was akin to hopping from one obscurity to another. It was also reassuring to confirm small towns like this still existed in China, to know not everyone had run off to chase their China Dream in homogenous megacities. Mangui was notable for its quiet, for its somber dreaminess and blemish-free skies, for its soft snow and the ghostly glances of its dogs and diffident inhabitants.

"Listen, the only sound is our boots crunching in the snow," I said to Teacher Cui as we walked across town.

"That and the occasional wok fire," he noted.

We walked through the deathly calm to the train station to get a sense of things as it was the only landmark in a town. It had been painted vermillion and fronted by a rock with the characters *'Wenming'*, Civilization, chiseled into it.

We garnered from a framed paper timetable that the next train would come sometime after six the following morning.

"Another night on a *kang*!" said Teacher Cui, adding, "no snoring."

"Let's get some food," I suggested, rubbing my gloves together.

The light failed and a wind whipped across the Northeast. We retreated back into the town center where Walter Wang was busy booking us into the only hotel.

"We need to rise before the sun," Cui said. "Eat plenty. It's going to be a cold morning."

IV

"Who is this?" the bald ticket collector asked.

"That's Winston Churchill, he was the prime minister during World War II."

"And that's the Queen of England right?" asked the thickset food vendor. Together the pair looked like Chinese pub bouncers, not railway workers, but they were exhibiting the curiosity of hardened collectors of the spare change I had in my wallet from a previous trip to Europe.

"Yes, right, Elizabeth the Second."

"Who is this on the twenty-pound note?"

"Adam Smith."

"Who is he?"

"He was an economist from Scotland."

"Let me have look," the bald ticket collector said. He passed his gaze over the note and returned his gaze to the blue-hued Churchill depicted on the fiver.

"I like this one better. But why is only worth five pounds? Churchill should have more value."

"How much is this worth in Renminbi?"

"Almost fifty, interjected Wang, adding, "I have some Euros too," before introducing another currency to the conversation.

"This one looks like a logo from Xi Jinping's Belt and Road Initiative," the ticket collector quipped.

"What does this say?" asked the food vendor, still clinging to the twenty-pound note like it was Willy Wonka's golden ticket.

"Bank of England," I translated.

"Wow, amazing. Look at that comrade, England Bank..."

The two Manchurians, who'd probably never ventured further than Beijing, soon started negotiating as to which note they wanted and how much they should pay us in Chinese yuan.

"I think I'm going to take this one," said the bald ticket collector.

"I want the twenty-pound note but it's 200 *kuai*," complained his colleague.

The transaction was interrupted when a railway matron sporting a Communist Party pin badge on her lapel came over to break up the party.

"What are you boys doing?" she asked in the tone of a headmistress. "Don't you have any work to do? Come on, leave the poor *laowai* alone."

They departed, leaving Wang and Cui to their game of drafts and me to sip from my tea flask and daydream. Beyond the plastic sheeting-tapped to the windows, the spines of winter trees lined up like soldiers from a skeleton army. Chinese Siberia was as monotonous as actual Siberia. I felt weary for the first time on the trip. After two nights spent on rigid *kangs* breathing human farts, I began to dream of a change of clothes and the familiar scent of my bed.

But peace and quiet was a fleeting condition on Chinese trains, even on the frontier line. A few stops ahead at Genhe — a town that laid the bold claim to being 'China's coldest' — a man boarded our carriage wearing old army fatigues and a carrying plastic sack fashioned as a rucksack.

Seeing me, he sat down opposite and began his pitch.

"Nice to meet you, foreign friend. I'm called Yao Gan. Let me show you my ID card, I'm for real," he said, noticing I already suspected him to be a snake oil salesman of some kind.

"You foreigners, you all have a bit of money don't you?"

"Hmm, I see you're from Inner Mongolia," I said, reading from his ID card in an attempt to parry any ideas he had about forcing my wallet open.

"That's it, my great homeland, as wide as the sea, as open as the sky. I have the blood of Genghis Khan," he said, flexing his muscles.

"Really?" I asked, as it said, "Han ethnicity" on his ID card.

"Yes, I'm Mongolian on my mother's side."

"Let me show you something from the grasslands, foreign friend, you're going to love this."

He pulled out a plastic bag and I anticipated a fragment of the Great Khan's battle axe or something akin. But he brought out a pebble instead.

"There you go," he said, as if he'd just gifted me the elixir of immortality.

I examined the stone, which appeared to be like any stone you might find anywhere. But Yao was a dedicated and creative salesman, showing me rock after rock with the same measure of excitement the railway workers had expressed for some rouge notes of Western cash.

"See what that looks like?"

"Not really…"

"A face, see the eyes, the nose…"

"What about this one?"

"I don't know…"

"It's a bird, see the wings? And this one looks just like a camel, who'd have thought it, it's uncanny," he remarked.

I entertained him, as he entertained me, and we haggled over the price of his non-precious stones for a while, until the novelty of meeting a foreigner faded with the reality that I wasn't going to buy any of his novelty pebbles.

"Here's my stop," he said, as we pulled into another frozen outpost, "*Zaijian*, foreign friend." Then turning to the spartan occupants of the carriage, he waved. "Goodbye, all of you, see you again, who'd have thought it, a foreigner up here in the Deep North, take care, ladies and gentlemen," he said, making a spectacle of his departure, "Adieu."

"You rascal, get off," shouted the carriage matron, who recognized him.

"See you next time," I called.

"*Zaijian, Laowai.*"

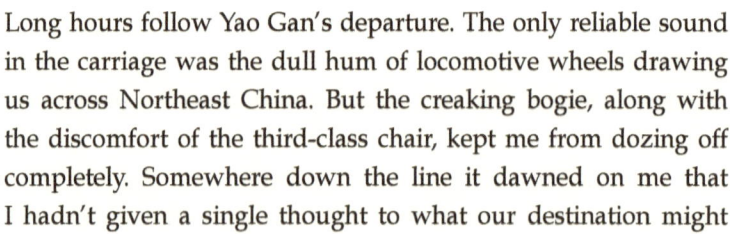

Long hours follow Yao Gan's departure. The only reliable sound in the carriage was the dull hum of locomotive wheels drawing us across Northeast China. But the creaking bogie, along with the discomfort of the third-class chair, kept me from dozing off completely. Somewhere down the line it dawned on me that I hadn't given a single thought to what our destination might be. That was Wang's business. Each wily farmstead, hovering raptor or snow drenched hillside we passed, helped solidify my conceit that we were rolling further from the path trod by foreign travelers, which made it a worthwhile endeavor in and of itself. I lost my gaze in this Chinese winter wonderland, my thoughts drifting through past episodes of life, long buried traumas and the sadness of failed relationships, which surfaced like buoys released from the ocean floor. Yet there was also something cathartic in this simple process of moving forward, moving towards the unknown, maybe to nowhere, the sense that moving was enough.

Ten hours after leaving Mangui, Wang gestured for us to alight.

Standing outside the station gate next to a car with a welcoming grin, was Tian Cheng, Walter Wang's apprentice, whom we'd met in Harbin days ago.

"What are you doing here? Is this your hometown?" I asked.

"No, I've come to meet you guys," he replied, relieving me of a backpack, which he planted in the boot of a car.

We drove to a town called Meitian, which ominously translated as 'coal field'. Snow had been piled on the edge of the road reaching higher than the crooked wooden houses common to this part of China. Only the chimneys were visible, breathing coal smoke into pale blue skies.

Eventually, the road aligned with a small branch railway cutting through the snowy wastes.

"I hope the light holds," said Wang.

"It's still a short while before sundown," said Tian,

"Look there, up ahead!" cried Wang.

"I see it, I see it," said Tian excitedly.

On the horizon it emerged, puffing steam, a great black beast of a machine. The car skidded to a halt and everyone alighted.

HARMONY EXPRESS

"What the hell is that?" I called at the three men running into a flaxen grass field.

"A steam locomotive," said Wang, adding a little later, "They started making this model in the 1960s back in Tangshan, it's an imitation of a Japanese-American Mikado 6."

Shunt by shunt, it crawled forward as each of its coal hoppers were filled with a loading facility hanging overhead. It was slow, heavy work, involving a lot of noise. As it drew closer, we encountered a metal monster, all pipes and levers, dust and filth, the last of the Iron Roosters, still alive in Inner Mongolia. Only the red wheels and rust gave it any color,

"This one dates to about 1983," yelled Wang, over the noise of the engine.

The hunk of metal appeared at home in a region where progress appeared to have frozen with the winter. The engine driver was a contented sort, a round-faced man wearing his China Railway cap in reverse like a baseball player.

He waved as we documented his drive.

"He's Tian Cheng's friend," explained Wang, "he knew we were coming."

Once all the hoppers were full, he uncoupled the locomotive and started driving towards the depot at full speed. We followed along the side road, Wang and Cui hanging out the windows to shoot video. It was like 007 does trainspotting.

The sun was soon touching the horizon and through its fading glare, the steam blasting and glimpses of glowing coals from the engine looked menacing. No wonder the Chinese called the first trains dragons. They even hissed like great serpents.

Tian announced he'd found us lodgings. The temperature had dropped to minus 25 and everyone was feeling it.

"The place is not great, around here, you take what you can get."

"Doesn't matter, as long as there's a hot shower and food." I said.

"It's a worker's dormitory, there are no hotels in town."

Down a single corridor we found a series of tiny rooms with beds as hard as prison bunks, and a foul, communal bathroom.

Most of the building was empty but I passed a whole family packed into one room, some construction workers playing cards in another. The owner chain smoked nonchalantly but grew concerned when he heard I was a foreigner, not an ethnic minority, as he'd initially assumed.

"We don't have a license for foreign visitors," he said.

"Relax, it's just for one night," appealed Tian.

"I'll need to check."

He made a phone call while we shuffled inside, doing what you should always do when in doubt in China: keep calm and carry on.

Minutes later, a cop showed up.

"Where is he from?" he asked Tian and Wang, who leaped to my defense like lawyers, explaining I was just a traveler who come here to see a steam train and that there was no harm in this.

After listening to their long plea bargain, he asked, "When are you boys leaving?"

"Tomorrow."

"First thing."

"Okay, listen, I don't want him going outside, this is an industrial base and well, we can't have any white devils snooping about learning all of China's business. I suggest you have dinner in your room and get out of here quick smart tomorrow, understood?"

"Got it."

"Yes."

"No problem."

Then turning to me, Tian said, "Don't worry, Xiao Fei, we'll go out and get you some vegetarian dumplings."

V

The tracks attached the obscure border settlement of Manzhouli to the world at the tail end of the 19th Century, the first station on the Chinese Far East Railway, part of the Tsar's grand Trans-Siberian Railway scheme. It was also where the first train we took from Beijing was heading and had we stuck with it, instead of alighting at Tangshan, the trip would have taken us 33 hours, not 14 days. It was safe to say we'd taken the long way around Manchuria.

Manzhouli was where Peter Fleming entered China, describing it as "a small, wind-swept village, lying in a vast, but naturally no less wind-swept plain".

Standing on an iron railway bridge, I viewed a century of change shaped into towering neon-lit hotels sporting faux Russian onion domes. This was not a Russian town on Chinese soil like central Harbin, but an imagined one, a Chinese simulacrum of Slavic kitsch, exotic enough to attract the Chinese north and familiar enough to bring the Russians south where they could enjoy its bewildering array of culturally mismatched attractions. Streets were signposted in Chinese characters, Cyrillic and Mongolian script, leaving English in fourth place (if at all). Downtown, Russian-style bistros outnumbered Chinese eateries two to one, but even the Chinese establishments exhibited some decorative quality of their northern neighbor, be it an oil painting of Lenin or a photo of a topless Russian blonde or simply a loudspeaker broadcasting their wares in Russian, on repeat. On our first night, we ate at a local attempt at fusion dining, dumplings and borscht, fried rice and gherkins, a choice of vodka or baijiu to wash it all down with.

Manzhouli Park was entered via a made-to-look-old Russian-style gate and centered on a pink Russian-style domed tower.

At the foot of the tower my phone rang. It was a Shenzhen number.

"Hello CC."

"Hi Xiao Fei"

We exchanged some standard questions about one another's well-being before she said, "I have some news."

I somehow knew what she was going to say. "Is it mine?"

"Of course not."

"Will you marry the father?"

"Yes."

We talked for a while longer but there was little else to say.

After the call, I stepped down onto frozen grass feeling bruised. The wind howeled and I felt, for the first time, the pervasive cold of the Northeast biting at my bones.

The park, like so many in China, had been left half-finished — construction materials abandoned on the flower beds, a few forlorn kids' rides coated in dust. On the edge of the grass stood the vestiges of old Manzhouli, a few brick houses connected by unpaved roads that smelled of pig shit, showcasing the inequality still endemic whenever you strayed from the hubbub of any commercial center.

"Are you OK Xiao Fei?" asked Teacher Cui, who'd caught some of the conversation.

"*Mei ban fa*," I said, "No way out."

———∞———

The next day, I got up after a restless night, but resolved to put on brave face. After breakfast, the three of us hopped a cab to check out some peripheral sites. We chanced upon the enormous

Manzhouli Matryoshka Scenic Area, a Russian nesting doll theme park on a scale little witnessed elsewhere in the world. Some of the dolls were over 30 meters high and when combined with palaces, entertainment and light shows, well, the need for any Chinese visitors to stray a few meters more into actual Russia was rendered null and void.

The theme park was a stone's throw from a tax-free shopping center and it was evident cross-border commerce was the city's lifeblood. Trade was evidenced on the main pedestrianized strip, Zhongshan Road, where rows of shops vended made-in-China-on-the-cheap electronics, pleather handbags and other fashion accessories to Russians and Mongols. Much of the produce was bought in bulk, carried by mules with packed suitcases and sacks to the North where products were resold.

But there were Russian wares on sale too, mostly big fur hats, animal pelts and military wares like binoculars and hunting knives for wannabe outdoorsmen.

The lines of freight cars hauled up on the railway line told of large-scale business between the two countries. Freight trains bound north were packed with TVs and household appliances while southbound trains were heavy with raw materials, especially timber.

I wrote in my diary, "No wonder China can protect its northeastern forests so well if Russia is so busy culling its trees and wild beasts."

All historical interest was found trackside, dating back to when this was little more than a railway town and Russia was the dominant force in the neighborhood. Wang led Teacher Cui and me on a tour of old water towers, woody warehouses and transport buildings, most of which were rundown and half-forgotten, until, tired and thirsty, we strayed into a so-called Irish Bar in search of some good beer. Inside, a group of Mongolians were singing karaoke. The rest of the clientele were red-eyed Russians downing shots of vodka.

After a few pints, over which we plotted our route back to Beijing, I overheard English being spoken, popping my traveler pretentions like bubble gum.

I went over and introduced myself to the English speaker, a nervous young man with glass lenses so thick his eyes looked like those of a dead fish staring up from a frozen fishmonger's counter.

"Excuse me, I just overheard you talking on your phone, are you from the UK by any chance?"

He was skinny, pale to the point of transparency, his nose freckled orange. "Yes, I am. I'm from a small village in Somerset, you probably haven't heard of it."

"Well what do you know, I'm from South Wales, just down the road. What on earth are you doing here in Manzhouli?"

"I've already been here for three years. I love it," he said, blinking like most people wave. "I hate big cities; I've never been to Beijing and only go to London to get to Heathrow."

"Really. Well it's quite of an out-of-the-way place to base yourself. How do you make ends meet up here?"

"I teach English, I'm making big money," he said, rubbing his fingers together like a London banker. Then to underline his success story, he added, "My girlfriend is a Russian dancer."

RAIL JOURNEY TO THE WEST

I

In great britain, The Railway Hotel would likely have been a quaint inn serving soggy sandwiches near a 19th Century stone bridge. In the People's Republic of China, it was a tobacco-perfumed business hotel deep within an enormous station building. I found it by way of two crowded lifts connected by a corridor of massage parlors, hair salons and Cantonese-style canteens, all, it seemed, components of a clandestine fun land luring weekenders from Hong Kong.

It could be a genuine pleasure watching trains coming and going from one's balcony, which is why I'd booked a night there. But my room had neither a balcony nor a view of anything but the upper floors of Luohu district's towers. The only way to know when a train pulled out for Zhuzhou or Zhengzhou was by the walls shaking like we were experiencing a low-magnitude earthquake.

In anticipation of my destination, I browsed the first chapters of Peter Hopkirk's *Trespassers on the Rooftop of the World*, then went out to get a foot massage, returned with a carton of noodles and promptly fell asleep watching a documentary about Hubei Province's golden snub-nosed monkeys.

The following morning, I was washed and fed a good hour before the train's scheduled departure. I unfolded the map of China I still traveled with and placed it on the floor. China's Far West was not just a symbolic blank canvas: it was literally a featureless blob on an otherwise dynamic page representing a very large and crowded country. The region was so featureless as to be notable. I even found myself examining the page closely to check that the cartographer hadn't accidentally smudged Qinghai Province's dimensions out of existence by mistake. But this was no print error. A province the size of France and Belgium combined was home to only half as many people as Paris. Only some blue circles representing plateau lakes, as well as the black and white dotted line denoting a railway, made the place look any more interesting than the moon.

This spectacular emptiness posed some intriguing questions, most obviously, if the Tibetan plateau really was such an inhabitable void, would LZD and I find anything worthy of comment?

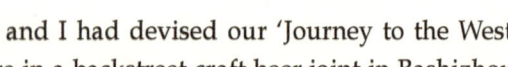

LZD and I had devised our 'Journey to the West' some weeks before in a backstreet craft beer joint in Bashizhou — Shenzhen's zestiest tumbledown migrant neighborhood. LZD was an artist of some repute, but the year's business had been, by his account, dismal. "I've hardly anything left Xiao Fei," he'd complained of the money he'd earned by selling prints from a photo series called *The New Chinese* to a wealthy art collector. "Since *The New Chinese* came out, none of my commercial clients want anything to do with me, I'm too dangerous, business has all but dried up."

You'd think an artist working in a one-party-state with a strong Confucian bent might have known a biting critique of society was bound to condemn him to nationwide notoriety, even if it did win him acclaim in the left field art world. But LZD had appeared somewhat surprised by his decline in fortunes that ran contrary to his rise as Chinese photography's *enfant terrible*.

"Then what have you done all year?" I asked earnestly.

"Drank beer and read books," he'd said, while taking a Baisha cigarette from the pack, habitually tapping it on the table before popping it into the right side of his mouth.

As one drink turned into several, darkness descended upon Bionic Brew's outdoor terrace. Neon blazed through the thick moist air holding the glow like a spotlight in a dusty theatre.

"Well I'm thinking of going to Lhasa," I'd half suggested.

The prospect of visiting the mystical Himalayan kingdom had tempted me many times in the past but I'd always found some excuse not to voyage there. I knew in my heart that a Tibet railway odyssey would elicit similarly strong emotions as holidaying in other disputed territories would, a weekend birding in Kurdistan or kite-surfing off Western Sahara, perhaps. One got pretty good at forgetting about the Tibet issue when you lived in China. As one Beijing expat put it to me, "China feels so dynamic, the people so optimistic, it's hard to consider such ugly happenings playing out thousands of miles away."

Chinese people seldom, if ever, grasped the consensus in the West that the CCP had been waging a campaign of brutal oppression against the Tibetans, repeating the Party line that China's mission was a civilizing one, bringing hospitals, electricity and even the railway to the rooftop of the world. Bookish friends would point out that during the Yuan and Qing dynasties, Tibet was very much part of the Celestial Empire, which was true, though this perspective neatly overlooked the fact that both epochs had been foreign-ruled empires that had subsumed China as well as Tibet. Furthermore, the Qing had awarded considerable autonomy to its western acquisitions, even adopting Tibetan Buddhist practices, as the Lama Temple near my apartment in Beijing demonstrated. Even those most critical of the Party rarely exhibited much sympathy for the separatist inclinations of Tibetans, complaining that the Han Chinese too lacked basic human rights and could be subject to similar levels of violent recrimination. "Consider Tiananmen," they'd say. "You think we have it better?"

The proposed journey elicited mixed emotions and had I not been firmly under the influence of Bionic Brew's signature IPA, I might have proposed travelling somewhere less synonymous with ethnic strife. But LZD was surprisingly keen.

"We should go, I'll take the pictures and you can write a story for one of those silly foreign travel magazines."

"I'll need to get a travel permit," I'd slurred, highlighting the difficulties of traveling to Tibet

"Don't you have a China visa?" LZD asked, raising his eyebrows up above his spectacles as he often did.

"Tibet requires separate documents."

"Oh, the government is afraid you foreigners will run amok up there. They're so paranoid," he said, laughing sardonically. "Maybe we should go to Qinghai first? That way we can get used to the high altitude while you process your documents and if you don't get permission to go to Tibet, we can still kick around the plateau. I hear there are plenty of Tibetan towns in Qinghai anyway."

"I've never been there and I don't know anyone who has."

"Sounds ideal."

"Let's drink to the plan, *ganbei*."

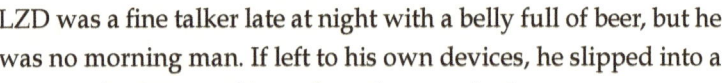

LZD was a fine talker late at night with a belly full of beer, but he was no morning man. If left to his own devices, he slipped into a nocturnal existence akin to that of a vampire bat.

When we were called to ticket inspection, he was still nowhere in sight. I began to concede to destiny, a sole passenger to what Abrahm Lustgarten called 'China's Wasteland Province' in *China's Great Train*. But as we shuffled forward, the distant murmur of chaos echoing down the hallway relieved me of my consternation.

LZD bumped through the throng, sweating profusely and clearly in a state of great agitation.

"Oh fuck, Xiao Fei!" he said, panting. "I thought I would die, the traffic was terrible, I've run here from the International Trade Building."

At least he was dressed for it. He was wearing a tracksuit similar to Bruce Lee's in *Game of Death*, paired with my corduroy bucket hat. "You left this last time you stayed at my house," he said, planting the hat on my head.

"Are you drunk?"

"Not really."

"You sound it… you smell it, oh for fuck's sake!"

"I had to stay up all night otherwise I'd miss the train, so I had a few bottles of Tsingtao, it was you who booked this stupid early train. I'm not getting a morning train ever again."

I waved the ticket at him, shouting, "This is the only train that goes to Xining, once a day, Guangdong to Qinghai daily fucking service."

"I thought we were going to Lhasa?"

"We are, or might be, via Qinghai, remember the plan?"

"Well that sign says that we're going to Urumqi South. I think you've gone the wrong way."

"This is the Z230, it goes through Xining enroute to Urumqi."

"Okay, well, anyway, I brought the oranges."

"What?"

"The oranges."

He was referring to a net containing eight or nine large oranges roped to his suitcase like an old woman's shopping cart.

"Well thank god for that," I replied, sarcastically.

"Don't be a fool, Xiao Fei, you're always saying that I need to be more sensible, we will be travelling at high altitude, the fruit will help us, they are rich in vitamin C, that's just plain science."

Before we'd made it out of Shenzhen, LZD was face-down, snoring like a lion that had swallowed a trombone, leaving me the task of making polite acquaintances with our new neighbors. We were flanked by two groups of travelers whom I soon learned neatly personified what we were leaving behind, and what we were straying towards: On one side, four Hong Kong bicycle enthusiasts kitted out in brightly colored bandanas picked at a carton of (what appeared to be) braised roadkill but what was probably pork (I hoped). They explained they were heading to Qinghai Lake for some high-altitude cycling. On the other side, a congregation of burly, headscarf-adorned Muslim Hui women wearing hooped golden earrings were returning to Qinghai burdened with umpteen plastic shopping bags after a retail binge in Hong Kong. The carriage soundscape was a veritable clash of the dialects; the Hui women gossiping in guttural, Central Asian-tinged Mandarin, the Hongkongers hiking through the octaves as they debated the issues of the day in tonal Cantonese.

After some inconsequential chitchat, I perched window-side to enjoy my old commute from Shenzhen to Guangzhou rolling by like a favorite film. Because we were travelling on a green train, there was ample time to digest the minute details of the Delta megalopolis in all its chaotic glory. I lazily absorbed a few hours of factories, scattered fish farms, brown gushing fords and tropical fruit plantation until prayer flag-like laundry waving from the windows of some massive apartment blocks signaled that we'd reached the Guangzhou outer-suburbs.

The train slowed to a crawl along the century-old Kowloon-Canton through train route, affording intrusive views of the happenings of the day: Shirtless coolies dragging produce-heavy wheelbarrows between the traffic; a massive wholesale market erected trackside near Taojin; African merchants bartering with Cantonese sellers over watch straps and football jerseys — every minute measured in money. Guangzhou was China's great bazaar, its status as an unrivalled city of trade exemplified not only by modern malls but also by the trappings of its international heritage that included one of China's oldest mosques and stately colonial villas along the Pearl River. It flourished well over a thousand years ago as a Maritime Silk Road port and centuries later, under the Qing, it had been the only city permitted to do business with the outside world. It was a tradition continued with the biannual Canton Fair, the world's largest commodities market.

As we pulled into Guangzhou Station, one could almost smell the fumes of enterprise rising with the smog, for Old Canton exhibited the side effects of its capital addiction; skies tinged chemical-yellow, bumper-to-bumper traffic and plastic waste coating any patch of ground not in use by humans.

I finished lunch in the dining car and returned to our carriage to discover LZD still sleeping. While the train trailed the pea-green Beijiang (North River) through the karst mountain scenery of Yingde, I resolved to write up my notes. But a few pages in, I was interrupted.

"I can't read anything you're writing," said a voice from over my shoulder.

Every second railway carriage on a Chinese train had an attendant charged to keep it clean, usually a seasoned old hag determined to slap your ankles with a mop. Managing the needs of carriage number eight, in a rare break with tradition, was a pretty young thing not yet embittered by the monotony of her occupation.

"Most people can't, it's not your fault," I said of my spider-web scrawl.

"I even struggle with pinyin," she said of China's official system of romanization.

"Where are you from anyway?"

"Fulan," she said, meaning Hunan and exhibiting in plain terms why pinyin, which related to the standard Northern pronunciation, had long puzzled her. "But I live in Shenzhen," she added.

"So do most Fulanese," I quipped of a city LZD, a Hunanese, called *Hunan de zhimindi* – Hunan's colony.

We exchanged names and Miss Zhang posed some standard questions, asking what on earth I was doing riding a train through south-central China towards one of the least hospitable places on the planet.

"I like train travel," I told her. "It offers a good perspective on the world. You have an interesting job. Do you solely work on this route or…"

"Yes," she said with a sigh, "but we get days off in between."

I'm reassured to hear this. When taken from end to end the Z230 travels 4,657kilometers for two and a half days, making it China's fifth longest railway in terms of distance, a serious slog.

"What happens when you get to Urumqi?"

"They put us up in our work unit's hotel near the station. The climate is so dry it burns my skin and I come out in a rash."

"How did you get this job?"

"A year ago my father set it up, he had a connection in the railway bureau. I'd wanted to work on a high-speed train but the expectations are much higher and I didn't meet the criteria."

"That's a pity. But if it's any consolation, I prefer the green trains; slow and steady wins the race."

She laughed and I briefly wondered if she was flirting with me. "You soon get bored, going back and forth, but what can I do? I have to work."

Somewhere beyond Chenzhou, LZD peeled himself off his bunk, fumbled for his glasses and then crash landed on the carriage floor.

"Where the hell are we?" he asked, dusting himself off.

"Hunan."

"Oh, I've been here before," he said, before disappearing down the carriage for a hit of nicotine.

When he returned, LZD had filled his flask with tea and mopped his face so thoroughly that water was trailing down his glasses. He also made a new friend.

"This is Blue," LZD said. "We met in the queue for the toilet, turns out he smokes Baisha cigarettes, too."

Chen 'Blue' Yi must have been six feet tall, a giant by South China's standards, though he was cursed with an adolescent face and was prone to giggle girlishly, qualities that diluted the authority his stature might have otherwise commanded.

"You're tall," I remarked.

"*Wo yiqian shi yi ge* basketball player," he said, blending Chinese and English.

"Do you still play?"

"No, I've been doing business in recent years. I've made good money, *wo nali dou qu guo*, England, America..." he explained, once again mixing English nouns with Chinese phrases, a habit I find, frankly, disorienting though it was becoming commonplace in certain circles.

"And where are you heading now?" LZD asked.

"Lanzhou," he replied, in a tone similar to that of a child who was heading to school on exam day.

"Are you going there for business?" I inquired.

He appeared taken back by this question. "Business, well, you could say it's a kind of business, a thing, a thing that I really have to do…"

We agreed to rendezvous with Blue later on in the restaurant car for an evening beer then spend the afternoon eating LZD's oranges and playing chess on a bamboo board I'd picked up in Vietnam. The train slugged stoically north through the endless villages of Hunan until darkness descended and only the clackity clack of the wheels could be known.

When we arrived in the dining carriage, Blue was nowhere in sight.

"Let's eat," said LZD, "I need some breakfast."

He ordered the spiciest dishes on the menu, reminding the waitress, to add 'extra spice'. The eye-watering vapor of chili peppers permeated the carriage long before plates of red hot tofu and century eggs arrived. We delved in, LZD munching through the tongue-torching banquet as if he was eating cornflakes. I was soon sweating profusely and having to spoon white rice into my mouth in a vain effort to dilute the inferno.

We were nursing warm cans of Tsingtao when Blue made a belated entrance in the company of a box full of beer.

"What the hell is that?" I asked.

"I thought you said stop by tonight for a drink?" he said, dumping the crate on the table with the pride of a fisherman arriving with the day's catch.

"I meant a drink," I said gesturing to the mini cans LZD already had. "One…"

"No problem," interrupted LZD, already dishing out the cans and cigarettes. "We can have a few, Xiao Fei, be polite."

We worked our way through half the box before we were

told to leave the restaurant car by a less-than-impressed railway matron. "We're closing!" she said, holding a broom with poise that suggested there would be no negotiation.

"It's fine, come to my carriage," said Blue, "I have a lower bunk."

The carriage lights had already been turned out, so our party continued on Blue's bunk by torchlight. If we were annoying the surrounding passengers, nobody said anything, exercising either remarkable restraint or perhaps the ability to sleep through any old racket in the world's noisiest country.

"So what do you have to do in Lanzhou?" I asked when the booze had numbed my inhibitions.

"Ah, well you see, I've been a bad boy."

"What do you mean?"

"I've made a lot of money but I've spent it on, um, naughty things. My wife, she's my sweetheart but she's furious with me..." He began to well up. "I don't want to divorce; we have a child..."

Blue pulled a picture of himself sat beside an absolute heartbreaker of Changsha beauty from his wallet. "I love her very much."

"I can see why."

"Anyway, it was she who sent me to Lanzhou. She says I have to get myself together for the sake of the family, for the sake of myself."

Blue looked visibly troubled, so I didn't inquire further. Eventually fatigue took hold and I left the two Hunan natives chatting in the carriage and stumbled off to bed.

I spent the following morning gazing dreamily into the farmhouse flecked hills of arid northwest China until LZD arose. After his habitual smoke and face-washing ritual, he was keen to offload Blue's story onto me.

"Blue told me he had a substance abuse problem," LZD explained, while pouring himself a cup of black tea.

"But he drank all those beers?"

"Exactly."

"So why is he going to Lanzhou? Do they have a treatment facility there?"

LZD laughed. "No, you silly foreigner. Blue is heading to a lamasery."

"What, like a temple?"

"Exactly, he's going to a Tibetan Buddhist lamasery to repent and dry out." LZD couldn't help but chuckle at the thought.

He told me the name, which recalled the monk I'd met in Yufeng Lamasery with Richard He in Lijiang.

"Why doesn't he go to a Zen Buddhist temple, I'm sure there's one in his neighborhood in Changsha, wouldn't that suit a Han person more?"

"Xiao Fei, you should understand by now, Chinese Buddhism is corrupt. Lots of Han people follow Tibetan Buddhism these days. It's like Christianity or consumerism, you know, an exotic import from elsewhere. Nobody believes in anything *Chinese* anymore, we've lost faith in ourselves."

I motioned for him to be quiet. "Be careful," I whispered. "A lot of soldiers came aboard while you were asleep this morning. I think they're going to Xinjiang."

LZD nodded affirmatively and soon disappeared down the carriage with his trusty Canon and packet of Baisha, presumably to try for some clandestine snaps of the troops.

We were navigating our way through the mighty loess plateau, forging a path along the Wei River, the largest of the Yellow River tributaries, a landscape of dried earth flaking like an old man's scalp. The Chinese called it *huangtu* — yellow earth, and it colored the river nut-brown. The land looked tough as hell to farm, which was perhaps why every second farmhouse appeared to have been abandoned. The Wei valley, like the central plain, had been integral to the genesis of Chinese civilization, nurturing several of its fabled ancient capitals, most notably Xi'an. But in the age of sea trade, people had moved to the coast and many of the stepped hillside fields were fading from sight, Mother Nature's land reclamation, a haunting sight, suffuse with a somber beauty.

In time, we reached the sprawling cityscape of Lanzhou where the Yellow River ran like chocolate and the glassy highrise totems stabbed a cloudless sky. Blue came to our carriage and bade us farewell. We exchanged contact details and wished him well.

"*Zaijian*, British guy," he called from the platform in his signature brand of Chinglish.

Advancing through a tapestry of lowland vegetable patches, corn and cabbages that quilted southwest Gansu like a crochet blanket, the only sign of life beyond the train was the occasional goat.

At a little after 6:00 p.m, we crossed the Gansu-Qinghai border, a milestone commemorated by Tibetan prayer flags decorating hillsides windswept and barren. The train began to climb a steep gradient, growling through tunnels and traversing grand valleys on shaky metal bridges until sunset brought down the curtain.

Pretty Miss Zhang was collecting litter from our carriage. "You boys should get your things together; we'll be arriving in Xining shortly."

She was right. We'd traveled 2,500 kilometers from a low-lying delta to the cusp of the Tibetan plateau, over 2,000 meters above sea level. Young Miss Zhang still had 2,000 kilometers more to go.

II

Located many miles from the heart of the great and empty realm that is Qinghai, for most of history, the city of Xining was a backwater clinging to the wrong side of Gansu Province like a pimple. Tellingly, historian Peter Hopkirk called it "the last town in China", which it probably felt like when Tibet and Xinjiang were territories only tenuously under Beijing's control, if at all.

Though there had been a settlement for over two millennia, Xining seldom made more than cameo appearance in the Grand Chinese drama, an obscure Silk Road layover, one where the Chinese, Muslim and the Tibetan worlds ostensibly met through trade.

Xining was made the capital of the newly forged province of Qinghai 1928, but it would be practically run by the Ma Clique for most of the Republican era, a dynasty of Muslim warlords who fought off Tibetan and Japanese attacks only to abdicate when, in 1950, the People's Government was declared. This brief epoch was remembered in the Ma Bufeng Mansion, a building complex in the East District dating back to the 1940s.

Paul Theroux described Xining of the 1980s as a "frontier town" of "square brown buildings on straight streets, surrounded by big brown hills," but three decades later it had seen major investment aimed at turning it into a modern Chinese city befitting its capital status. This had resulted in its "square brown buildings" being supplanted by rectangular white buildings, the asymmetric horror maintained, just on a grander scale. Only a few rammed-earth dwellings remained in the poorer quarters, buildings that would no doubt be bulldozed as soon as developers got around to it. In many ways, Xining reminded me of a poor-man's Shenzhen running on an east to west axis between the north and southern hills. Only the thin, high-altitude air and the sporadic appearance of maroon-robed Tibetan monks or bearded Hui Muslims reminded us that we'd travelled across the better part of the country to get here.

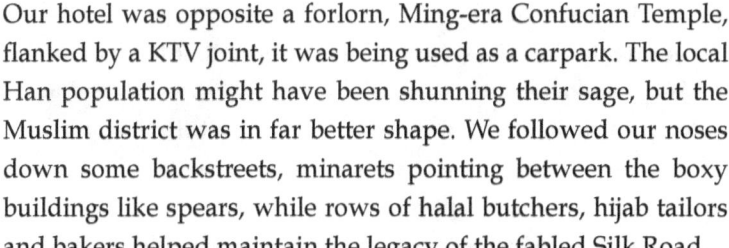

Our hotel was opposite a forlorn, Ming-era Confucian Temple, flanked by a KTV joint, it was being used as a carpark. The local Han population might have been shunning their sage, but the Muslim district was in far better shape. We followed our noses down some backstreets, minarets pointing between the boxy buildings like spears, while rows of halal butchers, hijab tailors and bakers helped maintain the legacy of the fabled Silk Road.

If you happened to be anemic, Xining was the place to dine, we learned at lunchtime. Evidently, the eating culture evolved so visiting merchants could get their monthly carbohydrate allowance before trekking off into the wilderness. LZD and I slurped down thick strings of wheat noodles paired with oil-drenched dishes; the gravy mopped up with batons of bread and concluded with sweet yak milk yogurt for dessert. LZD — a southern rice eater — was soon grumbling about the amount of wheat we were tasked with digesting. "Let's get hotpot," became his habitual evening cry.

Xining might have been superficially short on distractions but China was so old you never knew what you might discover, evidenced when we stumbled upon a 700-year-old place of worship by way of a local shop selling plateau delicacies like yak jerky and wolfberry tea leaves. The shop's backdoor led straight into the courtyard of Dongguan Great Mosque, a bastard child of various epochs, mixing Chinese, Arabic and even Tibetan architectural components, culminating as a rather hodgepodge affair. But the ancient men walking and chatting in the courtyard were anything but eclectic, sporting goatees, long tunics, dark spectacles and matching walking canes, they were the adherents to one creed, Islam.

As the congregation gradually swelled, I lost LZD, distracted by an impressive work of Islamic wood sculpture, until a speaker crackled into life, broadcasting the call to prayer. I checked my phone. It was Friday.

Suddenly, there was real purpose to the gathering, the chitchat deflated as prayer mats were laid out in neat rows. I stood to the side and watched with intense curiosity. But this was no liberal Yunnan, I soon discovered, when a stern tap on the shoulder put an end to my vicarious pleasure.

"Are you a Muslim?" a sharp-faced man holding a walkie-talkie asked me in gruff, northwestern Mandarin. He gave me a look that suggested I could soon end up in one of Qinghai's infamous gulags if I didn't toe the line.

"No, I'm not," I conceded.

"Then you'll have to leave."

Outside, a tide of cloaked men flowed towards the distorted commands of the mosque's antiquated broadcast system. The only non-Muslims were cops, on foot, on motorbikes, or wedged into backup cars, four apiece. There were several plainclothes personnel too, easily recognizable because of their radios and the fact they were all tall enough to play in the NBA.

Clearly a major security operation was underway, which reminded me of the recent news story from nearby Ningxia that authorities tried to demolish the Weizhou Grand Mosque, which had apparently been built without planning permission. The

Hui community resisted, leading to a protest that exemplified deteriorating Han-Muslim relations. Tellingly, a red banner suspended across the front of the mosque proclaims "All Ethnic Minorities Are Part of One Chinese Family."

The sound of struggle caught my ear, and I swung around to see two men escorting a troublemaker out. It was LZD.

"All right, that's enough, I said I'm leaving," he said, aggrieved by his unglamorous eviction.

"Can you believe these bozos? I showed them my Shenzhen Photographers Association card and they still won't let me stay. Assholes!"

"Many mosques around the world are out of bounds to non-Muslims on Fridays," I said. "I wouldn't take it personally."

"Bullshit! Remember when we were in Xi'an a few years ago? We were allowed inside that mosque then!"

"The Great Mosque of Xi'an is a top tourist draw. They were selling entrance tickets and novelty hats."

"Well it's your article that will suffer, honestly, I was right up in the rafters. The angle was perfect," he said, before scrolling through images on the back screen of his camera in search of a good snap.

Over ensuing days, we made a go of Xining's other attractions, a few mountainside Buddhist temples, some street markets and the provincial museum, which housed an effusive celebration of Communist Party achievements in the region. I caught a few captioned photographs of the Xining to Lhasa railway in various stages of construction, which conjured some interest. But overall, it underlined my conviction that the city was essentially a place of departure.

We made slow progress, because LZD was unwell,

complaining both of altitude sickness, which he was medicating with increased tobacco intake, and jetlag, on account of the unnatural shift I was forcing him to make from a nocturnal to a more diurnal existence. Every evening, unable to sleep, he slipped away for a drink at LOFT 2008, a small craft beer joint run by an affable local called Jack, only to return in the early hours grumbling about the state of China, human civilization and the universe more generally. "*The New Chinese*, that's all they'll remember me for … fucking stupid country … stupid art world … nobody sees what I see… I'm China's best photographer… fuck them…" were the pre-slumber mumblings before the snoring started.

The decision to leave Xining was an easy one, though where we'd head next was complicated. My Tibet travel permit might take some time. "There are no guarantees, Mr Thomas," said Miss Wang from the travel agency.

LZD, ever the bohemian, suggested we should just "roll with it." So our fate was to be left in the hands of the gods, or more specifically, Xining Coach Station's daily timetable.

"We'd like to book tickets please," I told a humorless hog of a woman seated behind a thick glass screen.

"Where would you like to go?"

"Where can we go?"

"You missed that one… sold out… nope, nope. Ah, the Yushu bus leaves at 11:30 a.m."

"I've read about Yushu," I told LZD. "It sounds like an interesting place."

LZD leaned over my shoulder and inquired, "How long does the bus take?"

"It's not far. Around eight hours."

"Eight hours!" he yelled.

"Sometimes more, it depends on the traffic."

"On the plateau?"

"There are a lot of wild animals out there, and heavy trucks, some pilgrims…"

"Is there a train?" I asked.

"Just a bus."

"Then we'll take two tickets," I said, determined to get beyond the city limits before LZD drove me insane.

I liked long-distance Chinese bus journeys only a little bit more than food poisoning, especially when the driver had a lot of religious icons in his cabin and there was no functioning toilet.

As we rolled out, the uniform suburbs hinted at little promise, but as buildings gave way to open country, our passage become the emptiest of empty roads, enchanting us in ways I had not prepared for. All I could do was scribble notes in my notebook as we bounced along the open highway somewhere on the rooftop of the world.

> *We've set sail across an oceanic expanse of undulating grass that is, I've no doubt, how Qinghai earned its name, "Verdant Sea." We pass Hekazhen "the first town on the grassland" at 14.45; the jagged peaks in the background are snow-capped. The driver seems to be having trouble with the gears. Thankfully he needn't make many changes on this table top. This is truly god's country, signified by pyramids of prayer flags and sacred Tibetan words embossed on hillsides – as the sedentary decorate their houses so nomads decorate the earth. We pass yurts and primitive dwellings scattered across the great plain like dots of pepper on a lettuce leaf. Sometimes we pass roadside Tibetans prostrating themselves every few steps on the tarmac. At*

HARMONY EXPRESS

15.51, we enter a white realm of snow and ice, the air is thin and I'm breathless sitting down. At 16.23, we pass Duocuo, an immense blue lagoon. There are no more yurts, villages or towns now, just snow, tundra and the wafer of blacktop we're trailing on. At 17.00 we stop for a toilet break, there are no service stations anymore, "men to the front, women to the back", the driver said.

With each mile the scenery gets a little more spectacular. Seeing another vehicle is an event. I'm having to gulp my breath down. A sweet Tibetan girl says we're higher than 3,000 meters and may reach 4,000 before the day is done. At 17.22 the sun bursts through the clouds reflecting on the snowy hills like a biblical painting. Just past 18.00, there are more huge, empty lakes at Madoi. Water looks to be the purest in the world. LZD is giving a running commentary. "Look, there's a lake... are there fish up here? I hope so, I love seafood...those yaks are totally black... look, another snow mountain, look a temple... the colors of the sky are amazing, purple and orange." But mostly there are no mountains, yaks or lakes, just space, nothingness, on and on. Night falls fast. The moon is huge and pink. But our caravan is alone, hundreds of miles from anywhere. If we hit a yak and skidded into the tundra what would happen? One of the passengers is chanting with prayer beads in hand, maybe he's warding off the road spirits.

Drizzle greeted us at Yushu, dampening expectations after our fantastic, if exhausting road trip. There was general chaos around the bus as hoteliers tried to hustle business and motorbikes splashed through puddles as they collected people. Given the weather, LZD and I reasoned we had little bargaining power, so we followed a huge a Tibetan up a flight of stairs into what was effectively his house.

"Fifty yuan per night, very good room," he insisted in nearly incomprehensible Mandarin as he showed us past his sleeping wife and child into a room unfit for swine. There was no lock, the wallpaper was peeling and the battered beds look like they'd been salvaged from a skip.

"What do you think?" I asked LZD in a gloomy tone. A cockroach scurried through the room. The Tibetan didn't flinch.

"Forty yuan," said LZD

The man grunted affirmation.

"It's fine, Xiao Fei, I've slept in plenty of places like this before," he said, pressing his hands on the concrete mattress to check for dust or lice. "I only go upmarket when I travel with you," he scoffed. "Come on, drop your bags, we'll find something better with the dawn. Let's grab a bite to eat, I wonder if they have hot pot around here."

Neither of us slept much past dawn, not even LZD. Stiff and sore, we set out on foot. Every building of Gyêgu, as the Tibetan's called Yushu Township, was colored pastel pink, orange, yellow or blue, every window and door frame embellished by decorative patterns. When compared with Xining's charmless tower blocks, it was a delightful place to explore and we soon shook off our fatigue.

Settling on the only guesthouse in town with a shower, we strolled off into the hills so LZD could take some panoramic shots and we soon ended up trespassing on somebody's garden, an act that might have had us shot or beaten in many parts of the world. A mother and her three children came out of the kitchen to see what a Welshman and a bespectacled Hunanese shutterbug were doing standing in their backyard.

"Taking pictures," I tried to explain. She couldn't speak any Chinese, though her kids could.

"Welcome to Tibet," said one of the girls giggling.

"Thank you," I said, before turning to LZD. "Isn't the border with Tibet a hundred miles from here?"

"Yes, but I think these Tibetans have a slightly different idea of geography."

He was not wrong. The Tibetan world actually spilled across the plateau in all directions. Sam van Schaik's *Tibet: A History* began with the question "Where is Tibet?" before noting that ethnographic Tibet "overlaps with four Chinese Provinces — Qinghai, Sichuan, Gansu and Yunnan — and the Himalayan kingdoms of Bhutan, Nepal, Sikkim and Ladakh," the latter locations explaining why taxis in Yushu tended to blast music from Mumbai, not Shanghai.

The lady of the house offered us some barley cakes, our introduction to a gastronomic tradition that made all food taste like sawdust. Both of us obliged, chewing on these floury biscuits until all the spittle in our mouths was exhausted and we nearly suffocated.

"They're great," I gasped, trying to smile without belching out too much barley dust.

She smiled back as only Tibetans can, disarming us of any bad feeling.

We crossed to the opposite side of town where we got to Yushu's hillside focal point, Jiegu Monastery, an imposing red structure topped with a lavish golden roof.

With LZD busy shooting pictures, I followed a path between the monk's residences to a hilltop pavilion where I sat to survey Yushu like one of the eagles coasting the thermals overhead. It was a town on a palpably human scale. It reminded me of an antique European town, the monastery positioned like a cathedral in medieval France or Spain. But it was the rhythm of the place that gave Yushu its ancient spirit; pious, unhurried, convivial. I watched monks sip tea, merchants hawking Nepali cloth and handsome women with plaited hair hand washing clothes, all engaging in the street with a measure of intimacy all but lost in great metropolises like Shenzhen, or even Xining.

There was such a lived-in vibe to Yushu that it was a great surprise to discover that almost everything was ostensibly new. On the eastern edge of town LZD and I came upon a monument commemorating a catastrophe that had turned Yushu into rubble. Composed of a grey stone clock sculpted to appear cracked and broken, the time 7.49; the date April 14, 2010, LZD and I learned of a devastating 7.1 magnitude earthquake that killed almost 3,000 people and injured 12,000. It was a visceral reminder the Indian Subcontinent was still driving into the rest of Asia at great geological speed, some five centimeters a year, pushing the mountains ever higher and occasionally shaking them like a giant's maraca.

———∽———

"*Om Mani Padme Hum*," chanted the faithful spinning prayer wheels as they circled a vast pile of engraved bricks known as mani stones. Some prostrated themselves on the ground, other, more casual adherents, were apparently out for a devotional stroll. According to local lore, a Tibetan Buddhist master named Jiana had built a small mani stone pile in Yushu some three centuries ago. Since then, locals had continued the tradition, with devoted artisans adding mantra-engraved stones to the pile daily—there were said to be around 200 million mani stones in the region when we visited, though nobody could be sure. How would you begin to count?

We followed the pilgrims on their clockwise tour of the

temple-mound. Dogs, goats and cows joined the mani stone pilgrimage.

Notwithstanding the rustic trappings of our setting, it was clear Tibetans were no grubby peasant clan. In fact, they appeared to take their appearance very seriously, the women in particular sporting trinkets and jewelry—beads, bangles, earrings, silk accessories—while Tibetan men were often bearded and wearing heavy duty woodsman gear—solid boots, sheepskin jackets and cowboy hats—the kind of clobber you'd want if you made a living wandering a treeless moonscape in the company of hairy cows.

Roadside, I got chatting with a local rock carver named Dorje who was selling his mani stones. "I've been here for ten years," he told me. "I carve stones and sell them to pilgrims who add them to the pile. People come from all over Yushu," he said, which was all the more impressive when one considered the autonomous prefecture was 188,794 square kilometers and most of its inhabitants were nomadic.

It was no surprise to discover the primary site of worship in earthquake-prone Yushu was an enormous pile of bricks. That said, it was a great novelty to enjoy a promenade in what, in other places in the world, would constitute a building site, while the general fanfare and enthusiasm the Tibetans brought to the occasion were infectious.

When LZD and I eventually reconnected, he was busy snapping his camera at a giant prayer wheel turned by an ancient lady chanting like a spell caster. He was in seventh heaven, the first alcohol-free good cheer I'd witnessed since we left Shenzhen.

"This place is amazing to photograph," LZD said, flicking a Baisha cigarette onto his lip with a sense of sincere satisfaction. Casting my eyes across this great assemblage of red, green and blue prayer stones, Buddha effigies, stupas and flags, all bathed in a superb Himalayan light, I could see why any photographer worthy of their Canon would be happy with this subject matter.

During the day, we chanced upon two Taiwanese backpackers, Xiao An and Jia Yi, who invited us to dinner at a Nepali restaurant. Over curry, they'd inform us they were hiring a driver to visit a scenic area in the morning. "Would you like to join us?" Xiao An asked.

LZD and I, who had conducted no research and had no plan whatsoever, glanced at one another.

"Of course!" declared LZD.

"Why wouldn't we?" I asked

The following morning, we rendezvoused with the girls just in time to set out into the wilderness. We were soon rolling through an undulating grassland bisected by crystalline streams and bordered by the greatest mountains on earth. Majestic black yaks dotted the grasslands, grazing near the tents of invisible shepherds and pyramids composed of prayer flags. The only structures with any permanence were stupas and shrines.

After a few hours' drive, our vehicle turned into a rocky gorge. But what awaited us was an ambush of color with more prayer flags flying through the valley than there were union jacks in London during the Queen's Diamond Jubilee.

While LZD had been stalking the streets of Yushu for a nightcap the previous evening, I'd done my homework, reading up on the curious episode of history commemorated there. In the 6th Century, after centuries of turmoil, Chinese Emperor Taizong was busy managing his Tang Empire, scarcely aware the son of a powerful *tsenpo*—divine king—Songtsen Gampo, was equally busy establishing a Himalayan empire of his own. Songsten was a formidable leader, extending his domain from his base in the

Yarlung Valley to incorporate much of wild Western Tibet as well as the green pastures of Amdo.

But what was a great prince without a princess befitting of his power? After subsuming or forging allegiances with all the minor kingdoms in the neighborhood, Songsten sent his right-hand man, Gar Tongtsen, to the Tang court in Chang'an (present-day Xi'an) to request a bride, a common diplomatic gesture in medieval Asia, just as it was in Europe. When Gar returned empty-handed, Songsten sent in the troops who humiliated Chinese forces, teaching Taizong a valuable lesson about who the new kids on the block were. Gar was sent to Chang'an again in 641 where he proved a charming ambassador. He returned with two brides, one for himself and one for Songsten, namely Princess Wencheng.

The marriage inaugurated an era of cooperation and peace between the two empires, even if the Chinese maintained a haughty sense of superiority. "According to Chinese historians, once the princess arrived in Lhasa, she set to work civilizing the Tibetans, convincing the Tibetan nobility to swap their felt and fur clothes for Chinese silk, and to abandon the old practice of painting their faces red," wrote Sam van Schaik. "According to the Tibetan historians, however, the princess's greatest contribution was Buddhist in nature. She brought with her the statue of the Buddha, the first to arrive in Tibet, which was placed in a special temple called Ramoche. Later it was moved to Lhasa's principal Buddhist temple, the Jokhang, where it remains to this day."

Tibet was not yet the holy Buddhist kingdom it would become. But as culture and society had become increasingly wedded to religion, so too had the legend of Princess Wencheng grown.

We were travelling along hallowed ground in rural Yushu, following the path she forged enroute to Lhasa, hence, the trappings of veneration decorating the mountainside like a crazed child let loose with a box of Christmas decorations.

Leaving the vehicle behind, we followed signs that led us to a perilously narrow hillside path festooned with more prayer flags. Several Tibetans were performing a kora—a practice that binds meditation with pilgrimage and requires the practitioner to circumambulate a sacred site, in this case a temple dedicated to Princess Wencheng, located at the foot of the hill.

We followed suit, scrambling up the gravelly hillside, while privately contemplating the prospect of a fatal fall. Overhead, hungry eagles circled ominously and one Tibetan I got chatting with told me, "When we die we leave our bodies on the hillside to be eaten by the birds. We wouldn't want to remain in one place like somebody in a grave," he said, describing a sky burial.

Back in the car, we drove deeper into the Leba Ravine, only to discover almost every rock and cliff face had been engraved with a mantra. "These are mountain mani," our driver said.

"These Tibetans are crazy," LZD declared while perilously hanging out the car window taking shots and smoking, "everything has to be made holy."

He had a point. It's not that church and state were fused, church and everything were wedded together in the Tibetan world.

We travelled deeper into the divine valley following another crystalline river. It was a superb journey, made all the more cheerful by the company of the girls, who were as vivacious as they were kind. Xiao An and I forged quite a bond and I noticed a bit of flirting.

After some time driving, we came upon a particularly picturesque stretch of greenery on the riverside, where we stopped to wash our hands and faces.

"That's better," I said.

"Why?" asked Xiao An.

"I haven't had a proper shower since we arrived, our hotel only offers a Japanese drip torture device."

"Tibetans use bathhouses, you need to go out for a good wash."

It was a sound piece of advice, one that I would adhere to throughout my Tibetan sojourn.

I heard some humming coming from the bushes. Pushing my way through, I came upon a Tibetan crouched riverside quietly chipping away at the rocks. LZD was already with him, taking photos, but he remained indifferent to our presence. We had no means to communicate but with a smile, an expression Tibetans mastered long ago.

And so we watched him meticulously engraving stones with sacred text "a 1,000-year-old tradition," I wrote in my notebook, "which feels strangely contemporary".

When he finished a stone, he didn't save it but tossed it back into the stream and began another. Yet there was method to the madness, we soon learned, when downstream we came upon a river junction where the water of one river silted brown and the other river running clear as jade converged. A gaudy riverside monument and sign explained we'd entered "the sanjiangyuan" a vast national park where three mighty rivers, the Yellow, the Yangtze and the Mekong began. The message of the mani stones was washed downstream, through the oldest of civilizations, across China and Southeast Asia, thousands of miles to the distant sea.

III

The scale of Qinghai meant simple day trips evolved into mini quests in which we bounced on a country bus for five hours, then clung to the back of motorbike for two more before hiking the remaining leg up a muddy hill, just to photograph a lamasery at a particularly scenic bend in a river. Anywhere that tickled our interest we attempted to visit and ended up logging a catalogue of firsts: getting caught in a yak jam; wandering across a meadow pock-marked by the holes of the fat mountain mice called piki that live like rabbits; bearing witness to a mass monastic debate, an ancient ritual that involved exaggerated movements and clapping as the monks perform a philosophical discussion; stopping for lunch in monastic towns so remote even LZD was a curiosity to the local Tibetans. Everywhere we turned reason was turned on its head, dealing us a hand of improbably good cards. I felt LZD's spirit rising by the hour as he detached from the months of solitude that had proceeded our journey, the tonic of travel working its magic in real time.

It helped that we were trespassing on a realm like no other. In his introduction to *Trespassers on the Rooftop of the World*, Peter Hopkirk went to great lengths to explain how geography sculpted the Tibetans, writing that much of this ancient seabed turned "storm-swept table land" stood above the tree line that "denied those amenities and everyday materials, such as wood," to cook at an altitude where water boils slower and "at a lower temperature than at normal altitudes". On the plateau, "one can suffer frostbite and sunburn simultaneously". Frozen for half the year, much of the tundra turned to swamp in the summer while explosive winds could "knock a rider off his horse".

Perhaps the weirdest feature of the plateau was its innumerable great lakes, vestiges of an ancient sea lifted towards heaven by tectonic activity, which, "because of violent squalls that sweep across them, they are too dangerous to navigate. Most of them being brackish, moreover, they are of little use to the thirsty traveler."

The greatest of these brackish lakes was the eponymous

HARMONY EXPRESS

Qinghai Lake, China's largest, a veritable inland sea 3,000 meters above the actual sea and covering 4,000 square kilometers. A gentle surf lapped the shores, and the lake was fringed by rocky peaks making the blue water even more vivid against a brown-grey backdrop. There was a ring road popular with cyclists and a few tourist villages on its coast but most of the lake's perimeter was stony turf inhabited by wild birds and the occasional goat, yak or pony.

Leaving LZD to seek a hillside vantage point one glorious afternoon, I rented a bicycle and peddled several miles around the lake in a rare state of complete contentment. China was a country where, as Paul Theroux observed, "The rarest landscape of all is free space," and I found myself in one such aberration, in the company of no one and nothing, the noise of humankind remembered only as the lyrics to an annoying old radio song.

The next evening, we camped for a night in a yurt in the Haixi Mongol and Tibetan prefecture on the plains leading up to another great brackish lagoon, Chaka Salt Lake. A loud horn awakened us to the frozen morning, a freight train rolling across the plain towards the lake, where it entered an old Mao-era salt mining facility to load up on the white stuff, which was destined, no doubt, for lowland dinner tables.

We followed the track across the plain to an adjacent scenic area where a tourist train following a narrow-gauge track delivered us to pearly white beaches of salt lapped by crystal clear waters that mirrored the sky like glass. Despite the cold, we couldn't help but go in for a paddle.

"Hey look, Xiao Fei," said LZD pointing to a white cloud reflected in the lake. "The world is upside down."

Our travels eventually led back towards the Gansu border,

rolling down a road that followed the Yellow River, branching off along the Longwu Valley and winding into a pastoral ravine, location of the artists' town of Tongren (Rebgong in Tibetan).

The sour smell of yak butter hit us as soon as we alighted the bus. LZD was buzzing with excitement. A painter by training, he was keen to see what this famous center of Tibetan art was all about.

We found our way to an absolute palace of a building invoking both Stalinist grandeur and classical Tibetan esthetics, The Rebgong Art Museum.

Being something of a Sinophile, I learned, in no way qualified me to understand the artifacts within. The claim that Tibet was just another expression of Chinese culture was contradicted by any number of things: Tibetans' Indian-based script, the habit of drinking tea with butter, religion and their general dislike of the Chinese. But if you needed some unequivocal proof Tibetans don't roll like the Han, head for your nearest plateau art gallery. Instead of the all-too-familiar black-and-white ink paintings or calligraphic verse that dominated Middle Kingdom galleries, we were confronted with terrifying masks, rainbow-colored robes, intricate clay sculptures and the wildly colorful thangka paintings that made Tongren famous.

"Look, there's a green Bodhisattva!" LZD exclaimed excitedly "and this thousand-armed Avalokiteśvara is purple, this would take years to paint, just look at the detail! Incredible…"

Thangka meant recorded message, I'd read, and evolved as an aid to Buddhist teaching. Essentially, each work was an intricately painted decorative scroll depicting episodes from the Buddha's life, or a mandala, a figurative representation of the universe. The art form had assumed a life of its own over the centuries and while it remained, in essence, religious, there were recognized masters and celebrated masterpieces that were sought after by religious and secular collectors alike.

We absorbed depictions of Tara, the 'mother of liberation', who protected adherents from 'the eight dangers,' the four harmonious animals (elephant, monkey, rabbit, bird) that looked as though they belonged in a storybook for kids, while awesome three-eyed wisdom deities glared at us from some of the most fantastical thangka portraits. There was a real blend of sophistication and simplicity in each frame, masterworks of craft and technique depicting the celestial and macabre imagery of antiquity, a juxtaposition that made thangka painting utterly compelling. One needn't be an expert to realize that, just as the Han Chinese turned the Buddha into a well-fed rich guy, so too had the Tibetans tailored the story of the Enlightened One to their own traditional outlook. As van Schaik put it, the pre-Buddhist Tibetan world was already "swarming with spirits, demons and minor deities". When Buddhism finally triumphed in Tibet it didn't vanquish the ghouls and goblins of old, "it accommodated itself to this world, which remained fundamental to the lives of most Tibetans."

"That was amazing," said LZD, as he emerged from the museum, sparking up a celebratory cigarette.

The sun was already dipping behind the majestic hills of the Longwu Valley but we decided to taxi over to the older quarters of Tongren before dinner to see if we could unearth anything of interest.

The five-minute drive transported us centuries back to a hillside district of wood and rammed earth dwellings that surrounded the imposing Rongwo Monastery, a vast and ancient site of Buddhist worship. While LZD followed his nose to a good photographic site, I learned from the monastery entrance sign that it was founded in 1301 by the Sakya Sect, who later converted to the Gelug Sect, making it "the biggest Gelug monastery in

Qinghai". Chinese association was, of course, writ large: "Ming Emperor Xizong bestowed the monastery a tablet and in 1996 the State Council listed the monastery as a key cultural relic." What the sign neglected to mention was that the monastery had been the epicenter of several major anti-government protests, the last of which spilled over from Sichuan Province in 2012, culminating in several acts of self-immolation that drew crowds of 6,000, shouting slogans demanding freedom and calling for the return of the Dalai Lama.

Now all was eerily calm, the air scented in incense, only the chime of bells and voices chanting from within altered the peace. The monastery was about to close but I was allowed to poke around the various prayer halls until a security guard ushered me towards the door.

Outside, I ran into LZD keen to show me some dazzling photos of the old town he just taken, before saying, "Let's get hotpot, I've got a date with an old friend who is coming to dinner."

I was unaware that LZD knew anyone in Tongren but the Chinese invariably had a university classmate or an old work colleague living in the most unlikely of locations, so I didn't question his unexpected announcement.

But when we got to the restaurant, Blue was already dining in the company of a friend he'd made in Gansu.

"Blue! What the hell are you doing here?"

"Surprise!" he said in English before ordering me a beer in Chinese. "Please have a seat. It's good to see you again, British brother."

"I thought you were locked away in a monastery."

"I saw you guys were travelling here via LZD's social media feed so I decided to escape for an evening. The temple is only a few hour's drive from Tongren."

"What's it like?"

"Dreadful. I spend all day banging my head against a cold floor," he complained while feeding some prayer beads through his fingers nervously. "I've no idea what the monks are saying, I can't speak Tibetan, I just copy the sounds. And the food the monks eat tastes like shit," he said, before grabbing a pair of chopsticks and delving into a bubbling, Sichuan pepper-laced broth. As LZD opened a bottle of Tsingtao, I sensed it was going to be a fun first night in Tongren.

Outside Guomar, piles of yellow wheat were drying in the sun roadside while a few solar-powered lamp posts stood out like beacons of modernity in this otherwise antiquated scene. The village proper appeared to be perched on a small hillside, but after closer inspection, the realization that it was, in fact, a manmade rammed-earth citadel began to dawn on us.

"The village is walled," said LZD, before engaging with an elderly Tibetan lady carrying a baby on her back in a cloth sling. He asked her about thangka artists, but her grasp of Chinese was limited, so she did what all Tibetan's seemed to do on such occasions, which was to laugh and smile. He shrugged. "Shall we just have a look around?"

We walked the earthen perimeter until we found the main gate but soon lost one another in the twisting streets, like mice lost in a laboratory maze.

"This is a labyrinth of a place," I called to LZD, whom I could see standing on a flecked rampart he had mounted to try and get some perspective, and perhaps, a good shot.

"I know," he hollered back, "it's great."

It was hard to say exactly why this village was fortified but I was aware that we were in the territory of Amdo, according to a Tibetan map, which had had a long and bumpy history as a frontier zone sandwiched between two civilizations, so it was easy to imagine why they might feel the need to protect themselves.

Whatever the reasoning behind the construction of this muddy warren, it was a fine place to wander around, wondrously disorientating in an age of right angles and symmetry.

When I eventually found my way out, Blue was standing by the car watching some locals pumping water from a nearby well. We crossed a stream together and walked to a large white stupa at the front of a sizable temple complex. Three giggly Tibetan girls with apple red cheeks and bright eyes had gathered outside. After some nervous debate, one ventured forth and offered me a pear, an invitation to chat perhaps, but they were soon prostrating themselves on the floor to pray to an effigy of the Buddha.

"You foreigners always get special treatment in China," remarked Blue sardonically. I offered him a bite of pear in solidarity but he declined.

We performed the kor, rounding the stupa in a clockwise direction, spinning prayer wheels to cast the sacred verse "Om Mani Padme Hum" into the cosmos and hopefully bank some good karma. It worked, as back at the village, we discovered LZD had made himself a guest inside the house of a local Tibetan artist. He introduced himself as Wendé Kar, a self-effacing and gentle-mannered man in his late thirties. His hairline was just beginning to recede, he had a tall nose and when he smiled, you couldn't help but smile too.

"He's a thangka artist!" exclaimed LZD, patting the man on the back and offering him a cigarette.

"Great, can we see your work?" I inquired, straight off the cuff.

"Um, actually my studio is on the edge of town, not here in

the village."

Before we followed our new friend back to Tongren, we bid farewell to Blue, who had to drive back to his retreat in Gansu or face the wrath of the lamas.

"It feels like you only just arrived and now you're going," said LZD.

"*Mei ban fa*," he said, "no way out".

"Maybe we'll see you in Changsha next time we're in Hunan?"

"For sure," he said, grinning at the prospect, "dinner's on me."

Blue and his driver skidded off down the road, beeping the horn while we hopped into Wendé Kar's vehicle. Immediately, we began quizzing him on how he became an artist.

"I started late, around fifteen years of age. I'm thirty-seven now. I always loved to draw but it takes a long time to become proficient in thangka painting, mastering the form is far more rigorous than, say, the ink painting the Han Chinese do."

He took us into a ground floor apartment in a modern high-rise building on the edge of town. Inside, atop a yellow and red patterned carpet, sat four of his students diligently painting to the accompaniment of Hindi-pop.

We spent some time admiring the work, which included a wild red depiction of a three-eyed demon.

One of the artists, a handsome twenty-five-year old called Rinchen Dorje, took the initiative to chat. "We come here for ten hours a day," he explained. "Without patience you could never do this. Every family has a house temple and inside every temple there's a sculpture or thangka painting. This is important work."

The muddy Longwu River fed flower-coated meadows that were so picturesque and uncorrupted as to resemble a child's painting.

I speculated the natural world must have inspired thangka's vivid sensibilities. We crossed a bridge to the other side of the river to find the twin villages of Upper and Lower Wutun, or Sengeshong, where we wandered from house to gallery, meeting the local artists.

Of all the artists we befriended, a plump, forty-four year-old monk named Tenzin proved to be one of the most charming. He invited us into his home, which, like most Tibetan dwelling in the area, was comprised of a flower-filled garden overlooked by a wooded terrace area where much of the day-to-day activity took place.

Nyima Tenzin was not a painter but a sculptor. "I've been doing this for twenty-five years," he explained as he etched details into the face of a man wearing glasses.

"Who is that?"

"You mean you don't know? That's the Dalai Lama."

I'd read the Dalai Lama had been born in the nearby village of Taktser, or Hongya as the Chinese call it. Any image of the 'wolf in monk's robes' was banned in the Tibetan Autonomous Region, and I'd imagined here too, but apparently it was a rule sporadically enforced and widely flouted. I ask Nymia if he was worried.

He shrugged. "I'm not bothered, everyone here has his photo of him in their house shrine."

Images of 'His Holiness' were not limited to people's homes, we soon learned, when we went to explore the epic Wutun Temple, which, like the village, was also divided into lower and upper sections.

Upper Wutun had more of a lamasery feel about it with monks going about their daily business. There was a gathering of worshippers when we arrived, all women and kids, who'd laid out a picnic table, which they picked at between periodic chants led by a local guru.

We attempted to go inside some of the large temple halls but found doors were locked. Eventually, a monk came over waving some keys. LZD and I exchanged a glance. "No photos were allowed," the monk warned, as he opened the first of three epic shrine chapels. The smell of incense mixing with wood and the yak butter of candles wafted out, that unmistakable Tibetan smell-scape. Within there were incredible wall murals, giant and elaborate effigies of the Buddha and the Bodhisattvas, as well as the Dalai Lama himself, framed and revered.

"We communicate with him," the monk explained to me.

"How?" I asked, half-imagining he meant via prayer.

"WeChat."

"What, the Dalai Lama has WeChat?"

"No. But his associates do, so we get all the news. He's in the USA right now."

IV

"Hi LZD, what's up?"

"Where are you, Xiao Fei?"

"I'm in my office. Fancy a cup of coffee?"

"You and cafés, you live in them. I'll pass, I haven't been up for long. What about going out for a beer with me tonight?"

"I told you, I came here to travel and write, not to be your drinking partner."

"If I'd have known you were going to be so boring I might not have come. Come on, let's call it my leaving party. You can write when I'm gone."

"Your train is not scheduled for a few days yet, LZD, this celebration is premature."

"I thought you British were fun, I stand mistaken."

"We are fun, what are you talking about?"

"Listen, I was out shooting some pictures yesterday when I found a great restaurant just off Huimin Street."

"Not hotpot again? My intestines can't take much more of the stuff," I appealed.

"No, something different. My treat tonight, Okay? If you want to come out afterwards we can head over to Jack's bar, if not, we can just go back to the hotel, how does that sound?"

"Okay, but let's not go wild, the altitude leaves me dizzy. I find myself feeling drunk after a couple of cups of tea."

"Relax comrade, let your hair down for a change, life is short..."

"All right, see you in a couple of hours, send me the address."

"Will do, *zaijian*."

Click.

I placed my phone on the table and gazed about the pokey little coffee shop that had become my de facto office since we'd returned to Xining. Shelves were piled high with Chinese-language editions of *Lonely Planet*, old maps and Tibetan knickknacks adorned the walls. It smelled of wood and pu'er tea. The light struggled to penetrate the narrow windows and my desk lamp flickered on and off intermittently. The waitress was an impossibly cute 20-something who wore her hair in plaits, as was popular during the Mao-era. She seamlessly deflected all my romantic advances with kung-fu efficiency but kept my teapot filled with hot water. I could not complain.

The café had also become a sanctuary of sorts. On the road, LZD had been an adventurous spirit but since we'd returned he was back on the bottle. It didn't help that my travel papers were still being processed, which was why I'd urged him to go ahead to Lhasa without me. I was trying to make my enforced hiatus in Xining count, arising early, taking regular swims in a nearby leisure center and reading up on all things Tibet over heavily caffeinated afternoons. But LZD could not acclimate to an ordered urban life, sleeping in, drinking out, unable to indulge in some down time.

As dusk fell, neon lights flickered into life and the streets clogged with Xining denizens on their way home from work. As it was Friday, the restaurants were filling up fast. Perhaps it was that end-of-the-week vibe pervading the city, but while my taxi struggled through the rush hour, I began to reason that maybe LZD and I needed a good blowout, a male bonding session, a last hurrah. He was clearly tense, or perhaps bored, and I owed him for accompanying me to such out-of-the-way places.

The restaurant he had hit upon was a two-story establishment with a golden Mao statue at the door and pictures of rural Hunan on the walls. No wonder he was so keen to dine out.

I found him seated upstairs already ordering from a colorful menu decorated with a chili pepper motif, the unofficial symbol of Hunan.

"Hey, Xiao Fei, over here. This place is great, lots of vegetarian stuff, really spicy, you will love it."

"Cool, you order, you know what I like."

"We'll have this dish and this dish," he said to the waitress. "What about some green beans? Oh, and something with potatoes, my friend here is British, that's all they eat over there."

"Sour and spicy potato shreds?" the waitress suggested.

"Perfect."

"Look what I found today," LZD said, as soon as the waitress departed. He pulled a bottle of liquor out of his bag and placed it on the table.

A bolt of terror ran through my liver like an electric shot. "That's not baijiu is it?"

"No, no, highland barley wine, look at the bottle, made in Qinghai. It's the local drink, you know, when in Rome…" He unscrewed the bottle and poured two big glasses.

Before long, we were high on over-spiced spuds and Xining-made rocket fuel for the soul.

"You need to forget that stupid Hunan girl in Shenzhen," LZD asserted, waving his finger at me. "She was a cheat. She never loved you, you were just her foreign toy. Find a nice Tibetan woman. I imagine a Welsh-Tibetan child would be the first in history."

"Haha, that could be an idea, but I'm not sure I could adapt to the local cuisine in the long term."

"That's true, not much variety for a plant-eater like you. Perhaps a Han lady would be better. A northeastern girl, they eat a lot of potatoes in Manchuria."

"And what about you?" I retorted. "Any love in LZD's life?"

LZD had had his heart broken at a tender age. A decade ago, when he'd lived in Beijing he'd embarked on an affair with a beautiful, unhappily married woman. At the time he'd held two prestigious jobs, one as an art teacher at a university and one as a photo editor for a magazine. But when the girl's husband found out, he literally chased LZD out of town. Though he'd lingered in the Deep South since, with stints in Guangzhou and Shenzhen, he'd been unable to hold down a steady job or forge a long-term relationship. His rise in the art world had been meteoric, but it hadn't translated into real money. He'd known little financial stability or human affection in the years since we first met in Shenzhen, when I'd been a magazine editor.

"The last few months have been pure solitude. I've barely seen any men, never mind women," he explained. "Occasionally my friend Shi Jie pops over for a drink but that's about it."

"Nothing else happening in your life?"

"There's a student in Beijing I've been chatting to online. She's a fan of my work. But I think she might be too young, plus, I can't very well go and live in Beijing again, can I?"

"Well she might be worth a visit, you can stay in my apartment, and it's near the Lama Temple."

"That might be a good idea. But I can't stand Beijing, it's far too political for me and the food is almost as bad as Tibetan cuisine."

He took a gulp of barley wine then switched tack. "Xiao Fei, I received some good news today," he says sparking a celebratory cigarette. "A Japanese publisher wants to produce a book of *The New Chinese*."

"That's great," I said, raising a glass for a toast. *The New Chinese*, which LZD shot in Shenzhen, had won him awards and even exhibitions overseas but he'd also had pictures pulled from gallery walls in Shanghai by angry officials. He was lambasted by the conservative art establishment, after one prominent critic called the work 'rubbish' and he'd lost a lot of commercial clients who were unwilling to be associated with an artist who dared ridicule China's economic ascent. A published book would be a well-deserved reward for a creative talent far braver than most of his contemporaries.

"Of course, it can't be published in China," he continued, "but at least it will be out there in the world."

"Well, I'll buy a copy of your *New Chinese* book," I told him.

"I'll give you a discount. Cheers."

By the time we stumbled into Jack's bar, the pair of us were already too intoxicated to hold much of a conversation. LZD perched himself at the bar to talk with the owner while I intruded on a table of fashionable local urbanites. It felt nice to kill a few dizzy hours with this crowd, which revealed a different side to

Xining to me, one more urbane. They entertained me, as any kind Chinese group would, and kept my glass filled until I gradually become aware that my English, never mind my Mandarin, didn't make a whole lot of sense.

"Come on LZD, time to call it a night," I said, dragging him from his barstool perch.

We stumbled out into the cool autumn air and flagged a cab. LZD sat up front chatting with the driver, I dozed in the back. When we arrived outside our hotel, I was completely wiped out. I wandered into the lobby, up the stairs and fell fast asleep before I was even undressed.

Screams, yells and a series of jabs to my rib cage awoke me from my drink-induced coma.

"You fucking idiot, where have you been, you asshole, you shitbag…"

I leaped up and instinctively went for the throat of my antagonist, rolling onto the floor, invisible objects smashing in the tussle. It was almost a minute before I realized I'd pinned LZD to the ground and he was suffocating.

"Oh shit!"

I hurriedly grab a glass of water from the bathroom to try to help stop him choking to death.

"So sorry old friend. Are you Okay?"

"Xiao Fei, you fucking prick! You stupid cunt! You could have killed me. I'm no longer your friend, you've caused me way too much trouble, how dare you, how fucking dare you?"

"What trouble? What are you talking about?"

LZD began to throw his belongings into a bag. "I'm not even willing to stay here with you. You're no kind of friend. See you around."

He walked out the door, slamming it behind him and leaving me utterly bewildered as to what has just gone down.

Morning did little to shed light on the situation. As far as I could recall, I'd gone to bed only to be awoken when LZD attacked me. But what made things even stranger was that on my phone I found hundreds of missed calls and messages from friends all over China enquiring as to my well-being

I lay prostrate, hung over, nauseous, bruised and bemused. "We'd had a good night, why had he attacked me?" I kept ruminating. LZD was my best friend in China, maybe on earth. He'd seen me through the good times and the bad. He introduced me to some of China's greatest artists, gallerists and critics, travelled with me by train to his hometown Anhua — a fantastic railway adventure that preceded this one by many years. He'd helped open my eyes to China in ways I couldn't have imagined and always treated me as an equal. And now, because of some silly drunken scuffle, we were no longer friends. Worse still, the world and his wife appeared to know about it.

I couldn't say this behavior was entirely out of character. LZD had been a big drinker since I'd known him. He romanticized booze and delighted in the chaos it could unleash. When he chanced upon some illegally translated copies of Charles Bukowski's books, he'd lapped them up like baijiu, and the banned-in-China bar room bard had helped justify a new wave of drink-fueled misadventures. His drunken antics could be hilarious but occasionally LZD's debauchery had led him to dark places, warranting apologies to those he'd hurt. Whenever I suggested he calm down, he would retort with political justification, "If you were from this fucked up country, Xiao Fei, you'd become a drunk, too."

But all this was part of his yin-yang character profile, the spectacle-wearing avant-garde poet, painter and photographer, the drunken, chain smoking, spicy food-scarfing cynic. And unlike most of us, he didn't try to hide the contradictions that composed his uniquely flawed character. He embraced them. It was his authenticity that had always shone through. This was a man who never passed a beggar without dropping a coin, even if he stayed up most nights drinking Tsingtao he could hardly afford. So how could things have gotten to this muddled state?

I lay there for some hours feeling beaten-up inside and out. Eventually my phone rang.

"Hi Xiao Fei, it's me, where are you?"

"I'm still in the hotel."

"Listen, I, well I fucked up last night. Let me come over and explain."

It turned out it had all been a huge misunderstanding. When I'd alighted from the taxi and stumbled off to bed in the hotel, LZD had turned around to find me gone. His boozed brain had been so inebriated he'd believed he'd left me behind at the bar and had ordered the taxi back to Jack's place. When he hadn't found me there he'd ordered another beer from Jack then set off walking around Xining looking for me, even visiting the local police station. He then called mutual friends across China to see if I'd been in touch. He became quite hysterical at the prospect of having lost me in a Chinese frontier city, so, when he found me fast asleep in the hotel room he'd naturally flipped out.

"I'm so sorry." he said.

"No I am, I shouldn't have grabbed you."

"Not to worry. We're both still alive. You should probably call a few people and let them know you're Okay."

"I will."

"I'm going to take a shower. Then let's go out and get some fresh air. This hotel room smells like old cabbages."

"Good idea, LZD."

And just like that, harmony was restored.

HARMONY EXPRESS

I saw LZD off a few days later at the train station. I felt sad that he was leaving me behind. As absurd as our scuffle had been, it showed he cared. I also sensed he wasn't in the best of mindsets. But we'd shared such an amazing journey around Qinghai. I hoped this would be our enduring memory, especially if I was unable to visit Lhasa.

"Do you have somewhere to stay in Lhasa?" I asked him.

"Remember Young Wang?"

"The long-haired hippie guy from Henan?"

"Right. Well he's opened a guesthouse up there."

"Good to know you'll be in good company. If I make it to Lhasa, I'll stop by."

"Still no news from the travel agency?" LZD asked, stubbing out his last cigarette.

"They said they'll know for sure within a day or two. I'm nervous. I'd hate to have come this far only to be refused entry to Tibet. You know me, I like train travel and writing about it. Feels like this train is somehow significant."

"Sky train to the third pole," he said, "choo-choo," and began walking towards the station doors.

"Don't be late," I called after him. "And go easy on the beer."

"Comrade Xiao Fei, if you came from this fucked up country you'd understand, it's not a choice. See you in Lhasa, old friend. The first round is on me."

SKY TRAIN TO THE THIRD POLE

I

Rolling out of Xining evoked some conflicting emotions. I was relieved that I had been granted Chinese permission to visit the Tibetan Holy City, Lhasa, yet, as the suburbs gave way to wilderness, I felt an unexpected hint of sadness at leaving a city that, charmless as it might superficially be, had served as a base since arriving on the plateau. Time spent there had unearthed some charm. Browsing Xining's eclectic street markets had been ethno-curio heaven; its hillside temples blissful oases; and the amazing restaurants of the Muslim quarter rejuvenating after days sustained on Tibetan barely cakes and service station snacks. Despite its status as a provincial administrative center, I realized, only as I left, that Xining retained the qualities of the Silk Road layover town that had shaped it over the centuries, affording bed and board to wanders who passed from the world within to the world without.

My nostalgia faded with the passing miles as the plateau captured my attention. LZD and my misadventures had largely taken place on the plateau fringes. But the Qinghai-Tibet railway arced its way right across the Himalayan table top, covering a distance not much short of the epic Shenzhen-Xining journey that had brought us up here in the first place.

Gone were the endless track-side factories of sultry Guangdong or the streams of villages flowing amongst the claret hills of Hunan. Beyond the window, there was just the yellowed grass of earth's rooftop savannah, rippling until it met a horizon shaped like crocodile teeth on the planet's highest hills.

A good indication of the plateau's vastness was expressed in the time it took to get from station to station, some four hours until our next stop at Delingha, a further three to Golmud. Between them there was almost nothing.

This vacant spectacle should not be misinterpreted as any kind of Arcadia. Should the train have broken down, few passengers would have lasted long in the windswept upland beyond our tightly sealed, oxygen-fed carriage. The air was so clear one could see for miles in every direction and there were no perceivable wells to drink from nor trees to shade beneath. If anything did hove into view it was invariably a skeleton: the carcass of a yak picked clean by scavengers, or Mao-era military facilities crumbling like ruins after a war. Even the prayer flags had been stripped of their prayers, white cotton sheets clinging to the rocks signaling man's surrender.

I thought about those first foreign adventurers who'd attempted to get to Lhasa, the original Forbidden City, people like the eccentric Thomas Manning from Norwich who, "haunted by the idea of China", sailed from Guangzhou to Calcutta in early 1811 wearing Vietnamese silks. In the company of a Chinese Catholic named Zhao, he crossed the Bhutan-Tibet border unchallenged and after months of hard travel set eyes on the holy Tibetan capital, the first Englishman ever to do so. Manning felt Lhasa was dirty and poor but he nonetheless won an audience with the six-year-old Dalai Lama before the 'amban' who governed Tibet on behalf of Beijing imprisoned him. He remained incarcerated for an entire winter while orders from the Jiaqing Emperor were awaited. The decision was to have Manning escorted to the border in chains and deported. Yet this lunatic somehow survived his ordeal to make it back to Blighty to tell the tale.

THOMAS BIRD

In the decades that followed Manning's adventures, China was opened along its coast by aggressive foreign merchants through naval wars and lopsided treaties. But adventurous cartographers, botanists, mountaineers, missionaries, spies, soldiers, gold prospectors and travel writers still dreamed of infiltrating the mystical citadel atop the roof of the world. They approached from all directions. Their motives differed but what they confronted made equals of them all: wolves, earthquakes and smallpox haunted a country that persisted, quite literally, off the map and was peopled by god kings, despotic monks, resolute border guards and armed bandits, a people so strange they slept huddled in a ball, stuck their tongues out to communicate a greeting and got altitude sick only when they went downhill.

Many died in the attempts that followed Manning. It was the audacity and might of Imperial Britain then that eventually brought Lhasa into worldview, a mission led by Lord Curzon, a veteran of the Central Asian Great Game that had been playing out between the Chinese, British and Russian empires at the tail end of the nineteenth 19th Century.

Basing his fears of having to confront the Tsar's army in Tibet on, frankly, scant intelligence, Curzon began petitioning Parliament in 1902 to take action on the pressing need to head off the Russian bear before it could establish a lair in the Tibetan stronghold. Orders from London were largely negative, however, until the hawkish clique in India found a motive when Lhasa refused to recognize a Himalayan trade agreement signed in 1883 between Britain and Beijing. All efforts to move goods between British India and Tibet were sabotaged, any incursion on Tibetan terrain stubbornly repelled, so the Tibet Frontier Commission was sent to rectify Britain and Tibet's trade relations. Despite its polite pretensions, the Frontier Commission was a military unit of over a thousand heavily armed troops led by Raj-born Francis

Younghusband, already a decorated geographer as well as a proponent of some questionable theories on race and religion.

Younghusband was simply charged with the vague objective of achieving 'satisfaction' for the British Empire. After a few false starts he would achieve this 'satisfaction' with the battle (some say massacre) of Guru. The Tibetans hauled up outside this obscure hamlet were armed only with aged matchlocks and pictures of the Dalai Lama they believed would protect them, no match for Enfield rifles and maxim guns that could fire hundreds of bullets a minute. The Tibetan ranks were brutally cut down after a Tibetan rifleman accidentally triggered the British attack when his gun went off. Those who survived the bloodbath simply walked away, unable to fathom what they had... just encountered or why their god had abandoned them. To their credit, British soldiers set to work rescuing the fallen Tibetans who littered the ground like a field of poisoned rabbits. They then advanced on to Lhasa, fighting further skirmishes along the way including the battle for Karo Pass, noted for being a battle fought at a greater altitude than any other engagement in history.

The British eventually got to the Holy City and although the Dalai Lama fled to Mongolia, they achieved what they wanted, namely a treaty with Tibet signed in 1904. Although they then fell back behind Indian lines, clear warning shots had been fired in both St Petersburg and Beijing's directions. Furthermore, the British had proven to the wanderers of the world that Lhasa was not the impregnable fortress many had imagined it to be.

The legacy of this invasion would linger in the hearts of Chinese for decades, transforming their attitude towards Tibet. No longer could it be regarded as a loosely controlled protectorate. Its strategic location and its inherent backwardness made it a liability that threatened the safety and sovereignty of China itself.

Though chaotic years followed the collapse of the Qing Empire, leading to 50 years of de facto Tibetan independence, in 1950, the Red Army would arrive to 'liberate' Tibet from 'serfdom', reclaiming it for China's 'big family'.

Justifying their actions with a Marxist read of history, the Chinese have channeled the same ruthless sense of superiority that they had been subjected to at the hands of Europeans, when dealing with their own 'nationalities'. This time, Tibet would not be permitted the autonomy it craved, leading to decades of bloodshed, vulgar human rights abuses and Han incursion. It would be the Reds, not the Russians nor the Brits, who would ultimately lay the railway to Lhasa, constructing a symbolic umbilical cord from the "Motherland" across the permafrost, connecting Beijing and its wayward mountain cousin via the highest railway anywhere in the world.

Chairman Mao was credited with dreaming up the Qinghai-Tibet Railway project. But due to the chaos of his Great Proletarian Cultural Revolution, the first section would not be completed until after his death, when, in 1984, Xining was finally linked with obscure Golmud, a nowheresville in the middle of Qinghai that swiftly became a jumping off point for a generation of hippies heading to Lhasa.

When Paul Theroux travelled from Xining to the railway terminus at Golmud, the train was powered by steam and took 30 hours, compared with just seven hours for me. "It was a horrible train," he wrote, before reporting on a scuffle between the passengers and the fact that it "ran out of water an hour after it started".

I felt somewhat spoiled by my cozy second-class bunk in a carriage fitted with whispering overhead nozzles to regulate oxygen levels to prevent altitude sickness. There was a barrel of piping hot water at the end of each carriage, should my tea flask need a refill. "The world has changed," I wrote in my diary, "but the Qinghai desert has not".

Dipping in and out of Theroux's final chapters as we rolled towards Golmud was like receiving a real-time commentary of the passing scenery beyond the window, "square mud-walled villages looked like habitations left over from the Neolithic age" scattered across a plain of stones that is "hellish and memorable" as we rolled deeper still into the "roughest land I had seen in China…"

But Theroux's description of Golmud as "hardly a town," just "a dozen widely scattered low buildings" no longer rang true.

Though the suburbs were still composed of some earthen dwellings the likes of which Theroux described, modern Golmud was so new and neat it looked as though it was transplanted from a model town factory onto the plateau by a helicopter. It had the same unnatural appearance as a bald man who has had a head of hair woven into his scalp, and I immediately felt queasy. I couldn't help but feel the leafy boulevards were somehow in breach of earthly laws, that a manifestly middle-class, semi-prosperous settlement, had no place on this plain of rock and skulls.

I dropped my bags off at my hotel then took a walk. Golmud was composed of charmless, block-shaped compounds. There were 'aunties' dancing in the plaza, couples in matching his-and-hers tracksuits, pushing babies in pushchairs, young girls clapping at shop doors to attract customers and street hustlers hawking everything from turnips to mobile phones. It was so much like a Chinese Truman Show, I wondered where the backstage area was.

I eventually came upon a large market vending made-in-Guangdong clothes and technical gizmos, though nothing of local manufacture. Chinese brand name stores and restaurants dominated the heart of Golmud. Indeed, the only thing out of the ordinary was the glare of the plateau light, the dust blowing in from the desert beyond and thin air that made a short walk feel like a marathon.

There were no tourists whatsoever and the stares I was garnering were deeper and longer than the usual point-and-stare one expected when traveling China's backroads.

I walked into a hot pot place, where one sat at a counter and ingredients were delivered on a conveyor belt, sushi train-style. I was halfway through dinner when a woman in leather boots and unusually bushy eyebrows approached me.

"What are you doing here?" she asked abruptly.

"I'm sorry?"

"You, what are you doing here?"

"Eating dinner," I replied, somewhat taken back.

She rummaged in her bag. "You know who I am?"

"Should I?"

She continued to rummage through her bag, becoming quite exasperated. "Well, I can't find my ID but I'm a cop." She said, adding, "police" in English.

"I see," I said, trying to remain cool.

"Where are you staying?" she asked.

"The Seven Days Inn," I replied, "on the main drag".

"And why did you come to Golmud?"

"I'm on my way to Tibet, I thought I'd stop for the night to break up the journey and check out Golmud, which I'd been reading about. Lovely place by the way, very friendly."

She asked to see my paperwork, including my passport, onward-bound train ticket, Tibet travel permit, health certificate and reservations in Lhasa, which she proceeded to photograph with her phone.

"I'm sorry, have I done something wrong?" I asked.

HARMONY EXPRESS

She ignored me and began calling people, presumably her superiors. I listened in. She, like everyone else, spoke standard Mandarin. There was no dialect, which implied the majority of the population had arrived recently. "I have a foreigner here, says he's staying at Seven Days Inn, yes, that's right…"

She turned to me. "The hotel has not reported your arrival."

"Well they scanned my passport," I said.

I was not allowed to finish dinner. Instead, I was escorted back to my hotel, where, after further debate and the arrival of two uniformed policemen it was confirmed that I'd broken no law in booking my room, nor had the hotel staff neglected to process the correct paperwork. But no apology was offered.

"Best you don't stray too far from the hotel until your train arrives tomorrow," I was warned, before the police departed.

The following morning, walking around looking for some breakfast buns, I began to notice every second building was embossed with the Chinese army logo, armed guards stood rigid on street corners and camouflage-painted military jeeps were not an usual sight in the traffic. Evidently, the Chinese had constructed a garrison town here between Tibet and Xinjiang. No wonder the cops were suspicious.

I began to feel very self-conscious. "I'm a travel writer," I told myself, "not a journalist" but would the Chinese authorities know the difference, or care? My Tibet permit said "teacher," a flagrant lie invented by the agency, creating a story I would have to stick to for the duration of my Tibet sojourn. But a Chinese-speaking foreign teacher was rare, and why would one waste his precious holiday in Golmud when he could be surfing off the coast of Hainan? I began to wish I hadn't sent LZD on ahead. He was right to have panicked in Xining when he'd lost me.

A Mongol cab driver pulled over by the side of the road where I was walking and worrying privately.

"Hey, foreigner, fancy going to the Kunlun Mountains?"

"How much?"

"500 *kuai*."

"I can't afford it, and anyway, I have a train to catch this afternoon. I'll probably just check out Golmud's sights.

"There's nothing to do here," she said in the guttural Mandarin of a people who traditionally sang from the throat. "The Chinese flattened the old town way back and built all this," she said, waving at the prosaic streets, apparently as repelled as I was. "I'm a native here," she added. "My family has farm land, but we're a minority now."

I liked her. She sported beautiful big beads around her neck and despite the wrinkles born of the severe climate, her high cheekbones suggested she'd been a real looker in her day. But mostly I was attracted by how casually she spoke to me. She didn't wear suspicion in her eyes like the other inhabitants of Golumud.

"Well, where should I go to kill a few hours?" I asked, leaning closer to the car.

"You could walk around Jiangjunlou Park?"

"Fair enough. How much?"

"Five yuan, hop in."

Jiangjunlou Park, proved to be a dust-plagued public garden commemorating the place where General Mu Shengzhong, who, I learned, oversaw the construction of the Qinghai-Tibet Highway, had once lived. As well as the general's old house, there were some exhibition halls concerning the plateau highway, Golmud city development and the Qinghai-Tibet Railway. None were remarkable, though grouped together, I got it: The city grew as a strategic junction, a pit stop for the military and the engineers tasked with placating Tibet from the 1950s onwards.

I wandered aimlessly around landscaped gardens, which were tatty and half-finished, the flowerbeds littered with food packaging like Wild West tumbleweeds.

The ominous sound of a circling chopper broke what was left of my resolve to explore further. I wondered if it was looking for the nosey Welsh scribe whose incessant wanderings had brought him to the wrong side of the tracks? Retreating to my hotel, I closed the curtains and waited out my remaining hours in dark seclusion until the Lhasa-bound train came to liberate me from this horrible little highland town.

II

As I nervously awaited to board the train on Golmud's nondescript concrete platform, I reflected on a news story from two dozen years ago when poker-faced then-President Hu Jintao opened the Qinghai-Tibet Railway. He addressed workers and select journalists to give the Qinghai-Tibet Railway's inaugural speech: "The opening to traffic of the Qinghai-Tibet Railway is another magnificent accomplishment we have achieved in our socialist modernization drive," he'd said, describing the railway as, "a long-cherished dream of generations of the Chinese people," before underlying his point by saying, "The project was not only a magnificent feat in China's history of railway construction, but also a great miracle of the world's railroad history."

Despite the flagrant jingoism, the Chinese really had achieved what the many scientists had deemed impossible. The challenges of building a 1, 200-kilometre stretch of railway across the top of the world were enough to make any right-thinking railway surveyor light a cigarette, lie down and try to forget about the whole silly idea. The winter up on the plateau, for starters, was so tempestuous it had helped earn Tibet the 'third pole' moniker. Put simply, if you don't get pulverized by golf ball-sized hail stones or whipped by gusts of mountain wind strong enough to blow a small child away, you might very well lose a few toes to frostbite.

If the weather didn't get you, the altitude might. Acute mountain sickness was not something you wanted to deal with when laying a railway line, or for that matter, doing anything at all. It could affect almost anyone who was above 2,000 meters elevation, irrespective of age, physical fitness or previous experience working at altitude. Severe headaches and chest pains, intense fatigue and nausea are sure signs you need to go back down the hill. But given that much of Tibet was flat, getting to a lower, safer elevation was not easy and the nearest clinic might be three days away. Such extreme conditions accounted for why Tibetan shepherds reported railway workers being buried trackside. Nobody knows how many of these poor men and women died but this being China, we could assume the number was not low.

The environment posed serious challenges for engineers too, the biggest problem being 869,000 square kilometers of permafrost, which was the largest frozen soil region outside of the poles, according to Abrahm Lustgarten's book, *China's Great Train*. Permafrost freezes in the winter but becomes boggy swampland in the summer. For a railway engineer this implied that in a typical year the ground could rise and fall by as much as 30 centimeters. Exacerbating the problem was the inconsistency of the thawing patterns, with areas frozen hard in some places and softer in others, an unpredictable lay of the land aggravated by human-induced climate change, particularly as the Tibetan Plateau was heating faster than anywhere else in China.

To overcome those seriously uncertain foundations, innovative thinking was required and a full seventh of the route had been built on bridges, as if traversing running water. The additional concrete boosted the overall cost to nearly US$4.5 billion (equivalent to the GDP of the Maldives today), at a time when poverty remained widespread throughout China.

Yet even with such provisions in place, this remained the largest continental plate collision zone on the planet and the specter of a massive earthquake was not an abstract one, as reconstructed Yushu had illustrated to LZD and me.

Which was why, as my train rolled into view, horns blaring, I couldn't help but feel a touch disappointed at the routine nature of it all, even if I was pleased that the promise of leaving shithole Golmud had at last materialized.

As I climbed aboard, I discovered the interior of the carriage had been decorated with Tibet-style carpets; the walls adorned with traditional Buddhist motifs. This was the first time I'd seen anything like this on a Chinese train, which were all mutually bland and functional. But what a great idea! Why couldn't the Sanya train be decked out in coconuts, the Harbin train painted with ice blue Russian murals? In China, homogeneity almost universally trumped regional expression, so when the mold was broken, however briefly, one was inevitably taken aback.

It did, however, feel right that the mold should be broken on a train bound to the capital of the most idiosyncratic people I'd met on or off the Chinese railroad — several of whom were lying prostate beneath my bunk, fully dressed in garish robes, their plaited hair splayed out on standard-issue China Railway pillows like a sun god's, and all of them sharing a satisfied expression that suggested a good bed was not a customary experience.

I attempted to get acquainted. "Ni Hao," I said, but all the Tibetans did was giggle. Finding a seat by the window was easy in the company of these languid herders, so I perched myself tableside to continue my reread of *Riding the Iron Rooster*, which concluded with Theroux's journey from Golmud to Lhasa by road. It was a hilarious, if grueling episode, a two-day road trip from hell in the company of whimpering Miss Sun and the incompetent driver Mr Yu, who got altitude sick and crashed the car. The author certainly earned his travel stripes by enduring a frigid night in a vomit-stained guesthouse so cold that, "everything that I had that could freeze had frozen." Alas, his brilliant observations did not translate into clairvoyance when he wrote, "The main reason Tibet is so undeveloped and un-Chinese — and so thoroughly old-fangled and pleasant — is that it is the one great place in China that the railway has not reached," before underlying this poignant insight thus: "the Kun Lun Range is a guarantee that the railway will never get to Lhasa."

As we left the station behind, a flock of cranes lifted off the tawny grasslands before the snow-covered Kunlun Mountains, which stood stoically to the side of the railway like celestial guardians, as if overseeing our passage into the great nothing.

But I couldn't help but look back down the line as well. I'd travelled so much on China's trains. What had I been running from and where had I been running to? The motives had faded along the way. A broken heart, a deep Chatwinian restlessness, insatiable curiosity, escape from routine, an aspiration to rewrite the *Iron Rooster* for the high-speed age. All seemed inconsequential in this strange world where the train had brought me. I felt further from suburban South Wales than at any time before. I often described China as another planet to British friends. But Tibet made me feel I really had boarded a spaceship and we were now rolling down the runway on Mars.

HARMONY EXPRESS

I walked to the end of the carriage to fill my tea flask and wash my face. I noticed in the mirror my skin has browned in the alpine sun and was flaky from the all-pervasive dryness. My lips were scarred by sores, my hair was shoulder-length and matted after weeks of bad showers and crappy beds. In my dungarees and Grateful Dead t-shirt, I looked both younger and older than I should at this age. And my eyes appeared utterly road weary, something I hadn't noticed before.

A stiff gulp of tea helped ground me a little, no wonder the Tibetans had imported it from the Chinese throughout the centuries that preceded the arrival of us Brits, who also came in search of a good brew.

Beyond the train, the great flats of wind-dusted permafrost-tundra were gradually disappearing into the dusk. This barren land scarcely sustained more than a few hearty herdsmen, yet it had the allure of the Medusa: Look into it long enough and you'd start to see yourself out there staring right back at the passing train, statuesque.

I slept early and without dinner. At some point during the night we crossed the Taggula Pass, which, at 5,702 meters marked highest railway in the world.

I was awakened the following morning by an overly cheerful broadcast concerning the railway construction, anecdotes related in Chinese and English that were another unique facet of the Sky Train: "The temperature often drops to 20 below zero at night, so it is easy to catch a cold while going to the toilet," said a woman in robotic English. "To solve the problem, the railway company installed toilets with electrical heaters inside…"

The Chinese were as proud of their Sky Train as they were of their Great Wall or Three Gorges Dam. Yet to stare at the empty wastes rolling by was to dwell on the pertinent question, namely, why? Perhaps it was just part of their proud history of building the biggest of things, even if, like the Wall that was easily bypassed by invading Manchu cavalry, or the Three Gorges Dam that submerged millions of homes, the reasons for doing it were dubious at best.

Officially the idea of China's Drive West was sold on poverty alleviation and on its completion in 2006, the railway did initially make good on this promise, ushering in a regional tourist boom, with 2.5 million visitors arriving in the first five months. This triggered above national average growth over the years to come in Tibet, which in turn, led to the radical remodeling of Lhasa with hotels, paved roads and condominiums, a transformation mockingly dubbed 'Tibet's Second Invasion' by critics.

Two years on, during China's coming-of-age Olympic year of 2008, however, things soured between the Chinese and the Tibetans as monks gathering in Lhasa to commemorate the anniversary of the failed 1959 revolt became protesters who turned violent. China called it a 'riot,' Human Rights Watch accused Chinese security forces of indiscriminately shooting civilians and torturing detainees. In the following months, and years, protests rippled across all-Tibetan populated regions, unrest which Beijing dealt with ruthlessly. These tensions had inevitably brought the curtain down on rampant Chinese speculation in Lhasa as national security took precedence over everything, including of course, tourism. The growth targets set for 2020, when the Tibet Autonomous Region was projected to have a population of 10 million, sustaining a tourist industry of 85,000 hotel rooms catering to visitors all across the plateau read like a bit of a joke. The autonomous region remained China's poorest province and was home to just over three million souls; 40 percent of whom were employed in subsistence agriculture. Though geographic surveys discovered major new deposits of minerals, this clearly hadn't translated into money for most Tibetans.

Beyond economics, it was probably more reasonable to consider the railway's strategic value. Since Younghusband intruded on Tibet, the Chinese had been preoccupied with the threat posed by its nearest big rival, India. As Tim Marshall, author of *Prisoners of Geography*, put it in cold, geopolitical terms, "If China did not control Tibet, it would always be possible that India might attempt to do so." China's major rivers began up on the plateau and a water-poor, over-populated country the size of the People's Republic could never allow a foreign power to control the taps.

Then there was the railway's role in nation-building. The Chinese understood just how vast countries like the US and Russia were forged by laying rail because much of the iron was laid by Chinese coolies. The Chinese also had first-hand experience of the colonizing power of a railway, when foreign powers laid tracks throughout China, as I'd witnessed in Yunnan, Shanghai, the Northeast and just about everywhere else I'd rolled.

They'd learned tough lessons. In the 1960s, the Communist Party drove the iron road northwest into Xinjiang. The railway brought a major demographic change. The Uighurs accounted for 73 percent of the population in 1950 but only 45 percent in 2000. In the capital Urumqi, they were just 13 percent of the population. The railway had enabled the Han Chinese to dominate the economy and subjugate the unruly minorities who, like the Tibetans, had risen up time and again against their Han overlords.

LZD and I had witnessed troops board our Urumqi-bound train. When viewed this way, Beijing's imperative to link the last piece of territory to the grid was political by design. No wonder the Dalai Lama reportedly described the Sky Train as an instrument of cultural genocide.

THOMAS BIRD

Passage to Lhasa followed the Kyi Chu, a northern tributary of the Yarlung Tsangpo River gushing through a brittle valley flanked by black jagged peaks ending in shards that viciously pierced the cotton wool clouds. This truly was a 'stone citadel', I realized, which went some way to explaining why it was arguably the last medieval city to fall to modernity. But fall it had, as the trappings of modern human society appeared trackside, electricity pylons and warehouses, roads and condos — sure signs we were heading to that quintessential hallmark of human civilization, the city.

Lhasa's allure to any world wanderer worthy of their boots was self-evident: its remoteness, its strangeness and despite the forces of globalization and Sinification, its isolation, whether maintained by oppressive Han bureaucrats or the insular Tibetan monks of old. It was 3,700 kilometers from Beijing and 284 kilometers from the nearest foreign capital, Thimpu, Bhutan. Even with the train, Lhasa was still the most out-of-the-way, bugger-of-a-place to get to on god's green earth.

I finally stepped down from my carriage feeling conversely weary and refreshed. But before I'd had time to take a whiff of Tibetan air, a security guard with a shrill whistle was pointing me to a large white tent where all foreign visitors must go to register their arrival with the police.

I was soon handing over all my documents to a cop again, which included the address of the three-star hotel the agency had booked for me, my itinerary, the name of my tour guide and the length of my stay, my mode of arrival and departure, as well as my passport, my China visa, my Tibet travel permit, my inside leg measurements and the kitchen sink I'd been carrying since Shenzhen.

"What job do you do?" he asked, while shuffling through my papers.

"Um, teacher…"

He looked at me for a long second, then continued to scan the bundle of documents before him.

After some minutes more, a red stamp and a signature signaled that I was free to go. But freedom didn't last long in Lhasa, only the length of the station forecourt, beyond which a cheerful Tibetan holding a sign splashed with the travel company logo asked, "Are you Mr Bird Thomas?" in Indian-lilted English.

"Yes, that's me."

"Welcome to Lhasa."

He put a white silk scarf around my neck, the traditional Tibetan welcome, then ushered me aboard a mini-bus packed with awkward-looking foreigners also wearing silk scarves. We chatted briefly as we rolled towards the Barkhor, the historic center of Lhasa. It turned out I was the only one who didn't arrive by plane.

As I dumped my bags in my room, I was finally able to digest the fact that I had arrived at the city atop the world. My heart was thumping like the double bass drum on a Motorhead record. *Was it the altitude or adrenalin?* I wondered. I'd been fretting since my run-in with the police in Golmud. It was not that I felt singular in attracting official attention. Theroux recorded various episodes of government harassment in his book, as do most other travel writers to have made China their canvas, so perhaps I should have felt fortunate I'd been able to roll to Lhasa largely unchallenged. But China had become markedly more oppressive in recent years. The renewed sense of Mao-era suspicion was especially evident on the frontiers. I'd felt it in Manchuria and I felt it in Tibet.

Of course, it would be the thought police who got you first, and often these mind cops were the paranoid by-products of one's own psyche, shaking you down without reprieve.

I tried to get myself together in order to fully enjoy Lhasa for my all-too-brief stay. But as I took a proper look at the glossy documents emailed to me by the travel company for the first time, a different sense of dread sank in. For the next few days, I would be a tourist.

III

Breakfast was standard Chinese buffet fare—cold fried rice, stewed tea and steamed buns—endured in the company of the motley band of Tibet bucket-listers I'd been grouped with. While chewing down the last few mouthfuls of lukewarm stodge, we were directed past the hotel's in-house altitude sickness room and onto the street to meet our guide. As soon as we stepped beyond the confines of the hotel, everyone put on coats with brand names that invoked snowboarding or rock climbing. The Dutch couple wiped zinc oxide across their cheeks as American football players apply eye black, the Australian gardener (whose name was Gardener) donned tinted sunglasses, the banker from Singapore sparked up the first of many gold-tipped cigarettes. As I toggled up my duffle coat, I sensed I was the more retrogressive member of the group.

When our guide arrived, I grew more at ease. She appeared modest and intelligent, not to mention beautiful, handsome really, with pointed cheekbones, a hazelnut complexion and brilliant eyes that were unmistakably kind.

"Okay, everyone, gather round, my name is Dechen, I'm a Tibetan and I'll be your guide. Now I know people have paid for different itineraries but for the first two days we'll all be together. Today, we'll be moving on foot through old Lhasa, tomorrow we'll take a minibus to the Deprung and Siri monasteries. Try to keep close, if you feel out of breath just let me know," before adding, "an American had a heart attack just last week." Glancing at the portly American in our party, I privately wondered if it was steamed bun-induced.

We were soon on the move through the dusty back streets of Lhasa, narrow lanes that smelled one-part yak butter to three parts juniper incense.

"Your English is excellent," I told her, as we passed a row of shops selling Tibetan bling—great silver rings bearing precious stones, turquoise amulets, hooped earrings and beady yellow bracelets.

"It's really my mother tongue," she said, "I grew up in India."

"Darussalam?" I asked her, the home of the Tibetan Government in exile and, of course, the Dalai Lama.

She nodded and gave me a wink before introducing our first destination, an old tea house. "As you can see, Tibetans love tea, it doesn't grow here but comes here from Yunnan along the old tea horse road but we serve it with butter to keep warm in the winter..." We peered inside a room dominated by men wearing *chumba* cloaks, some sporting cowboy hats, all discussing the issues of the day over glasses of thick yellow curd. "Would anyone like to try some?"

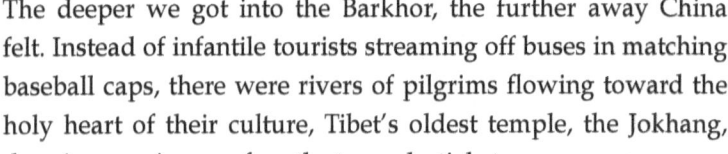

The deeper we got into the Barkhor, the further away China felt. Instead of infantile tourists streaming off buses in matching baseball caps, there were rivers of pilgrims flowing toward the holy heart of their culture, Tibet's oldest temple, the Jokhang, drawing a universe of moths to a celestial star.

"You can take photos here," said Dechen, "but certain places inside are prohibited."

"Why?"

"Some scenes from the Brad Pitt film *Seven Years in Tibet*

were secretly shot here, so the government doesn't want you to reproduce the scene."

The Jokhang translated as the 'chapel of the Jowo' because inside the Jowo Rinpoche was housed, the Buddha that travelled from Xi'an to Lhasa in the company of Princess Wencheng in the 7th Century. Having been through Yushu, I couldn't help but feel a strong affinity with her trail.

"They took two protesting monks away from here recently," Dechen suddenly confided in me, while the rest of the group posed for photos. "They haven't been heard of since."

It was an unexpected revelation, the likes of which she divulged throughout the two-day tour. Perhaps she had noticed my incessant scribbling in my notebook — too much detail to be the words of a humble diarist. Or maybe it was just that she was in the habit of telling anyone who looked like they might listen, just out of earshot of the security personnel, like a prayer flag or mani stone bearing a message from afar. Anyone who might listen, just out of earshot of the security personnel.

After squeezing us through the pilgrim-jammed Jokhang, we were herded on foot to Lhasa's singular iconic structure, one so imposing and beautiful that should it fall, the city would effectively be beheaded. Premier Zhou Enlai was credited with saving the Potala Palace from the Red Guards during the Cultural Revolution, as he was credited with protecting most marvels to have survived Maoist wrath. Whether it was Zhou or someone else, they deserved a posthumous world heritage award, for the red and white goliath that was the Potala Palace was absolutely marvelous. One hundred thirty meters high, comprising 13 stories, 1,000 rooms and enough prayer halls to house all the pilgrims prostrated outside the Jokhang, it made Buckingham Palace look like a holiday cottage in Clacton-on-Sea. And I couldn't help but notice that, just as Beijing's Forbidden City was as flat as the central plain that birthed Chinese civilization, so too did the Tibetans build their principal house to reflect their genesis, that is, on a hillside.

"The Potala Palace was first built in the 7th Century by Songtsen Gampo," said Dechen as she led us through a mandatory electronic bag scan. "But what you see today was reconstructed during the reign of the fifth Dalai Lama in 1645."

It was hell of a hike just getting up to the palace front door, especially at high altitude. From the ramparts, I caught my breath and cast my eyes across Lhasa. The mountains still dominated the frame, black and bare of vegetation, something like Mordor. Despite what I'd read of a new Chinese city, the place looked quaint when compared with eastern hellscapes like Wenzhou, though I'd no doubt what stood before was far more redolent of Tibetan culture. There was a generic plaza opposite the palace, Liberation Square, home to a vulgar public monument representing how one-sided Sino-Tibetan relations had become and I feared the palace was just another reminder of a 'feudal' past maintained for posterity and the tourist dollar. Atop the majestic Potala, a red flag fluttered.

Noticing I was trailing the group, Dechen waved me forward, "Come on, Thomas, keep up," before turning to her flock and continuing, "If you'd like to follow me into the white palace, we can explore the residences of the 13th and 14th Dalai Lamas…"

IV

"Hi, Xiao Fei, where are you?"

"Hey LZD, I'm in my hotel."

"Have you had dinner?"

"No, I've been walking around Lhasa all day, I was just taking a rest, there's no oxygen up here."

"Tell me about it, if I didn't smoke there'd be nothing in my lungs."

"Where are you staying?" I asked him.

"Since I left you in Xining, I've been staying at Young Wang's place. He's been quite the host, taking me to all the sites. Why don't you come over here? I'm cooking."

"Where is it? The guide told us not to leave the Barkhor after dark."

"It's outside the old town, you'll need to get a cab. I can send you the address."

"Then I really shouldn't, why don't you come downtown for dinner instead?"

"Will you chill out, when did you start following the rules anyway? Listen, nobody will stop you if you come, and if you do run into any problems, just give me a call, Young Wang has some connections with the public security bureau."

"Okay, I'll try, see you in about an hour. *Zaijian.*"

Click.

The temperature had plummeted with the darkness, a chill that suggested winter was living just over the next hill. I found the hotel gate already closed, but when I opened it the security guard didn't flinch.

The main street was illuminated by ornate lamps similar to the ones they had along the boulevards of central Beijing, which looked impressive on Chang'an Avenue but misplaced in Lhasa, like a chandelier dangling in a yurt. There were still pious pilgrims chanting and prostrating themselves on the pavement, their extraordinary ritualized crawl to the Jokhang not yet over.

I walked until I found a street with no police, no easy feat in Lhasa. I was wearing my scarf across my face, a vain attempt to hide my ethnicity that probably had me looking like an active member of al Shaabab. But when I flagged a cab, the Tibetan driver took one look at my eyes and said, "Foreigner, no, no," then sped away.

Disheartened, I began to trundle back to the hotel. But somehow I plucked the courage to do a U-turn and press on into the Lhasa night.

Eventually, a man driving a red, Chinese-brand Honga motorbike pulled over.

"Where are you going, *laowai*?" he asked in Sichuan-lilted Mandarin.

I showed him the address.

"Ten yuan."

I didn't even try to bargain.

We were soon racing through Tibet after dark, weaving in and out of the traffic and bolting through police roadblocks like outlaws heading for the state line. Just as I'd come to terms with imminent death in Lhasa, the headline 'Travel writer dies doing what he loves best' appearing in the *South Wales Echo*, the driver skidded around a corner and pulled up before an entrance barrier.

"*Da kai*!" he shouted at the Tibetan manning the barrier booth, meaning "Open up!"

It was promptly lifted and we whizzed into a residential complex at the end of which was the glowing entrance to Young Wang's guesthouse.

I paid the man and walked into the lobby with the jelly legs of someone who has just tried jet skiing on Qinghai Lake for the first time. The walls were half painted and there was an enormous straight-out-of-Tongren mural depicting a yellow deity with a green head riding on a cloud towards an elephant on a lotus flower.

"Who are you?" asked a Tibetan girl meekly.

"I'm Young Wang's friend."

"Oh, I see, well go on upstairs, they're all on the fourth floor."

I hiked up the stairs and then followed my nose to a kitchen where I found LZD in his signature pose, scraping chunks of tofu around a chili-pepper doused wok, a bottle of Lhasa Beer at his side to keep him cool amid the smoke and the steam.

Taking off his glasses to wipe away the water droplets with his sleeve, he announced smugly, "I told you, Xiao Fei, nobody would stop you. China is just this way."

"You were right," I conceded, though in reality, nobody had had a chance to stop us.

He came over and gave me a warm embrace. "Good to see you, old friend," he said, at once vanquishing any lingering animosity between us. I had long believed friendship in China meant more than it did in the West. This was proof.

"Anyway, how was your trip to Lhasa?" he asked, returning to stir the pan.

"Long," I tried to say while catching my breath. I decided not to tell him about my Golmud detour. "I went to Jokhang Temple and the Potala Palace today."

"That's pretty standard, I thought you were an explorer," he quipped, while handing me a bottle from the fridge.

"I told you, I can't go it alone. I have to follow a guide. Plus, I only paid for the cheapest itinerary on the brochure, I don't think they're going to take me on an off-the-beaten-path-adventure."

"Don't worry, we've had enough adventures, enjoy the tour. How many days have you got left?"

"Just one more, then I'll leave for Beijing the day after. What about you?"

"I've seen most of Lhasa. I'll stay a few more days then fly to Chongqing and try to pick up where I left off on the Yangtze

River." He was referring to a documentary photo project he'd been working on for some years, *From the Zi River to the Yangtze*.

"No rest for the wicked, aye?"

"Exactly. Now, make yourself useful and take this bowl across the corridor into the dining room. Don't worry, it's all vegetarian, I told these Tibetans a Welsh hobbit was coming for dinner and that according to Celtic tradition you people only eat leaves and beans. They're intrigued…"

Across the corridor I met Young Wang laying the table in the company of three guests.

"Hi Xiao Fei, long time no see," he said, shaking my hand. His skin had bronzed in Tibet while he sported a pair of Tibetan boots and some glittering Tibetan bling. The Western hippies Theroux met might have left the Holy City long ago, but disenfranchised bohemian Chinese find much to fetishize in the land of their ethnic minority comrades, just as the Laurel Canyon set in the '60s and '70s identified with Native American culture.

"Look at you, you've gone local," I said, patting him on the back.

"Haha, Tibetan culture is amazing, I've learned a lot since I came up here. What do you think of my hotel?"

"Very impressive."

"It's such a pity I'm not licensed for foreign guests, otherwise, you could stay. Lily has been with me for a month," he said, gesturing to a girl from Guizhou with dyed red hair sitting at the table devotedly smoking cigarettes.

"Take a seat," he said, gesturing to a wooden stool opposite two Tibetans. "Hey, everyone, this is my British friend, Xiao Fei," he began, before rolling out a compliment-studded introduction.

While LZD and Young Wang continued to serve a veritable banquet of delicacies, I got to know the guests.

"Nice to meet you," I said in Mandarin to the Tibetan couple opposite. "How should I address you both?"

The girl took the initiative. "I'm Dolkar and this is my boyfriend Kalden."

"Wow, you speak pretty good Chinese."

"I grew-up in Guangzhou, my family is from Garze, a Tibetan part of Sichuan, but my mother set up a business in the Pearl River Delta when I was about five."

"So when did you come to Lhasa?"

"Kalden is from here, but you know, for all Tibetans, Lhasa feels like home."

"Is it difficult living here?"

"Sometimes, you've seen the security people around here I imagine? But we get by."

"Yes, I'm not supposed to be here. I think if I was found even talking to you I'd get in trouble."

"We'd get into more trouble," Kalden replied, without altering his warm expression.

"Did you hear about the storm?" interjected LZD as he placed another piping hot dish on the table.

"What storm?"

"A huge typhoon has hit Hong Kong and Shenzhen, ripping up trees and knocking down houses. A few people have died. The Shenzhen Metro has been turned into a river. Old Huang's cat drowned."

"What about your apartment, LZD?"

"I don't know, I tried calling my landlord. I think I left the window open." He laughed. It's good to see his humor back, LZD the chef, the entertainer and the arch-dissenter, guns blazing.

"Well, we've had pretty good weather in Tibet," I said. "The gods have smiled on us…"

"Yes, it's really nice at this time of year but winter is around the corner and it gets really cold here," said Young Wang. "I mean, like, even colder than Beijing. This is about the last good week. You've timed your travels well."

We toasted a round of beers and began eating. Like any Chinese banquet, it was a spirited affair infused with boisterous laughter, cigarette smoke and clinking glasses. I didn't have much of an appetite, more a thirst, the dry air perhaps, or the anxiety I'd carried from Golmud. By the time a guitar was, handed around, I'd doused more bottles than anyone else.

"Xiao Fei has a Chinese song he wrote by himself," said LZD, putting me on the spot. "It's called *Wo Bu Shi Gaofushuai* – I'm Not Tall, Rich or Handsome."

I managed to get through two verses of this self-deprecating party-pleaser before laughter drowned out the chords.

"I'm too dizzy to play," I said, "I think it's the altitude. What about a Tibetan song?" I asked, trying to hand over the guitar.

"We can't play," said Kalden politely.

"Come on," said LZD, "ethnic minorities can all sing and dance, that's all the government ever lets you do on state TV."

"Yeah, sing a folk song like you did last time you visited," asserted Young Wang.

The pair looked a touch nervous, they glanced at each other, then with a wave of the hand they began to sing with perfect pitch. I soon realized this was unlike anything I'd heard before. Good folk music was always rooted in the soil and best performed in the native language of a given place. This was as true of Ireland as it was of Mongolia. It was true when the train took me to see Wu Tiao Ren and Li Yihan in Guangdong. But never had it been truer than at this moment. Though I couldn't understand the words of the 'mountain song' I could hear the landscape of Tibet in the melody, the train rolling through the wilderness given an anthem worthy of its melancholy splendor. The female soprano reached into the high octaves like a soaring bird, the male part trailed the valley below, deep and sincere like a lone wolf. They hit more blue notes than a southern bluesman after a whisky-soaked breakup, yet somehow invoked a sanguine sense of hope. There was no tragedy in their chorus. I quickly pulled out my notebook and pen. As I looked at the black lines on the page they appeared blurry.

"The Tibetans are singing together," I managed to write, "in harmony."

About The Author

Thomas Bird fled the rain-soaked British suburbs for East Asia in 2005. Having cut his teeth in journalism as a magazine editor in southern China, over the last decade, Bird has written for a host of top international publications. A regular contributor to the *South China Morning Post* in Hong Kong, he has co-authored more than ten guidebooks including, most recently, *The Rough Guide to Thailand*. He likes train travel, craft beer and the teachings of Zhuangzi.